College Preparatory Mathematics 3

(Algebra 2)

Second Edition

Editors:

Steve Simon
 Lick-Wilmerding High
Robert Petersen
 Sacramento High
Judith Kysh
 The CRESS Center
 University of California, Davis
Sally Keszler
 Bear Creek High

Technical Assistance:

Bethany Sorbello
 CPM Educational Program
Thu Pham
 The CRESS Center
 University of California, Davis

Program Directors:

Tom Sallee
 Department of Mathematics
 University of California, Davis
Judith Kysh
 The CRESS Center
 University of California, Davis
Elaine Kasimatis
 Department of Mathematics
 California State University, Sacramento
Brian Hoey
 CPM Educational Program

Illustrator:

Kelly DeMartini

College Preparatory Mathematics
Algebra 2

Second Edition Editors: 1998-99

Bob Petersen...Sacramento High
Steve Simon.....................................Lick-Wilmerding High
Sally Keszler...Bear Creek High

Original Writers and Editors: First Edition 1992-95

Nancy Aaberg ....Yuba City High
Kathy Borst ....Anderson Valley High
Tracy Brown.....................................Luther Burbank High
Carlos Cabana...San Lorenzo High
Jonathan Compton...Belen High
John Cooper...Del Oro High
Kelly (Martin) DiLeo.........................Alhambra Senior High
Carmel Draper......................................Wood (Will C.) High
James Friedrich...Valley High
David Goodwin...Florin High
Carol Grossnicklaus......................................Oxnard High
Patty Hart ....Elk Grove High
Gail Holt...............................El Camino Fundamental High
Karen Junker...Florin High
Mark Kellman ....Luther Burbank High
Richard Melamed ....El Camino Fundamental High
Bob Petersen...Sacramento High
Steve Piekarski...................................C.K. McClatchy High
Rolf Schumann.............................Christian Brothers High
Jeanne Shimizu-Yost.....................................San Juan High
Clark Swanson...Sacramento High
Joel Teller................................College Preparatory School
Kathy Van Liefde...........................Christian Brothers High
Joe Veiga..Elk Grove High
Karen Wootton ....Will C. Wood High

and by

Judith Kysh & Tom Sallee, Project Co-Directors

Technical Assistance
Crystal Mills, Kirk Mills, Thu Pham, and Bethany Sorbello

3 4 5 6 7 8 9   03 02 01 00

Printed in the United States of America   ISBN 1-885145-64-0

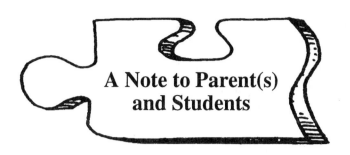

A Note to Parent(s) and Students

The authors of the College Preparatory Mathematics Series (CPM) are all high school and middle school teachers currently in the classroom. Working along with University mathematicians, they developed and tested these materials with the dual goals of teaching the core facts and procedures of Algebra 2 AND having the mathematics contained in the course make sense. These teachers are dedicated to helping more students successfully learn and understand college preparatory mathematics.

The text provides basic skills checkpoints. These problems are marked with the Milepost icon. If a student has difficulty with a Milepost problem, he or she should ask the teacher for the Milepost practice set for that skill.

To provide additional support for students, the authors have written a unit by unit, "Parent's Guide and Supplement to Math 3 (Algebra 2)." This document contains annotated solutions for key problems and makes suggestions about how to be successful in this course. Each unit's discussion is followed by additional practice problems. As an additional study guide, there is also a section in each unit with practice problems similar to those found on the SAT examination. Some schools make these documents available through the classroom teacher or school library. CPM sells the Parent Guide and Supplement for $15.00, including tax, shipping and handling. You may order this resource through the CPM website at *http://www.cpm.org* or mail your request for the "Math 3 Parent Guide and Supplement," **second edition**, with a check payable to "CPM Educational Program," 1233 Noonan Drive, Sacramento, CA 95822-2569. Allow ten days for delivery. This document can also be downloaded from the CPM website at *http://www.cpm.org*.

Sometimes students find that their Algebra 1 skills need more review than an Algebra 2 course provides. Another source is the CPM "Parent Guide with Review for Math 1 (Algebra 1)." This resource has numerous worked out examples, as well as hundreds additional practice problems arranged by topic. You may order it for $15 from the above address.

TABLE OF CONTENTS

iv

CONTENTS LIST BY LESSON

College Preparatory Mathematics
(Algebra 2)

Goals

Goals for Algebra 2 include all the goals stated for Algebra 1 and Geometry with emphasis on learning to:

- use problem solving strategies in conjunction with a knowledge of the inter-connections among algebra, geometry, and functions to analyze problems and formulate appropriate solutions and to extend current knowledge by making new connections;

- visualize, express, interpret, and graph functions (and their inverses, when they exist) and some relations in various positions in two dimensions. Given the graph, be able to represent it with an equation including the following:

linear	exponential	logarithmic	circles
quadratic	absolute value	simple rational	ellipses
other polynomial	sine, cosine, tangent	square root	hyperbolas

  as well as other functions and real world problems associated with graphs;

- use variables to represent relations from tables, graphs, verbally stated problems, and geometric diagrams and understand that algebraic relations can be tested by substitutions of numbers;

- solve any real linear or quadratic equation in one variable, mixed systems in two variables, and linear systems of equations in three or more variables;

- use ratio, proportion, and direct variation from numerical, geometric, and algebraic perspectives (percent, similarity, right triangles, slope, and probability);

- use the properties of algebra to reorganize algebraic expressions in order to put them into more useful forms;

- extend the use of trigonometry to the laws of sines and cosines and connect right triangle definitions with the trigonometric functions;

- construct convincing arguments and proofs to support or prove assertions and communicate mathematical ideas clearly using appropriate vocabulary;

- apply mathematics to problems in economics, biology, chemistry, and physics; and,

- use elementary probability and statistics to solve problems.

WHAT DO THE BARS REPRESENT?

The bars on the opening page for each unit represent the six main threads of the course, six major areas in which you should be making progress all year long. At the beginning of each new unit take a look at the each of the bars and ask yourself, "How am I doing? What are some of the things I now know for sure in this area? What do I need to do some more work on?"

Problem Solving: Continues to be a major focus for learning mathematics in Math 3. You should be developing your ability to integrate your use of basic strategies such as identifying subproblems, using guess-and-check, and making organized lists with the use of algebraic procedures and your knowledge of graphing.

Representation/Modeling: Learning to represent situations with diagrams, graphs, equations or other models has become a much more important aspect of mathematics since the development of technologies which can carry out algorithmic procedures once a situation is represented. Being able to represent situations in several ways and to move back and forth between representations such as graphs, tables, and equations is emphasized throughout the year.

Functions/Graphing: Math 3 is mostly about functions: linear, exponential, quadratic, other polynomial, logarithmic, trigonometric, rational, radical, and absolute value plus others that arise out of specific situations. You'll also need to know about some non-functions such as circles, ellipses, hyperbolas, and "sleeping" parabolas and about inequalities and their graphs.

Intersections/Systems: Intersections (and non-intersections) of graphs of functions (and non-functions) lead to systems of equations (and inequalities) which sometimes can be solved by algebraic means and sometimes cannot. You will build on what you know about solving linear and quadratic equations to solve 3x3 systems of linear equations, 2x2 pairings of lines, circles, parabolas and other polynomials that can be solved algebraically, and some pairings of these with exponential, logarithmic, and trigonometric equations for which you will have to use estimation and graphing or some combination of methods.

Algorithms: As you gain familiarity through practice with some types of problems that appear routinely as subproblems in other problems, you will need to develop facility with routine procedures, including the tried and true tools of algebraic reorganization as well as others of your own devising or choice. Procedures that should become routine are identified throughout the year, often with a note to include them along with examples in the your Tool Kit.

Reasoning/Communication: Includes developing the ability to give clear explanations, to make conjectures, and to develop logical mathematical arguments, proofs as well as derivations. Throughout the course you will practice articulating and justifying ideas orally, in writing in both mathematical and standard language, in diagrams, and sometimes in models.

UNIT 7

At the County Fair
POLYNOMIALS AND GENERAL SYSTEMS

Unit 7 Objectives
At the County Fair: POLYNOMIALS AND GENERAL SYSTEMS

In this unit you will investigate polynomial functions beyond linear and quadratic functions. You will go back to looking at where a curve intersects the line $y = 0$. Then you will investigate what happens when there are no real numbers to make a polynomial equal zero. This work leads to the introduction of imaginary numbers.

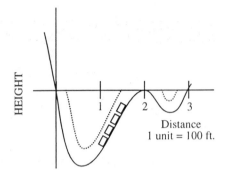

HEIGHT

Distance
1 unit = 100 ft.

In this unit you will have the opportunity to:

- explore polynomial equations and their graphs.

- find intersections of non-linear functions and other equations both graphically and algebraically.

- discover that some systems of equations cannot be solved algebraically. Their solutions can only be approximated by graphing and estimating.

- learn that other equations which, at first glance, could not be solved can be solved when we expand the set of numbers we can use.

- expand your thinking in order to work with numbers composed of real and imaginary parts.

- summarize the important ideas from the course.

Keep a graphing calculator handy—you will be surprised at how useful, even necessary, it will be in solving many of these problems, especially equations that cannot be solved using algebraic methods.

CF-0.   **THE GAME TANK** The Mathamericaland Carnival Company wants to make a special game to premiere at this year's county fair. The game will consist of a tank filled with ping pong balls. Most are ordinary white ones, but there are a limited number of orange, red, blue, and green prize ping pong balls. The blue ones have a prize value of $2; the reds, $5; the orange ones, $20; and the green ping pong ball (there's only one!) is worth $1000. There are 1000 blue ping pong balls, 500 red ones, and 100 orange ones. Fairgoers will pay $1 for the opportunity to crawl around in the tank while blindfolded for a set amount of time, trying to find one of the colored ping pong balls.

The owner of the company thinks that she will make the most profit if the tank has maximum volume. In order to cut down on the costs of building this new game, she hires you to find out what shape to make the tank.

PROBLEM SOLVING
REPRESENTATION/MODELING
FUNCTIONS/GRAPHING
INTERSECTIONS/SYSTEMS
ALGORITHMS
REASONING/COMMUNICATION

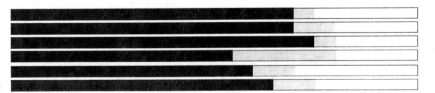

Unit 7

At the County Fair: **POLYNOMIALS AND GENERAL SYSTEMS**

INTRODUCTORY TOPICS

CF-1. Solve each of the following for x:

a) $(x - 1) = 0$ b) $(x - 1)(x + 1) = 0$ c) $(x - 1)^2 = 0$

CF-2. Sketch a graph of each of the following functions and indicate where each intersects the x-axis:

a) $y = (x - 1)$ b) $y = (x - 1)(x + 1)$ c) $y = (x - 1)^2$

CF-3.

> By this time in the course, we hope you have realized that the two previous problems are basically asking for the same thing. In the Parabola Lab, you discovered how to make a parabola "sit" on the x-axis, and you also looked at ways of making parabolas intersect the x-axis in two specific places. These x-intercepts for the graph of the function are often called the **ROOTS of the function** and sometimes can be found by factoring. Another name for roots of the function is **ZEROS of the function** because at the root or x-intercept, the value of the function is zero. Add **roots** and **zeros** to your Tool Kit.

CF-4. Find the **roots** of each of the following functions:

a) $y = x^2 - 6x + 8$ b) $f(x) = x^2 - 6x + 9$ c) $y = x^3 - 4x$

CF-5. For the equations in this problem, make tables from -2 to 2 and draw the graph.

a) $y = (x - 1)^2(x + 1)$ b) $y = (x - 1)^2(x + 1)^2$

c) $y = x^3 - 4x$ d) Do we have the parent graphs for these equations in the Parent Graph Tool Kit?

CF-6.

> The algebraic expressions in the previous problem are called **POLYNOMIALS**. Polynomials are expressions that can be written as a sum of terms of the form:
>
> (any number)$\cdot x^{(\text{whole number})}$. The highest power of x in any of these terms is called the **DEGREE** of the polynomial, and the terms are usually arranged with the powers of x in order, starting with the highest, left to right. The numbers which multiply the powers of x are called the **COEFFICIENTS** of the polynomial.

These are polynomial functions	These are not polynomial functions
a) $\quad f(x) = 8x^5 + x^2 + 6.5x^4 + 6$	d) $\quad y = 2^x + 8$
b) $\quad y = \frac{3}{5}x^6 + 19x^2$	e) $\quad f(x) = 9 + \sqrt{x} - 3$
c) $\quad P(x) = 7(x - 3)(x + 5)^2$	f) $\quad y = x^2 + \dfrac{1}{x^2 + 5}$

The general equation of a second degree (quadratic) polynomial is often written: $ax^2 + bx + c$. The general equation of a third degree (cubic) polynomial is often written: $ax^3 + bx^2 + cx + d$.

If the polynomial has degree n, we do not know how many letters we will need for the coefficients, so we use subscripts: $(a_n)x^n + (a_{n-1})x^{(n-1)} + \ldots + (a_1)x^1 + a_0$

This general polynomial has degree n and coefficients $a_n, a_{n-1}, \ldots, a_1, a_0$. For example:

in $7x^4 - 5x^3 + 3x^2 + 7x + 8$, n = 4, therefore . . .

$a_n = a_4 = 7, \quad a_{n-1} = a_3 = -5, \quad a_{n-2} = a_2 = 3, \quad a_1 = 7 \quad \& \quad a_0 = 8$

a) What is the degree of example (a) in the box above? example (b)? example (c)?

b) Why are (d), (e) and (f) <u>not</u> polynomial functions?

c) Find the degree and identify the coefficients a_0 through a_n for the polynomial in part (a) of the preceding problem. You need to do a subproblem to be able to answer this question.

CF-7. Describe the possible numbers of intersections for each of the following pairs of graphs. Sketch a graph for each possibility. For example, in part (b), a parabola could intersect a line twice, once, or not at all. Your solution to each part should include all of the possibilities and a sketched example of each one.

a) Two different lines. b) A line and a parabola.

c) Two different parabolas. d) A parabola and a circle.

CF-8.   Solve the following system: $y = x^2 - 5$
                                            $y = x + 1$

CF-9.   How did you solve the previous problem? If you did not use algebra, try to solve the
         system algebraically. Show your work or explain why it cannot be solved that way.

CF-10.   Describe the difference between the graphs of $y = x^3 - x$ and $y = x^3 - x + 5$.

CF-11.   Artemus was putting up the sign at the
         County Fair Theater for the movie "ELVIS
         RETURNS FROM MARS." He got all of
         the letters he would need and put them in a
         box. He reached into the box and pulled
         out a letter at random.

a)   What is the probability that he got the first letter he needed when he reached
      into the box?

b)   Once he put the first letter up, what is the probability that he got the second
      letter he needed when he reached into the box?

CF-12.   Which of the following equations are polynomial functions? For each one that is not,
         give a brief justification as to why it is not.

a) $y = 3x^3 + 2x^2 + x$ b) $y = (x - 1)^2(x - 2)^2$

c) $y = x^2 + 2^x$ d) $y = 3x - 1$

e) $y = (x - 2)^2 - 1$ f) $y^2 = (x - 2)^2 - 1$

g) $y = \dfrac{1}{x^2} + \dfrac{1}{x} + \dfrac{1}{2}$ h) $y = \dfrac{1}{2}x + \dfrac{1}{3}$

CF-13.   Sam thinks that the equation $(x - 4)^2 + (y - 3)^2 = 25$ is equivalent to the equation
         $(x - 4) + (y - 3) = 5$, because you can just take the square root of both sides of the first
         equation. Are the two equations equivalent? Explain why or why not.

CF-14.   Solve the equations below (remember "fraction busters").

a) $\dfrac{3x}{x + 2} + \dfrac{7}{x - 2} = 3$ b) $\dfrac{x - 7}{x - 5} - \dfrac{6}{x} = 1$

CF-15.   An arithmetic sequence starts out -23, -19, -15, . . .

a)   What is the rule?

b)   How many times must the generator be applied so that the result is greater than 10,000?

POLYNOMIAL FUNCTIONS LAB

CF-16.   **Polynomial Functions Lab (CF-16 & CF-17)** We are going to be doing an investigation of polynomial functions, but first we will do one example as a class. The example function we will work with is $P_1(x) = (x - 2)(x + 5)^2$.

a)   Graph the function on a graphing calculator using the standard viewing window.

b)   As you can see, we do not get the best view of the function in the standard window. We will use the zoom features of the graphing calculator to obtain a better view of the graph. What should we be looking for when we zoom? Start by zooming out. You may have to do this more than once to get the complete graph. Next use the box feature to select the portion of the graph which you would like to view. Sketch this graph on the second set of axes. It helps to label the important points of the graph such as the intercepts.

c)   Find the roots.

d)   On the number line mark the roots with open circles and then shade the regions where the function outputs are positive (the graph is above the x-axis).

e)   Describe the graph and its relation to the equation. Make sure that you include the degree and the intercepts as part of your description. Pay close attention to the way the function curves.

CF-17.   Use the approach you used for $P_1(x)$ to investigate the following five polynomials.

a) $P_2(x) = 2(x - 2)(x + 2)(x - 3)$ b) $P_3(x) = 0.2x(x + 1)(x - 3)(x + 4)$

c) $P_4(x) = (x + 3)^2(x + 1)(x - 5)$ d) $P_5(x) = -0.1x(x + 4)^3$

e) $P_6(x) = x^4 - x^2$

CF-18.   Sketch a graph of $y = x^2 - 7$.

a)   How many roots does this graph have?

b)   What are the roots of the function?

CF-19. Solve: $x^2 + 2x - 5 = 0$.

a) How many x-intercepts does $y = x^2 + 2x - 5$ have?

b) What are they?

c) Approximately where does the graph of $y = x^2 + 2x - 5$ cross the x-axis?

CF-20. Are parabolas polynomial functions? Are lines polynomial functions? Are cubics? Exponentials? Circles? In all cases, explain why or why not.

CF-21. **The County Fair Ferris Wheel**

Consider this picture of a Ferris Wheel. The Wheel has a 60' diameter and is drawn on a set of axes with the Ferris Wheel's hub at the origin. Use a table like the one below and draw a graph that relates the angle (in standard position) of the spoke leading to your seat to the approximate height of the top of your seat above or below the height of the central hub. The table below starts at -90°, your starting position before you ride around the wheel.

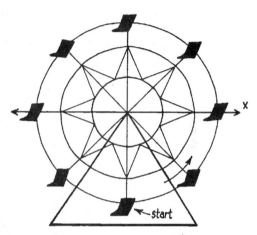

x, the angle measure	-90°	-45°	0°	45°	90°	135°	180°	....	270°
y, the height	-30'	-21.2'	0'						

a) The wheel goes around (counter-clockwise) several times during a ride. How could you reflect this fact in your graph? Update your graph.

b) What is the maximum distance above or below the center that the top of your seat attains during the ride?

CF-22. Graph the inequality $x^2 + y^2 \le 25$, then describe its graph in words.

CF-23. Find x if $2^{p(x)} = 4$ where $p(x) = x^2 - 4x - 3$.

CF-24. Start with the graph of $y = 3^x$, then write new equations that will shift the graph:

a) down 4 units.

b) to the right 7 units.

CF-25.   Look back at the work you did on the **Polynomial Functions Lab.** Then answer the
           following questions.

   a)   What is the maximum number of roots a polynomial of degree 3 can have? Sketch
        an example.

   b)   What do you think is the maximum number of roots a polynomial of degree n can
        have?

   c)   Can a polynomial of degree n have fewer than n roots? Under what conditions?

   d)   For each function below, state the minimum degree its polynomial equation could have

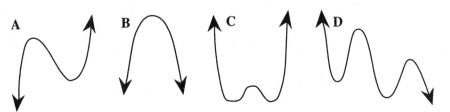

   e)   Which of the graphs above have a negative orientation? (They are opposite of their
        parent graphs.) Explain how you determine the orientation of a graph.

CF-26.   In the previous problem, we specified how to find the minimum degree. It may be
           possible that these graphs have a higher degree.

           Look at the graphs of $y = x^2$ and $y = x^4$.

   a)   How are these graphs similar? How are they different?

   b)   Could graph **B** (previous problem) have degree 4?

   c)   Could it have degree 5? Explain.

CF-27.   In the first example from the **Polynomial Functions Lab** $(x + 5)^2$ is a factor. This
           produces what is called a **double root**.

   a)   What effect does this have on the graph?

   b)   In $P_5(x)$ (problem CF-17, part (d)) there is a **triple root.** What does the equation
        have that lets us know it has a "triple root?"

   c)   What does this do to the graph?

CF-28. The following number lines show where the output values of each polynomial function (a), (b), (c), and (d) are positive, that is, where the graph is above the x-axis. Sketch a possible graph to fit each description. Note: each number line represents a different polynomial.

a)
-3 -1   4

b)
-5   0 2

c)
-1 1   4

d)
-2 -1   1 2

CF-29. Without using a graphing calculator, sketch rough graphs of the following functions. Refer to your Polynomial Functions Lab.

a) $P(x) = -x(x + 1)(x - 3)$

b) $P(x) = (x - 1)^2(x + 2)(x - 4)$

c) $P(x) = (x + 2)^3(x - 4)$

CF-30. Where does the graph $y = (x + 3)^2 - 5$ cross the x-axis?

CF-31. If you were to graph the function $f(x) = (x - 74)^2(x + 29)$, where would the graph of $f(x)$ intersect the x-axis?

CF-32. What is the degree of each of these polynomial functions?

a) $P(x) = 0.08x^2 + 28x$

b) $y = 8x^2 - \frac{1}{7}x^5 + 9$

c) $f(x) = 5(x + 3)(x - 2)(x + 7)$

d) $y = (x - 3)^2(x + 1)(x^3 + 1)$

CF-33. A sequence of pentagonal numbers is started at right.

a) Find the next 3 pentagonal numbers.

b) What kind of a sequence is formed by the pentagonal numbers?

1   5   9

c) What is the equation for the nth pentagonal number?

CF-34.   A circle with its center on the line $y = 3x$ (1st quadrant) is tangent to the y-axis.

a)   If the radius is 2, what is the equation of the circle?

b)   If the radius is 3, what is the equation of the circle?

CF-35.   A contractor working for the county failed to complete the new County Fair Pavilion within a specified time. According to his contract, he is compelled to forfeit $10,000 a day for the first ten days of extra time required, and for each additional day, beginning with the eleventh, the forfeit is increased by $1000 a day. If he lost a total of $255,000, how many days did he overrun the stipulated completion date? What kind of sequence do his fines form starting after the tenth day?

CF-36.   Sketch the graph of each function below on the same set of axes.

a) $y = 2^x$ b) $y = 2^x + 5$ c) $y = 2^x - 5$

NON-LINEAR SYSTEMS

CF-37.   Consider the equation $2^x = x + 3$.

a)   Discuss in your team methods you could try to solve this equation. How many different ways can you think of?

b)   Solve the equation.

c)   Be sure you found two solutions. How can you be certain there are no more than two?

CF-38.   When solving systems of equations, it is important to recall the significance of the solution. What does the solution represent in terms of:

a)   The equations?   b)   The graphs of the equations?

CF-39.   Consider the following system: $y = 2^x + 1$
                                                                                   $y = x + 6$

a)   What kind of equation is $y = 2^x + 1$?

b)   What kind of equation is $y = x + 6$?

c)   In how many points might a linear graph and an exponential graph intersect? Must they intersect? (This will tell us how many solutions we can expect.)

d)   Solve the system by any method that your team discussed for the previous problem.

CF-40.   Cindy needs to graph $y = \log_2 x$ and wants to use her graphing calculator. She figures that she can change the equation into exponential form by converting both sides to base 10, and then re-solving for y. Here is what she did:

$$y = \log_2 x$$

$$2^y = x$$

$$(10^{\log 2})^y = 10^{\log x}$$ (Remember that this is now log base 10.)

$$y \cdot \log (2) = \log (x)$$

$$y = \frac{\log (x)}{\log (2)}$$

a)   Will this work for any base? Show the method for $y = \log_7 x$.

b)   How would you change $y = \log_3 (x + 5)$ to be able to graph it on a graphing calculator?

c)   How would you change $y = \log_2 x - 3$ to be able to graph it on a graphing calculator?

CF-41.   Find where the graphs of $y = \log_2 (x - 1)$ and $y = x^3 - 4x$ intersect.

CF-42.   Solve $\log_2 (x - 1) = x^3 - 4x$.

CF-43.   The systems that you have been solving today are non-linear systems.

a)   What does "non-linear" mean?

Some non-linear systems may be **impossible** to solve algebraically; others may just be extremely difficult.

b)   What other methods do we have to solve these systems?

CF-44.   Sketch a graph of the equation $y = x^2 + 4$.

a)   Where does the graph cross the x-axis?

b)   Solve the equation $x^2 + 4 = 0$ and explain how this relates to the answer you found in part (a).

c)   What occurred when you tried to solve the equation in part (b) that let you know that it has no real solution?

For the function pictured at right:

a) Sketch one cycle. The **PERIOD** is the length of one cycle.

b) How long is the period of this function?

c) What is the difference between the highest and lowest value in the range?

d) The **AMPLITUDE** of a **PERIODIC FUNCTION** is one-half the distance between the highest and lowest value in the range. What is the amplitude of this function?

e) Put the definitions of amplitude and period into your Tool Kit.

CF-46.   Sketch the graphs and find the area of the intersection of: $y > |x + 3|$
                                                                        $y \le 5$

CF-47.   Determine if $x = -2$ is a solution to the equation $x^4 - 4x = 8x^2 - 40$. Show why or why not.

CF-48.

A circle with a radius equal to 1 is called a **UNIT CIRCLE**.

a) Draw a sketch of a unit circle centered at the origin. What is the equation of the circle?

b) What is the area of the circle?

c) What is the circumference of the circle?

CF-49.   Solve the following equation for x:

a) $\dfrac{x + 3}{x - 1} - \dfrac{x}{x + 1} = \dfrac{8}{x^2 - 1}$

b) In part (a) the result of solving the equation is $x = 1$, but what happens when you substitute 1 for x? What does this mean in relation to solutions for this equation?

CF-50. Sketch the circle $(x + 2)^2 + (y + 1)^2 = 9$ and the line $y = x + 4$ on the same set of axes. Find and clearly label the point(s) of intersection of the line and the circle. You may use your graph to estimate the solutions but show how to find the solutions algebraically.

CF-51. Sketch the circle $x^2 + y^2 = 25$, and the parabola $y = x^2 - 13$.

a) How many points of intersection are there for this parabola and the circle?

b) Find the coordinates of these points algebraically. Remember that the key to solving systems is to eliminate a variable.

c) Explain how the graph helps you with the algebraic solution.

CF-52. Solve this system of equations, and explain your method: $(x - 1)^2 + y^2 = 16$
$$y = 2^x$$

CF-53. Solve this system of equations. Be sure to sketch the graphs on your paper.
$$(x - 2)^2 + y^2 = 25$$
$$y = x^3 - 9x$$

a) How many solutions does this system have? Are you sure?

b) Zoom in or set up a new range with x-values close to -3, and y-values a little greater than zero. Now what do you think?

CF-54. Verify that the graphs of the equations $x^2 + y^3 = 17$ and $x^4 - 4y^2 - 8xy = 17$ intersect at (3, 2). Then:

a) give an equation of the vertical line through this point.

b) give an equation of the horizontal line through this point.

CF-55. The equation for the circle at right is $x^2 + y^2 = 1$.

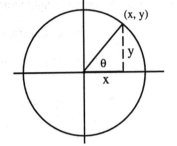

a) What is the radius of the circle?

In terms of the labels on the graph, what is:

b) $\sin(\theta)$?

c) $\cos(\theta)$?

d) $[\sin(\theta)]^2 + [\cos(\theta)]^2 = ?$

CF-56. Each year the Strongberg Construction company builds twenty more houses than in the previous year. Last year they built 180 homes. Acme Homes business is increasing by 15% each year and they built 80 homes last year.

a) Assuming that you don't have a graphing calculator with you now, what can you do to solve this problem with just a scientific calculator?

b) Write equations for each construction company and find the year in which both construction companies will build the same number of homes.

CF-57. Each of the dart boards below is a target at the County Fair dart throwing game. What is the probability of hitting the **shaded** region of each target? Assume you always hit the board but the location on the board is random.

a)

b)

c) 60°

d)

e)

f) 2
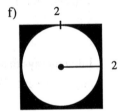

CF-58.   Use the graph at right to answer the questions below.

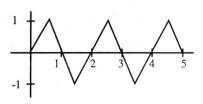

   a)   What is the **amplitude** of this function?

   b)   What is the **period** of this cyclic function?

   c)   How many **cycles** are represented on this graph?

CF-59.   A general equation is an equation that can be used to describe a group of equations or functions with similar characteristics (sometimes called a **family of equations** or **family of functions**). For example, circles with centers at (-3, 5) can be written as $(x + 3)^2 + (y - 5)^2 = k^2$. Here k can be any positive number. Find the general equation for each of the following and sketch a couple of examples of each type.

   a)   Lines parallel to $y = 6x - 7$.

   b)   All parabolas with a vertex at (4, 3).

   c)   All parabolas with roots of 2 and -5.

CF-60.   Choosing your own values for k, sketch on the same set of axes five different examples of graphs which fit the equation: $(x - 3)^2 + (y - 5)^2 = k$. Then describe the graphs in words.

CF-61.   Choosing different values for k and j, sketch three different examples of graphs which fit the equation $(x - k)^2 + (y - j)^2 = 9$. Then describe the graphs in words.

CF-62.   Sketch three different graphs which fit the equation: $(x - d)^2 + (y - 5)^2 = 16$ by choosing different values of d. Describe the graphs in words.

CF-63.   Julianna says that $\dfrac{a}{x + b} = \dfrac{a}{x} + \dfrac{a}{b}$. Fred is not sure; he thinks that the two expressions are not equivalent. Who is correct? Justify your answer.

CF-64.   The area of $\triangle ABC$ is 24 square inches. If $\overline{AB} \perp \overline{BC}$ and BC = 8 in., find AC.

INTRODUCTION TO COMPLEX NUMBERS
(WHEN GRAPHS DO NOT INTERSECT)

CF-65. Consider the graphs whose equations are $y = x^2$ and $y = 2x - 5$.

    a)   Use algebra to find the intersection of the graphs.

    b)   Sketch the graphs and label the intersection.

CF-66. Discuss the previous problem with your team. What happened when you tried to solve the system algebraically?

CF-67. Solve: $x^2 = 3$.

COUNTY FAIR INFORMATION BOOTH: HISTORICAL NOTE

In Ancient Greece, people believed that all numbers could be written as fractions of whole numbers (what we call rational numbers). Many individuals realized later that some numbers could not be written as fractions (such as the result you just calculated) and challenged the accepted beliefs. Some of these people were exiled or outright killed over these challenges. As you can see, the Greeks took their mathematics very seriously. It was known that for a one unit square, the length of the diagonal, squared, yielded 2; when it was shown that no rational number could do that, they accepted the existence of what we call irrational numbers, and invented symbols like $\sqrt{2}$ to represent them. The problem above also has no rational solutions; fractions can never work exactly. The rational (i.e., decimal) solutions that calculators and computers provide are only approximations; the exact answer can only be represented in radical form.

---

    a)   How do you "undo" squaring a number?

    b)   When you solved $x^2 = 2$, how many solutions did you get?

    c)   How many x-intercepts will $y = x^2 - 2$ have?

    d)   Write your solutions both as radicals and as decimal approximations.

CF-68.   Mathematicians throughout history have resisted the notion that some equations were not solvable. Still, it made sense that $x^2 + 1 = 0$ was not solvable, because the graph of $y = x^2 + 1$ has no x-intercepts.

a)   What happens if we try to solve $x^2 + 1 = 0$?

In some ways, each person's math education parallels the history of mathematical discovery. When you were much younger, if you were asked, "How many times does 3 go into 8?" or "What is 8 divided by 3?" you might have said, "3 doesn't go into 8." Then you learned about numbers other than whole numbers, and the question had an answer. Of course, in some situations you are only interested in whole numbers, and then the first answer is still the right one. Later, if you were asked "what number squared makes 5" you might have said "no number squared makes 5". Then you learned about numbers other than rational numbers, and you could answer that question.

Similarly, until about 500 years ago, the answer to the question "what number squared makes -1" was "no number squared makes -1." Then something remarkable happened. An Italian mathematician named Bombelli used a formula for finding the roots of third degree polynomials. Within the formula was a square root, and when he applied the formula to a particular equation the number under the square root came out negative. Instead of giving up, he got a brilliant idea. He knew the equation had a solution, so he decided to see what would happen if he pretended that there *was* a number you could square to make a negative. Remarkably, he was able to continue the calculation, and eventually the "imaginary" number disappeared from the solution. More importantly the resulting answer worked; it solved the equation he had begun with. This led to the acceptance of these so-called imaginary numbers, though the name stuck, and mathematicians came to believe that equations like the one above do have solutions. Of course, in some situations we are only interested in real numbers (that is to say not having an "imaginary" part) and then the original answer, that there is no solution, is still the right one.

COUNTY FAIR INFORMATION BOOTH: DEFINITIONS

The set of numbers that solve equations of the form $x^2 =$ (a negative number) are called **IMAGINARY NUMBERS**. They are not positive, negative, or zero. The collection (set) of positive and negative numbers (integers, rational numbers (fractions), and irrational numbers), along with 0, are referred to as the **REAL NUMBERS**. In particular, the imaginary number that solves the equation $x^2 = -1$ is named **i**, so $i^2 = -1$. In general, **i** follows the rules of real number arithmetic (e.g. $i + i = 2i$). The sum of two imaginary numbers is imaginary (unless it $= 0$); the same is true of the product of a real number and an imaginary number. In fact, multiplying the imaginary number **i** by every possible real number yields all the imaginary numbers. Record this information in your Tool Kit.

---

b)   If we let $i = \sqrt{-1}$, and we define $i^2 = -1$, then what would be the value of
$\sqrt{-16} = \sqrt{16i^2} = ?$

CF-69.   Use the definition of **i** to show that:

a) $\sqrt{-4} = 2\mathbf{i}$

b) $(2\mathbf{i})(3\mathbf{i}) = -6$

c) $(2\mathbf{i})^2(-5\mathbf{i}) = 20\mathbf{i}$

d) $\sqrt{-25} = 5\mathbf{i}$

CF-70.   Consider the function $y = x^2 - 4x + 5$. Its graph does not cross the x-axis, so the equation $x^2 - 4x + 5 = 0$ has no real solutions. Show that applying the quadratic formula to this equation yields the solutions $x = 2 + \mathbf{i}$ and $x = 2 - \mathbf{i}$. Check one of these solutions by substituting it for x and simplifying the result.

> The sum of a real number and an imaginary number, such as 2 + **i**, is neither real nor imaginary. Numbers such as these, which can be written in the form $a + b\mathbf{i}$, where a and b are real numbers, are called **COMPLEX NUMBERS**. These numbers constitute all of the "non-real" numbers. Each complex number has a real component, a, and an imaginary component, $b\mathbf{i}$. Note that according to this definition, the real numbers are also complex numbers; they are the ones with a 0 imaginary part. Record this definition in your Tool Kit.

CF-71.

> If all the numbers on the number line are real numbers, where are the complex numbers located? The real and imaginary parts are independent, so the complex numbers are a two-dimensional number system. To represent them, we need a plane. Real numbers are on the horizontal axis and imaginary numbers are on the vertical axis. Complex numbers are graphed using the same method that coordinate points are: the number $2 + 3\mathbf{i}$ is located at $(2, 3)$, the number **i** or $0 + 1\mathbf{i}$ is located at $(0, 1)$. The number -2 or $-2 + 0\mathbf{i}$ is located at $(-2, 0)$. This representation is called the **COMPLEX PLANE**. Enter this into your tool kit and include an example of how to graph complex numbers.

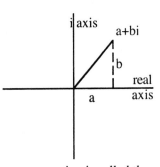

CF-72.   In solving the system at right, we need to solve the equation $x^2 = 2x - 5$. Use the Quadratic Formula to find a solution which includes **i**.

$$y = x^2$$
$$y = 2x - 5$$

CF-73.   Simplify the following (write in $a + b\mathbf{i}$ form):

a) $-18 - \sqrt{-25}$

b) $\dfrac{2 \pm \sqrt{-16}}{2}$

c) $5 + \sqrt{-6}$

CF-74. Explain why $i^3 = -i$. What does $i^4 = ?$

CF-75. Solve for x: $16^{(x+2)} = 8^x$.

CF-76. Is $(x - 5)^2$ equivalent to $(5 - x)^2$? Explain briefly.

CF-77. Evaluate each of the following:

i) $(\sqrt{7})^2$ ii) $(\sqrt{18.3})^2$ iii) $(\sqrt{d})^2$

a) Using what you observed above, evaluate: $(\sqrt{-1})^2$

b) What does $i^2 = ?$

c) Is this consistent with part (a)?

CF-78. Calculate each of the following:

a) $\sqrt{-49}$ b) $\sqrt{-2}$

c) $(4i)^2$ d) $(3i)^3$

CF-79. A function $g(x)$ that "undoes" what another function $f(x)$ does is called its inverse. In the last unit, for example, we saw that $\log_2 x$ is the inverse of 2^x. We often use a special notation for this relationship and, instead of giving the inverse function a different name, such as $g(x)$, write $f^{-1}(x)$ (read " f inverse of x"). In other words, whatever f does to x, f^{-1} undoes.

a) If $f(x) = 2x - 3$, then $f^{-1}(x) = ?$ b) If $h(x) = (x - 3)^2 + 2$, then $h^{-1}(x) = ?$

CF-80. Consider a circle located at the origin with a radius of 5.

a) If you make a quick sketch of this graph, how many points on the graph do you know are accurate? Explain.

b) Find other points which will satisfy the equation $x^2 + y^2 = 25$. To get you started, consider (-4, 3). Look for a total of 12 points with integer coordinates.

MORE WORK WITH COMPLEX NUMBERS

CF-81.   When a graph crosses the x-axis, these x-values are sometimes referred to as the **roots** of the equation (in other words, when $y = 0$). We have seen that solutions to equations can be real or complex, so it must be possible for **roots** be either real or complex.

    a)   Sketch the graph of $y = (x + 3)^2 - 4$. What are the roots?

    b)   Sketch the graph of $y = (x + 3)^2$. What are the roots?

    c)   Sketch the graph of $y = (x + 3)^2 + 4$. Find the roots by solving $(x + 3)^2 + 4 = 0$. Where does the graph cross the x-axis?

CF-82.   Show by purely algebraic methods that the graphs of $y = \frac{1}{x}$ and $y = -x + 1$ do not intersect. What are the complex solutions? Check the graphs on a graphing calculator.

CF-83.   Find the roots of each of the following quadratic functions by solving for x when $y = 0$. Do any of the graphs of these functions intersect the x-axis?

    a) $y = (x + 5)^2 + 9$.   b) $y = (x - 7)^2 + 4$.

    c) $y = (x - 2)^2 + 5$.

CF-84.   What do you notice about the complex solutions of the equations in the previous problem? Describe any patterns you see. Discuss these with your team and write down everything you can think of.

CF-85.   Look for patterns as you find the products for parts (a) through (d). Then use your pattern to answer parts (e) and (f).

    a) $(2 - i)(2 + i)$ b) $(3 - 5i)(3 + 5i)$

    c) $(4 - i)(4 + i)$ d) $(7 - 2i)(7 + 2i)$

    e)   Find a complex number by which you can multiply $(3 + 2i)$ to get a real number.

    f)   Find a complex number by which you can multiply $(a + bi)$ to get a real number.

CF-86.

The complex numbers 2 - 3i and 2 + 3i are called **COMPLEX CONJUGATES**. What is the complex conjugate of:

a)   4 + i?   b)   2 + 7i?   c)   3 - 5i?

Put examples of complex conjugates in your Tool Kit. Explain what happens when you multiply them and when you add them.

CF-87.   If $f(x) = x^2 + 7x - 9$, calculate:

a)   f(-3)   b)   f(i)   c)   f(-3 + i)

CF-88.   Verify that $5 + 2i$ is a solution to $x^2 - 10x = -29$.

CF-89.   Another useful tool in finding some inverse functions is a table. When the formula has only one x in it we can describe it with a sequence of operations, each applied to the previous result. Consider the following table for $f(x) = 2\sqrt{x - 1} + 3$:

	1st	2nd	3rd	4th
what f does to x:	subtr. 1	$\sqrt{}$	mult. by 2	adds 3

Since the inverse must undo these operations, in the opposite order, the table for $f^{-1}(x)$ would look like:

	1st	2nd	3rd	4th
what f^{-1} does to x:	subtr. 3	div. by 2	( )^2	adds 1

a)   Copy and complete the following table for $g^{-1}(x)$ if $g(x) = \frac{1}{3}(x + 1)^2 - 2$:

	1st	2nd	3rd	4th
what g does to x:	adds 1	( )^2	div. by 3	subtr. 2
what g^{-1} does to x:				

b)   Write the equations for $f^{-1}(x)$ and $g^{-1}(x)$.

CF-90.   Consider the following graph:

a)   What is the parent for this function?

b)   What are the coordinates of the locator point?

c)   Write an equation for this graph.

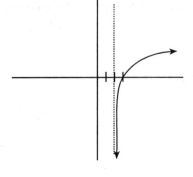

CF-91.   In one of the games at the County Fair, people pay to shoot a paint pistol at the target shown at right. The center has a radius of one inch. Each concentric circle has a radius one inch larger than the preceding circle. Assuming the paint pellet hits the target randomly, what is the probability it hits:

a)   the 50 point ring?

b)   the 20 point ring?

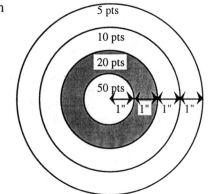

CF-92.   Kahlid is going to make a table to graph $y = \sqrt{x^2}$ but Aaron says that it would be a waste of time to make a table because the graph is the same as $y = x$.

a)   Use Kahlid's equation to make the table and draw the graph.

b)   As you can see, Aaron was wrong, but you did get a graph that you have seen before. What other equation has the same graph? Explain why this is reasonable.

FINDING THE EQUATIONS OF POLYNOMIAL FUNCTIONS

CF-93.   Find reasonable equations for each of the following polynomial functions:

a)

b)

c)

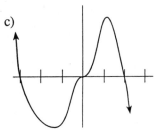

CF-94.   What is the difference between the graphs of the functions $y = x^2(x - 3)(x + 1)$ and $y = 3x^2(x - 3)(x + 1)$?

CF-95.   Find a possible equation for the graph at right:

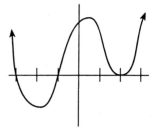

a)   If the equation were multiplied by 5, how would that alter the graph?

b)   The polynomial for this graph can be written as $P(x) = a(x + 3)(x + 1)(x - 2)^2$. Find the value of a if you know that the graph goes through the point (1, 16).

CF-96.   **The County Fair Coaster Ride**

The Mathamericaland Carnival Company has decided to build a new roller coaster to use at this year's county fair. The new coaster will have the special feature that part of the ride will be underground. The designers will use polynomial functions to describe various sections of the track. Part of the design is shown below:

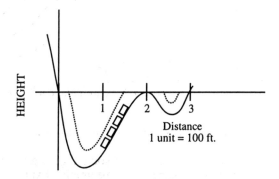

The numbers along the x-axis are in hundreds of feet. At 250 feet, the track will be 20 feet below the surface. This will give the point (2.5, -0.2).

a)   What degree polynomial is demonstrated by the graph?

b)   What are the roots?

c)   Find an exact equation of the polynomial that will generate this curve.

d)   Find the deepest point of the tunnel.

CF-97.   Write an exact equation for each of the following graphs.

a)

b)
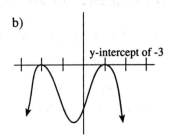
y-intercept of -3

CF-98. $y = \frac{1}{2}$ and $y = \frac{16}{x^2 - 4}$. Find the coordinates where the graphs of the functions intersect.

CF-99.   A circle is tangent to the lines $y = 6$, $y = -2$ and to the y-axis. What is the equation of the circle? Draw a picture!

CF-100.   Use algebra to solve the system of equations: $y = x^2 + 5$
          Confirm your solutions by sketching the graphs. $y = 2x$

CF-101.   You are given the equation $5x^2 + bx + 20 = 0$. For what values of b does this equation have real solutions?

CF-102.   The function $h(x)$ is defined by the operations in the following table:

	1st	2nd	3rd
what h does to x:	adds 2	$(\ )^3$	subtract 7
what h^{-1} does to x:			

a)   Copy and complete the table for $h^{-1}(x)$.

b)   Write equations for $h(x)$ and $h^{-1}(x)$.

CF-103.   Find the center and radius of the following circles:

a) $(y - 7)^2 = 25 - (x - 3)^2$ b) $x^2 + y^2 + 10y = -9$

c) $x^2 + y^2 + 18x - 8y + 47 = 0$ d) $y^2 + (x - 3)^2 = 1$

COMPLEX ROOTS

CF-104. Based of the following graphs, how many **real** roots does each polynomial function have?

i)   ii)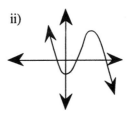

Something is added to each function and each graph is translated upward resulting in the graphs below. How many **real** roots does each of these polynomial functions have?

iii)   iv)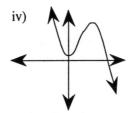

The polynomials in (iii) and (iv) do not have fewer roots. Polynomial (iii) still has **two** roots, but now the roots are complex. Polynomial (iv) has **three** roots: **two** are complex and only **one** is real.

CF-105. Recall that a polynomial function with degree n crosses the x-axis at most n times. For instance, $y = (x + 1)^2$ intersects the x-axis once, while $y = x^2 + 1$ does not intersect it at all. The function $y = x^2 - 1$ intersects it twice.

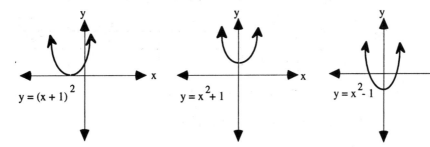

a)   A third-degree equation might intersect the x-axis 1, 2, or 3 times. Make sketches of all these possibilities.

b)   Why can't a third-degree equation have 0 real roots?

CF-106.   Now consider $x^3 - 3x^2 + 3x - 2 = 0$. Since the number of different real solutions is the same as the number of points of intersection of $y = x^3 - 3x^2 + 3x - 2$ with the x-axis, how many real solutions could this have?

   a)   Check to verify that $x^3 - 3x^2 + 3x - 2 = (x - 2)(x^2 - x + 1)$. How many real solutions does $x^3 - 3x^2 + 3x - 2 = 0$ have? How many non-real (complex)? What are all the solutions?

   b)   How many roots does $y = x^3 - 3x^2 + 3x - 2$ have? How many real and how many non-real (complex)? How many times does the graph intersect the x-axis? Check it out.

CF-107.   In our example with the parabolas (problem CF-105), $(x + 1)^2 = 0$ has one real solution, and $x^2 - 1 = 0$ has two real solutions.

   a)   How many solutions of what type(s) does $x^2 + 1 = 0$ have? Solve for x. How does this relate to the graph of $y = x^2 + 1$? Explain.

   b)   Consider the factors of the three polynomials: $(x + 1)^2$, $x^2 - 1$, and $x^2 + 1$. What is the relationship between the factorization and the number and kind of roots?

CF-108.   For each polynomial function $f(x)$, the graph of $f(x)$ is shown. Based on this information, tell how many linear and quadratic factors the factored form of its equation should have and how many real and complex (non-real) solutions $f(x) = 0$ might have. (Assume a polynomial function of the lowest possible degree for each one.)

 EXAMPLE:

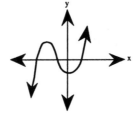

f(x) will have three real linear factors, therefore three real roots and no complex roots.

a)

b)

c)

d)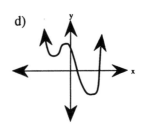

UNIT 7

CF-109. Make a sketch of a graph $f(x)$ so that $f(x) = 0$ could have the indicated number and type of solutions.

a)   5 real solutions.

b)   3 real and 2 complex.

c)   4 complex.

d)   4 complex and 2 real.

e)   For parts (a) through (d), what is the smallest degree each function could be?

CF-110.   Add some examples to your Tool Kit that illustrate the fact that the degree depends on the number of linear and quadratic factors and that the number of roots will be less than or equal to the degree of the polynomial since some factors may be repeated.

CF-111.   Consider the function $y = x^3 - 9x$.

a)   What are the roots of the function? (Factoring will help!)

b)   Sketch a graph of the function.

CF-112.   Which of the following equations have real roots and which have complex roots?

a) $y = x^2 - 6$

b) $y = x^2 + 6$

c) $y = x^2 - 2x + 10$

d) $y = x^2 - 2x - 10$

e) $y = (x - 3)^2 - 4$

f) $y = (x - 3)^2 + 4$

CF-113.   Graph the following system: $y = x^2 + 5$
                                              $y = 2x$

a)   Refer back to your algebraic solution in problem CF-100.

b)   How does your graphical solution relate to your algebraic solution?

CF-114. Raul claims he has a shortcut for deciding what kind of roots a functions has. Jolene disagrees. She says you just have to solve the quadratic equation to find out. They are working on $y = x^2 - 5x - 14$.

Jolene says, "See, I just start out by trying to factor. This one can be factored $(x - 7)(x + 2) = 0$ so the equation will have two real solutions and the function will have two real roots."

"But what if it can't be factored?" Raul asked. "What about $x^2 + 2x + 2 = 0$?"

"That's easy, I just use the Quadratic Formula," said Jolene. "And I get,...let's see, negative two plus or minus the square root of...two squared, that's 4, minus...eight..."

"Wait!" Raul interrupted. "Right there, see, you don't have to finish. 2^2 minus $4 \cdot 2$, that gives you -4. That's all you need to know. You'll be taking the square root of a negative number so you will get a complex result."

"Oh, I see," said Jolene. "I only have to do <u>part</u> of the solution, the part you have to take the square root of."

Use Raul's method to tell whether the each following functions has real or complex roots.

a) $y = 2x^2 + 5x + 4$ b) $y = 2x^2 + 5x - 3$

CF-115. Consider this geometric sequence: $i^0, i^1, i^2, i^3, i^4, i^5, ..., i^{15}$

a)   You know that $i^0 = 1$, and $i^1 = i$, and $i^2 = -1$. Calculate the result for each term up to i^{15}, and organize your answers so a pattern is obvious.

b)   Use the pattern you found in part (a) to calculate $i^{396}, i^{397}, i^{398}$, and i^{399}.

CF-116. Use the pattern from the previous problem to help you to evaluate the following:

a) $i^{592} =$ b) $i^{797} =$ c) $i^{10,648,202} =$

CF-117. Describe how you would evaluate i^n where n could be any integer.

CF-118. The management of the Carnival Cinema was worried about breaking even on their movie ELVIS RETURNS FROM MARS. To break even they had to take in $5000 on the matinee. They were selling adult tickets for $8.50 and children's tickets for $5.00. They knew they had sold a total of 685 tickets. How many of those would have to have been adult tickets for them to meet their goal?

CF-119. Sketch graphs of each of the following polynomial functions. Be sure to label the x- and y-intercepts:

a) $y = x(2x + 5)(2x - 7)$

b) $y = (15 - 2x)^2(x + 3)$

CF-120. Multiply each of the following:

a) $(x - 3)^2$

b) $2(x + 3)^2$

c) $(a - b)(a^2 + ab + b^2)$

CF-121. Show that each of the following is true:

a) $(i - 3)^2 = 8 - 6i$

b) $(2i - 1)(3i + 1) = -7 - i$

c) $(3 - 2i)(2i + 3) = 13$

CF-122.   The Mathamericaland Carnival Company wants to make a special game to premiere at this year's county fair. The game will consist of a tank filled with ping pong balls. Most are ordinary white ones, but there are a limited number of orange, red, blue, and green prize ping pong balls. The blue ones have a prize value of $2, the red ones $5, the orange ones $20, and the green ping pong ball (there's only one) is worth $1000. There are 1000 blue ping pong balls, 500 red balls, and 100 orange balls. Fairgoers will pay $1 for the opportunity to crawl around in the tank for a set amount of time while blindfolded, trying to find one of the colored ping pong balls.

The owner of the company thinks that she will make the most profit if the tank has maximum volume. In order to cut down on the labor and materials costs of building this new game, she hires you to find out what shape to make the tank.

The tank will be rectangular, open at the top, and will be made by cutting squares out of each corner of an 8.5 meter by 11 meter sheet of specially processed, heavy-duty transparent material.

We can model this problem by using a sheet of paper. You will need to write a report with your findings to the Carnival Company. The report needs to include the following:

a)   The data and conjectures found in the experiment making the paper tanks.

b)   A well drawn diagram of the tank with the dimensions clearly labeled with appropriate variables.

c)   A graph of the volume function that you found with notes on a reasonable domain and range.

d)   An equation that matches your graph.

e)   An estimate of the number of ping pong balls that will be needed and your adjusted recommendation based on this information.

f)   Your final conclusions and observations.

The following problems (CF-123 through CF-128) will help guide you through the various aspects of the project.

CF-123. Use a full sheet of 8-1/2" x 11" paper, which is the same shape as the material for the tank (at a slightly smaller scale!). Each member of your team should cut a different size square out of each corner. Measure the side of the square you cut out and write along the edge of the large piece of paper. Use either inches or centimeters. Your paper should look like the figure at right:

Fold the paper up into an open box (fold on the dotted lines). Then tape the cut parts together so that the box holds its shape. Measure the dimensions of the tank. Record the dimensions directly on the model tank.

CF-124. Make a table like the one below, then calculate the volume of your tank, write it on the tank, and record all of the data in your table. Next, add the data from each of the other members of your team to your table. Finally, get the data from four more students, possibly by having pairs of teams exchange data. Make sure that you consider "extreme" tanks, the ones with the largest possible cutout and the smallest possible cutout (do not actually try to build them; that would be physically impossible. You cannot cut a square that is 1/100th of an inch on a side, but you can **imagine** cutting a square out of each corner zero inches on a side.)

Tank height	Tank width	Tank length	Tank volume

a) Discuss with the other members of your team (experimenting if you wish) what happens if the cutouts are not square.

b) Examine the data in the table from the different sizes of cutout squares and discuss it with your team. Make some conjectures about how to find the maximum volume.

c) Label the height as x. Using x for the height, find expressions for the length and the width.

d) Find an equation for the volume of the tank.

e) Sketch the graph of your function by using the roots and determining the orientation.

CF-125. Graph the function on your calculator. Make sure you find appropriate values for the range on the graphing calculator.

a) Make a large accurate graph on graph paper with appropriate labels. Locate and label the points from your data table on the graph. (What did 'x' represent?)

b) Find the maximum for the volume and the dimensions of the tank that will generate this volume.

CF-126. Use your graph and your tank model to carefully answer the following questions.

a) Which points on the graph represent tanks which can actually be made? Explain.

b) How are the dimensions of the tank related? In other words, what happens to the length and width as the height increases?

c) Make a drawing of your tank. (You may want to use isometric dot paper.) Label your drawing with its dimensions and its volume.

CF-127. The carnival company decides to follow your recommendation on the dimensions of the tank and to fill the tank to a depth of 1.2 meters in order to avoid losing the ping pong balls that might bounce out. At the retail price of six for $2 the ping pong balls would cost a fortune, but the carnival owners have found a bargain on army surplus ping pong balls at $20 per case of 1000. A standard ping pong ball has a diameter of 3.7 cm (1.45 inches). Estimate the number of ping pong balls they will need and the cost.

CF-128. The company realizes that it was overly ambitious (or greedy) in planning a tank with maximum dimensions. They have only budgeted $8000 for ping pong balls. They decide to reduce the size of the tank, but keep the tank proportions the same.

a) Find the dimensions of the reduced tank, if the new height is 1.2 meters.

b) The company decides that it will only fill the new tank to a level 0.4 meters below the top, to keep the balls from bouncing out. Can they fill the new tank with ping pong balls to a level of 0.8 meters for under $8000?

c) Based on your scaled down tank, what is the probability of winning a prize?

CF-129. A polynomial function has the equation: $P(x) = x(x - 3)^2(2x + 1)$. What are the x-intercepts?

CF-130. Sketch a graph of a fourth-degree polynomial that has no real roots.

CF-131. In this unit you have learned that the roots of a polynomial correspond to its linear factors; for each root $x = a$ there is a factor $(x - a)$ and vice versa. This makes sense to Elijah, but one day he found himself puzzled.

"Can you factor $x^2 + 4x + 1$?" he asked his friend Kelly.

"Let me see. . .two numbers that multiply to make 1 and add up to 4? Don't think so!" he said.

"But look what happens when I graph it. It crosses the x-axis in two places, so it must have two linear factors, right?"

"It should. Let's see what the roots are."

a) Find the roots of Elijah's equation as accurately as you can.

b) Using what you have learned in this unit, what should be the factors of $x^2 + 4x + 1$?

"Wow," said Kelly, "It works! There *are* two numbers that multiply to make 1 and add up to 4."

c) What are the numbers to which Kelly is referring?

In the past, when you were asked to factor, it was understood that you were only to use integers as the coefficients in your factors. This restriction meant that many expressions were unfactorable. If we allow other numbers (such as fractions and irrationals) as coefficients, many more expressions can be factored. In fact, if we allow complex numbers as coefficients, every quadratic polynomial can be factored!

Use Kelly and Elijah's method to factor the following polynomials:

d) $x^2 - 10$

e) $x^2 - 3x - 7$

f) $x^2 + 4$

g) $x^2 - 2x + 2$

CF-132. Draw a unit circle (that's a circle with radius 1) centered at the origin.

a) Find the circumference of the circle. Keep your answer in terms of π.

b) What is the length of the arc that lies in the first quadrant? Answer in terms of π.

c) What is the measure of the angle formed by the positive x- and y-axes?

d) What is the length of the arc that lies in the first and second quadrants?

e) What is the measure of the angle that forms the arc?

f) Suppose the arc has length 2π. What is the measure of the angle that forms the arc?

CF-133. Sketch a graph of the following system: $x^2 + y^2 \le 25$
$x - 2y > 5$

CF-134. **PORTFOLIO: GROWTH OVER TIME—PROBLEM #1**

On a separate piece of paper (so you can hand it in separately or add it to your portfolio) explain **everything** that you now know about the function below. Be sure to add everything that you have learned since the last time you did this problem, and don't leave out any important information that you included in your earlier attempts.

$$f(x) = x^2 - 4 \quad \text{and} \quad g(x) = \sqrt{x + 4}.$$

CF-135. Growth Over Time Reflection. Look at your three responses to the growth-over-time problem above. Write an evaluation of your growth based your responses. Consider the following when writing your answer:

a) What new concepts did you include the second time you did the problem? In what ways was your response better than your first attempt?

b) How was your final version different from the first two? What new ideas did you include?

c) Did you omit anything in the final version that you used in one of the earlier problems? Why did you omit that item?

d) Rate your three attempts by making three bars like those below and shading each bar to represent how much you knew on each attempt.

First Attempt:	
Second Attempt:	
Final Attempt:	

e) Is there anything you would add to your most recent version? What would it be? Discuss this with your team.

CF-136. Consider the equation $x^2 = 2^x$. Use inspection and a graphing calculator to answer:

a) How many solutions does the equation have?

b) What are the solutions?

CF-137. A polynomial function has the equation $y = ax(x - 3)(x + 1)^2$ and goes through the point (2, 12). Use the coordinates of the point to figure out what 'a' must equal and write the specific equation.

CF-138. **Unit 7 Summary Assignment**

Identify with your team five main topics from this unit. For each topic, rewrite or create a problem that represents the main ideas in that topic. Carefully solve and explain the solution to each of those five problems so that someone else, someone who didn't know what to do, could use these problems and solutions as example problems to help them through the unit. This should be done on a separate sheet of paper to be included with your portfolio.

CF-139. Find the width of the river in the figure at right if AB is 33 meters.

CF-140. Verify that $x = -2 + 5i$ is a root of the quadratic function $y = x^2 + 4x + 29$.

CF-141. Carmel picks an integer from 1 to 12 as a value for c in the equation $y = x^2 + 4x + c$. What is the probability that his equation will have complex roots?

CF-142. A parabola has intercepts at $x = 2$, $x = -4$, and $y = 4$. What is the equation of the parabola? There are at least three ways to solve this problem. Show as many ways as you can.

CF-143. Solve each of the following quadratic equations.

a) $x^2 - 4x + 3 = 0$

b) $x^2 - 8x + 25 = 0$

c) $x^2 - 4x + 20 = 0$

d) $x^2 + 100 = 0$

CF-144. Write an explanation, including an example, of how to find out what f^{-1} does to x if you know what f does to x.

CF-145.   Find the point where the graph of $y = 2^x + 5$ will intersect the line $y = 50$. Find your answer to three decimal places.

CF-146.   Write equations for these circles:

a)   center (9, -3), radius 4

b)   center (-5, 0), radius $\sqrt{23}$

COURSE SUMMARY

CF-147.   **Course Summary Assignment**

Identify with your team at least six, but no more than ten big ideas from units 1-7. After describing each big idea, rewrite or create one or two problems that illustrate the main point(s). Just as you did in the Unit Summaries, solve and explain the solution to each of these problems. This should also to be done separately from your homework and should be included with your portfolio.

CF-148.   You are given the equation $ax^2 + bx + c = 0$.

a)   What are the roots of this equation?

b)   What part of the equation determines whether they are real or complex roots?

c)   When will the roots be real?

d)   When will the roots be complex numbers?

For any quadratic equation $ax^2 + bx + c = 0$, you can determine whether the roots are real or complex by examining the value of $b^2 - 4ac$, known as the **DISCRIMINANT**. The roots are real when $b^2 - 4ac \geq 0$ and complex when $b^2 - 4ac < 0$.

CF-149.   Solve for x and y in each of the following systems:

a) $2x + y = 12$
       $xy = 16$

b) $y = -2x + 12$
       $xy = 20$

c)   What is the difference between the graphs of the two systems? (If you are not sure, you may want to graph them.)

CF-150. Farmer Ted grows alfalfa and he has been losing more of his crop each month because of the growth of the rabbit population. Ted has been advised to have the rabbits destroyed, but he feels he can simply increase his production to compensate for the alfalfa destroyed by the rabbits. Currently Ted produces 600 tons of alfalfa each month and he plans to increase his production by 5 tons each month. Last month the rabbits destroyed 3 tons of the crop. The rabbit population around Ted's farm is increasing by 15% each month. If Ted allows the rabbits to continue to destroy part of his crop, at what point will they eat everything he produces? Write a system of equations to represent his dilemma and estimate how long it will take.

CF-151. A fifth-degree polynomial has exactly two x-intercepts. What does this tell you about the roots of the function? Try sketching several different examples.

CF-152. By looking at the graph of the function at right:

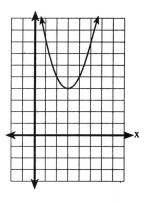

a) What can you tell about the roots?

b) What is the equation of the function if the y-intercept is 13?

c) Find the roots of the function you found in part (b).

d) Find the average of the roots. How does it relate to the equation?

e) Using the domain $1 \leq x \leq 4$, what are the maximum and minimum values of the function?

CF-153. Explain what the relationship is between the solutions of $3x = x^2 + 5x$ and the x-values where the graphs of $y = 3x$ and $y = x^2 + 5x$ intersect.

CF-154. If a system of equations has only complex number solutions, what do we know about the graphs of the equations?

CF-155. Judy claims that since $(xy)^4$ is x^4y^4, it must be true that $(x + y)^4$ is $x^4 + y^4$. What do you think? Explain your reasoning.

CF-156. Write the equation for the circle with center (-4, 7) that is tangent to the y-axis. Sketching a graph will help.

CF-157. If $f(x) = \frac{1}{2}\sqrt{3(x-1)} + 5$, then $f^{-1}(x) = ?$

CF-158. **TOOL KIT CHECK-UP**

Your Tool Kit contains reference tools for algebra. Return to your Tool Kit entries. You may need to revise or add entries.

Be sure that your Tool Kit contains entries for all of the items listed below. Add any topics that are missing to your Tool Kit NOW, as well as any other items that will help you in your study of algebra.

- Roots/Zeros of a Function
- Polynomial and Degree
- Amplitude and Period
- Unit Circle

- Complex Numbers
- Complex Plane
- Complex Conjugates
- Discriminant

UNIT 8

The Circle of Terror
CIRCULAR FUNCTIONS

Unit 8 Objectives
The Circle of Terror: CIRCULAR FUNCTIONS

What do all of the following situations have
in common?

- pedaling a bicycle
- the motion of the tides
- riding a Ferris Wheel
- your heartbeat
- the orbit of the Space Shuttle
- the length of each day (sunrise to sunset) as
  we move through the year from January to
  December
- the motion of a bouncing spring

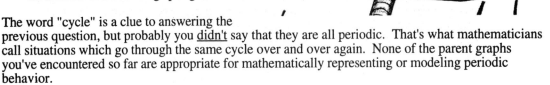

The word "cycle" is a clue to answering the
previous question, but probably you <u>didn't</u> say that they are all periodic. That's what mathematicians
call situations which go through the same cycle over and over again. None of the parent graphs
you've encountered so far are appropriate for mathematically representing or modeling periodic
behavior.

In this unit, before pedaling your bicycle off into the sunset, you will have the opportunity to:

- use a circle to create some very important cyclic curves.

- become familiar with the Parent Graphs of circular functions.

- use what you know about Parent Graphs and translating, compressing, or expanding
  their graphs to model a variety of situations.

- learn how "DEG" and "RAD" on your calculator are related to each other and explain that
  relationship.

The theme problem for this unit includes gathering data on an imaginary amusement park ride. You
will ride with Sally and Steve for several days in order to develop some very important and useful
ideas about circular functions. Read the problem below, then go on to problem CT-1.

CT-0.　　**THE CIRCLE OF TERROR** Great Hemisphere Amusement Park has a new
　　　　　ride for the new century. The Circle of Terror is a circular track, half above
　　　　　ground and half below. The track rises to a height of 1 kilometer and descends to
　　　　　a depth 1 km below the ground. Sally dares Steve to try it. Steve boards the ride
　　　　　at ground level, buckles in, and glances up to see a display that says, "ALTITUDE
　　　　　0 km." As the ride begins, he clutches the rail in front of him and focuses on the
　　　　　track ahead. Is there a relationship between the height of his seat and the distance
　　　　　he has traveled on the circular track?

PROBLEM SOLVING

REPRESENTATION/MODELING

FUNCTIONS/GRAPHING

INTERSECTIONS/SYSTEMS

ALGORITHMS

REASONING/COMMUNICATION

Unit 8
The Circle of Terror: CIRCULAR FUNCTIONS

THE CIRCLE OF TERROR (PART 1)

CT-1.　It's January 1, 2100, and Great Hemisphere Amusement Park has a new ride for the new century: The Circle of Terror. It is on a circular track, half above ground and half below, and it rises to a height of 1 kilometer and descends to a depth 1 km below the ground. Sally dares Steve to try it. Steve boards the ride at ground level and glances up to see a display that says, "ALTITUDE 0 km." As the ride begins, Steve

clutches the rail in front of him and focuses on the track ahead. He notices that the distance along the track is marked every kilometer, and to distract himself from his rising anxiety he begins to pay attention to the relationship between the distance he's traveled along the track and the altitude above or below ground level displayed on the panel overhead. At home later he found himself wondering about the relationship he observed while on the ride.

a)　Is the relationship between the distance traveled and the altitude a function? Does it matter which quantity is the independent variable and which is the dependent?

b)　There are four points at which you know Steve's exact altitude. What are they, and how far had he traveled when he was at each of those altitudes? Use your knowledge of circles to express these distances in exact form.

c)　Make a table of values for the function Steve observed. Use the diagram on the resource page provided to estimate Steve's altitude at the distances indicated and include the four points you found in part (b). Use negative numbers to represent altitude below ground level.

Steve's View

d)　We'll call Steve's function $S(x)$. Continue investigating this function. Be sure to include **all** of the usual information involved with investigating functions.

CT-2. Steve brought his investigation to school the next day. He wanted to convince his teacher that riding the "Circle" had been a mathematical experience. Sally looked at Steve's table of values for his function and decided to challenge him (she knew he didn't have a formula for his function).

    a) "So, what's $S(5.5)$?" she asked. Use the graph you made in problem CT-1 to estimate this value. Then describe what this tells about the Circle of Terror ride.

    b) Undaunted, Sally tried again. "Solve the equation $S(x) = \frac{1}{2}$," she said. Use your graph to solve Sally's equation.

    c) Explain what the solution(s) to this equation tell about the Circle of Terror.

CT-3. While Steve was presenting his investigation to the class, Sally interrupted, saying, "But we've already seen that kind of function. It's a third degree polynomial!"

    a) Explain why Sally might think $S(x)$ is a third-degree polynomial. Find a possible equation of the third-degree polynomial that looks like $S(x)$ on the domain of Steve's graph. Do you think that is the equation of $S(x)$? Why or why not?

    b) Cynthia thought $S(x)$ was made by gluing together two semi-circles. Do you agree? Why or why not?

CT-4. What is a Unit Circle? What is its equation? Check your Tool Kit if you don't remember.

CT-5. This problem is the Milepost problem for completing the square and stating the locator point of a parabola.

Write the equation in graphing form and sketch a graph of $y = 2x^2 - 4x + 5$. Then label the coordinates of all intercepts and write the equation of its line of symmetry.

CT-6. Find the equation of the parabola that passes through the points $(0, 0)$, $(3, 9)$, and $(6, 0)$.

CT-7. Find the inverse functions for:

    a) $y = \sqrt[3]{4x - 1}$ b) $y = \log_7 x$

CT-8. Find the x- and y-intercepts of $y - 7 = 3^{(x+4)}$.

CT-9.   Copy the triangles at right.

a)   Finish labeling the lengths of the sides.
      Use radical form to give exact values.

b)   The 30-60-90 triangle is also called a
      half-equilateral. Draw a picture to
      illustrate this, and explain how it can be
      used to help label the missing sides in part (a).

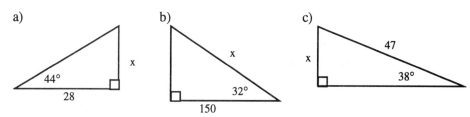

CT-10.   In each of the following triangles, find the length of the side labeled x:

a)   b)   c)

CT-11.   Calculate $(2 + i)(3 - 5i) - (1 - 4i)^2$.

THE CIRCLE OF TERROR (PART II)

CT-12.   Steve was now more
          curious than ever about his
          Circle of Terror
          investigation. He decided
          that his data was incomplete.
          Ignoring the queasiness he
          still felt from yesterday's
          adventure, Steve decided to
          head for the park and ride
          the "Circle" again to gather
          more information. He paid
          the ride operator double to
          allow him to make **two**
          complete circles instead of
          the usual one.

Reluctantly, Steve boarded the ride for the second time. To his relief, he noticed that the
data he collected for the first rotation of the ride had not changed. However, now, after
one complete rotation, he had to be careful. Help Steve out. He's terrified, his head is
spinning, and he must concentrate to collect the correct data.

a)   After one complete rotation, how far has he traveled along the track? (Give both the
      approximate and the exact distance.)

>>Problem continues on the next page.>>

b) After one complete rotation, what is his altitude?

c) When he passes the **1 km** marker for the second time, how far has he really traveled along the track? What is his altitude?

d) Continue the table of values of $S(x)$ to include the following values of x:
$2\pi + 1$, $2\pi + 2$, $2\pi + 3$, $2\pi + 4$, $2\pi + 5$, $2\pi + 6$, 2.5π, 3π, 3.5π, 4π.

e) On the resource page make a new graph of $S(x)$ that shows the data for distance traveled and altitude for Steve's second ride.

f) How does the new graph compare to the original one?

CT-13. Steve was excited with his findings and shared his new data with his classmate Sally. Intrigued by the investigation, Sally volunteered to gather more data. "Instead of going for a third rotation, I want to try something different," she said, " I wonder if the Circle of Terror goes in reverse?" "Oh no," said Steve. "That will make everything confusing. How will we be able to tell which points were collected when the ride was going forward, and which were taken when the ride is traveling in reverse?" "Simple," stated Sally. "We'll use negative numbers to represent distance traveled in the opposite direction." After talking with the ride operator, Sally climbed into a seat and made one complete revolution going in reverse.

Sally found that the ride was built to go in both directions, so there were also distance markers facing her as she went around in reverse. On the diagram on your resource page, add dots to show the distances around the circle as she traveled in reverse. Make a table of values that shows Sally's distances and altitudes using the opposites of all the x values you used in problem CT-1. Extend your graph from the previous problem to include these points.

CT-14. What is the domain of the entire graph of $S(x)$?

CT-15. Suppose we extend $S(x)$ to include all possible distances traveled along the track, in either direction, and the resulting altitudes.

a) Describe what this graph would look like.

b) The question Sally raised in problem CT-3 is an important one: could $S(x)$ be an example of any of the functions we know already? Explain why $S(x)$ cannot be a polynomial function.

CT-16.

A function like $S(x)$, which repeats the same pattern endlessly in both directions, is called a **PERIODIC FUNCTION**. The function pictured in problem CF-45 is also a periodic function, assuming that the pattern continues forever to the left and right. Add **periodic function** to your Tool Kit, and make sure you also have the definitions of **period** and **amplitude** from problem CF-45.

a) What is the period of $S(x)$?   b) What is the amplitude?

CT-17.   Copy the triangles and label the missing side lengths.

CT-18.   Find the measure of angle A.

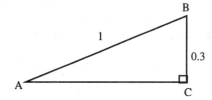

CT-19.   State the degree of $f(x) = (x + 4)(x + 1)^2(x - 2)$, then sketch its graph.

CT-20.   Find the equation of a polynomial that has the roots 3, 2, and -1 and goes through the point (1, 1).

CT-21.   On her way back from the amusement park Sally was going 80 miles per hour when she passed a parked highway patrol car. By the time she was half a mile past the patrol car, the officer was chasing her at 100 miles per hour. If these rates remain constant, how long did it take the officer to overtake Sally? Write an equation to represent this situation.

EVALUATING THE S(X) FUNCTION

CT-22.   **INTRODUCTION**

$S(x)$ will turn out to be a very important function, so you need to learn more about how the input and output values are related. You may already be irritated by the fact that you had to estimate from a diagram in order to make tables of values. In the next few problems you will learn how you can use your calculator to be more precise. You'll also discover a very close relationship between $S(x)$ and trigonometry.

To begin, evaluate $S(\frac{\pi}{3})$. (This may seem like a difficult number to use for x, but it turns out to be easier than numbers like 1 or 2.) The first thing you'll need to do is figure out where you are when you have traveled $\frac{\pi}{3}$ km around the circle. You already know that π km takes you around the upper semi-circle. Now see if you can find $S(\frac{\pi}{3})$. If you are not sure how to start, complete the steps below.

a)   On the diagram of the Circle of Terror on the resource page, find the point $\frac{\pi}{3}$ km around the circle. (Recall that $\frac{\pi}{3}$ is the same as $\frac{1}{3}$ of π.) Label this point A. If we think of the Circle of Terror diagram as a graph on a set of xy-axes with its center at the origin, what is $S(\frac{\pi}{3})$ in relation to the point A?

b)   Draw the line segment connecting point A to the center of the circle. What is the measure of the angle formed by that line segment and the x-axis? (Remember that you have traveled one-third of the way around the upper semi-circle. How many degrees are in the semi-circle?) Now can you find $S(\frac{\pi}{3})$?

c)   Next draw the line segment from point A straight down to the x-axis. The length of that segment is the value of $S(\frac{\pi}{3})$. Use your knowledge of trigonometric ratios to find that length. Use the diagram on your resource page to make sure your answer is reasonable.

CT-23.   Use the process from the previous problem to calculate $S(\frac{3\pi}{4})$. Again, $\frac{3\pi}{4}$ may seem like a strange number to use for x, but it turns out that numbers like this, expressed as multiples of π, are the distances around the circle that lead to central angles with convenient numbers for their measures. Remember that $\frac{3\pi}{4}$ is the same as $\frac{3}{4}\pi$ and that $x = \pi$ corresponds to traveling half way around the circle. Use the unit circle (on the resource page) which is divided into eighths.

CT-24. Now find the precise value of $S(1)$. If you are not sure how to begin, complete the following steps.

    a)   Write a fraction that represents the portion of the upper half of the Circle of Terror that Steve had covered when he passed the 1 km point.

    b)   Draw the line segment from the center to the point at the 1 km mark. Use your fraction from part (a) to find the angle between the x-axis and this segment. Don't forget there are $180°$ in the semi-circle.

    c)   What trigonometric ratio relates this angle to the y-coordinate (i.e. height) of the point at the 1 km mark? Explain how to use your calculator to find $S(1)$.

CT-25. You may have realized that you could find the value of $S(\frac{\pi}{3})$ without using trigonometry, once you found the measure of the central angle, because the triangle formed is one of the "special" right triangles. Show how to use a special triangle with hypotenuse equal to 1 (see problem CT-17) to find $S(\frac{\pi}{3})$.

CT-26. Calculate:

    a) $S(\frac{\pi}{4})$ b) $S(\frac{2\pi}{3})$

CT-27. Calculate:

    a) $S(4)$ b) $S(\frac{4\pi}{3})$

CT-28. In problem CT-2 you used the graph of $S(x)$ to approximate the solutions to $S(x) = 0.5$. Use the sine ratio or special right triangles to find the exact values of those solutions.

CT-29.   Complete the table of values for $f(x) = \dfrac{x^2 + 4x - 5}{x - 1}$.

x	-2	-1	0	1	2	3
y						

a)   Graph the points. What kind of function does it appear to be? Why is it not correct to connect all the dots?

b)   Look for a simple pattern for the values in the table. What appears to be the relationship between x and y? Calculate f(0.9) and f(1.1), and add the points to your graph. Is there an asymptote at x = 1? If you're not sure, calculate f(0.99) and f(1.01), also.

c)   Simplify the formula for f(x). What do you think the complete graph looks like?

CT-30.   The measure of ∠ROS in Δ ROS is 60°.

a)   The curved arrow represents the rotation of $\overline{OR}$, beginning at the positive x-axis. Through how many degrees has $\overline{OR}$ rotated?

Use the special right triangle relationships to give exact answers for the following in radical form.

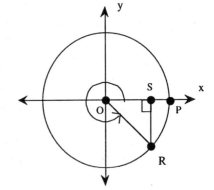

b)   If OR = 1, what is OS? SR?

c)   What are the coordinates of point R?

d)   Find the distance around the circle, traveling counterclockwise, from P to R. Now find S(x) for that value.

CT-31.   In 1998, Terre Haute, Indiana had a population of 72,000 people. In 2000, the population had dropped to 70,379. The city officials expect the population to eventually level off at 60,000.

a)   What kind of function would best model the population over time?

b)   Write an equation that would model the population.

CT-32.   A semi-circular tunnel is 26 feet high. A road 48 feet wide is centered under the tunnel. Bruce needs to move a house on a trailer through the tunnel. The load is 22 feet wide and 24 feet high. Will he make it? Draw a diagram and explain why or why not. Show all your work.

CT-33. Mr. Ron Keis, math teacher extraordinaire, loves challenging his talented Algebra 2 students. He writes the following problem on the board and tells his class, "No calculators please. Simplify. You have thirty seconds!"

$$\left(\frac{13^{12}}{14^{23}}\right)\left(\frac{27^3}{13^{11}}\right)\left(\frac{2^{10}}{27^4}\right)\left(\frac{14^{22}}{13}\right)\left(\frac{27}{2^9}\right)$$

Time yourself and simplify the expression. What is the answer? Did you meet the challenge?

CT-34. Verify that $3 + i\sqrt{2}$ is a solution of $x^2 - 6x + 11 = 0$.

SINE: A NEW PARENT GRAPH

CT-35. In previous problems you uncovered a relationship between the function $S(x)$ and the sine ratio you use to solve triangles. Each value of x leads to a point on the unit circle (radius = 1) and that point determines a central angle of the circle. The Greek letter θ (pronounced "theta") is commonly used to represent the measure of this angle.

a) Explain how to find θ when you know x.

b) Explain how to find $S(x)$ when you know θ. You will need to adjust your rule for each quadrant of the graph.

CT-36.

> The fact that values of $S(x)$ can be found from the sines of angles reveals the connection between the function $S(x)$ and the sine ratio. Because of this, the official name of the function $S(x)$ is the **SINE FUNCTION**, abbreviated **SIN X**, and in fact the sin key on a calculator can be used to find values of $S(x)$ directly for any value of x. However, the sin key operates in two different modes. You are familiar with the **degree mode**, and this mode is used to find missing sides and angles of triangles (though you will find later that it also can be used on the unit circle.)
>
> The mode that tells your calculator to interpret x as a distance traveled around the unit circle is called **RADIAN MODE**. Enter this in your Tool Kit, and make sure you know how to set the mode of your calculator. When your calculator is in radian mode, the sin key represents exactly the function we have been calling $S(x)$. Put your calculator in radian mode, and use it to check some of the entries in the table of values you made in problem CT-1.

CT-37. Take out your Parent Graph Tool Kit. Add **y = sin x**. Remember to include statements about domain and range, intercepts, asymptotes, symmetry, period, amplitude, etc. Sin x is the parent graph for most periodic (i.e. cyclic or infinitely repetitive) behavior. Not only does sin x go back and forth, changing directions at regular intervals, but it does so in a way that mirrors cyclic behavior in the physical world.

a) Imagine a pendulum swinging back and forth, or a train that shuttles between two stations, changing direction without turning around, or an athlete doing wind sprints in a gym, running back and forth as fast as he can and stopping at each end to touch the line on the floor. Where in its cycle will each of these back-and-forth travelers be going the fastest? Why? What must each of them do as they approach a turn-around point? What will they do just after they change directions?

b) Now look at your graph of sin x, and think about riding the Circle of Terror. When is the height, relative to the distance traveled, changing the fastest? How can you see this on the graph? When is the height changing slowly? How can you see that on the graph?

c)

> The periodic functions you are learning about in this unit are called
> **CIRCULAR FUNCTIONS**. Why do you think sine is called a circular function?

CT-38. Imagine the graph y = sin x shifted up one unit.

a) Sketch what it would look like.

b) What do you have to change in the equation y = sin x to move the graph up one unit? Write the new equation.

c) What are the intercepts of your new equation? Label them with their coordinates on the graph. It may help to look at the graph from problem CT-12 and imagine shifting it up one unit.

d) When you listed intercepts in part (c), did you list more than one x-intercept? Should you have?

CT-39. The graph at right was made by shifting one cycle of $y = \sin x$ over to the left.

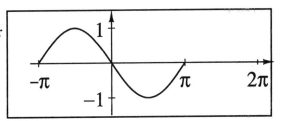

a) How many units to the left was it shifted?

b) Figure out how to change the equation of $y = \sin x$ so that the graph of the new equation will look like the one in part (a). Keep in mind that you may need to change the viewing window. If you don't have a graphing calculator at home, sketch the graph and check your answer when you get to class.

CT-40. You have seen that you can calculate values of the sine function (formerly known as $S(x)$) using right triangles formed by the radius of the unit circle. Values of x that result in 30°- 60°- 90° or 45°- 45°- 90° triangles are used very frequently on exercises and tests because their sines can be found exactly without a calculator. You should learn to recognize these values of x and find their corresponding central angles quickly and easily. The same is true for values of x that correspond to the x- and y-intercepts of the unit circle.

The central angles that correspond to these "special" values of x are: 30°, 45°, 60°, 90°, 120°, 135°, 150°, 180°, 210°, 225°, 240°, 270°, 300°, 315°, and 330°. What these angles have in common is that they are all multiples of 30° or 45°, and some of them are also multiples of 60° or 90°.

a) You already know that $x = \pi$ corresponds to $\theta = 180°$. So $\frac{\pi}{2}$, which is half of π, corresponds to 90°, and $\frac{\pi}{4}$, which is half of $\frac{\pi}{2}$, corresponds to 45°. Similarly, $\frac{\pi}{3}$, which is one-third of π, corresponds to 60°, and $\frac{\pi}{6}$, which is half of $\frac{\pi}{3}$, corresponds to 30°. Since all the special angles are multiples of 30°, 45°, 60°, or 90°, all the special values of x are multiples of $\frac{\pi}{6}$, $\frac{\pi}{4}$, $\frac{\pi}{3}$, or $\frac{\pi}{2}$. Thus, you can recognize a special value of x because it will have a multiple of π in the numerator, and 2, 3, 4, or 6 as its denominator. To find the corresponding angle for one of these values of x, think of the fraction as a whole number times $\frac{\pi}{6}$, $\frac{\pi}{4}$, $\frac{\pi}{3}$, or $\frac{\pi}{2}$, and then replace the fraction with its corresponding angle measure. For example: $\frac{5\pi}{6} = 5(\frac{\pi}{6}) \Rightarrow 5\ (30°) = 150°$.

b) Copy and complete the table below. Try to do the calculations in your head.

x	$\frac{5\pi}{6}$	$\frac{2\pi}{3}$	$\frac{3\pi}{4}$	$\frac{4\pi}{3}$	$\frac{7\pi}{6}$	$\frac{11\pi}{6}$
θ	150°					

CT-41.   Graph the system at right: $1 + x - y \geq 3x - 2y - 4$

$$y < 2x^2 + 1$$

CT-42.   Some function W(x) is sketched at right.
Make your own copy, then sketch the graph
of the inverse of W(x).

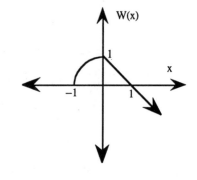

a)   Is the inverse a function?

b)   Explain.

CT-43.   Solve for x: $\dfrac{1}{ax} + \dfrac{1}{b} = \dfrac{1}{x}$

CT-44.   While trying to measure the height of a tree, Julie noticed that a 3.5 foot post had a 4.25 foot shadow. If the tree's shadow is 100 feet long, how tall is the tree?

CT-45.   Show and explain why the equation $2^x = 5 - x$ has only one real solution.

CT-46. Sketch a graph of at least one cycle of $y = \sin x$. Label the intercepts. With your team:

a) Write an equation whose parent graph is $y = \sin x$, but is:

   i) shifted 3 units up.   ii) reflected across the x-axis.

   iii) shifted 2 units to the right.   iv) vertically stretched.

b) Check your answers to part (a) with your graphing calculator. Then sketch each graph and label it with its equation. **For each sketch**, include the points that represent:

   i) the locator point (the start of the first cycle);

   ii) the end of the first cycle;

   iii) the middle point of the first cycle;

   iv) the point one quarter of the way through the first cycle (halfway between the first point and the middle point); and

   v) the point three quarters of the way through the first cycle (halfway between the middle point and the last point). This is important. Don't rush through it.

Note: We call the steps above the **FIVE-POINT METHOD** for graphing periodic functions. Here is how it looks when applied to $y = \sin x$:

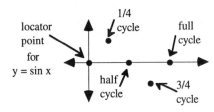

c) Write a general equation for $y = \sin x$. Explain what each letter that you use represents or how it affects the graph.

d) Add these examples to your Tool Kit. Be sure to list the five key points for each.

$$y = \sin\left(x + \frac{\pi}{3}\right) \quad \text{and} \quad y = \sin(x - 1)$$

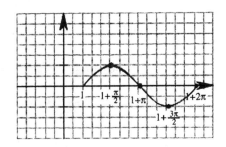

CT-47. Use the five point method to sketch each of the following graphs without using your graphing calculator. Label the coordinates of all five points.

a) $y = \sin\left(x + \frac{\pi}{4}\right)$

b) $y = -2 \sin (x - 1) + 0.5$

c) $y = 3 \sin (x + \frac{\pi}{3}) - 2$

d) $y = a \sin (x - h) + k$ (Put the locator at a random point and label the other four points in terms of h and k.)

CT-48. Find an equation for each graph:

a)

b)

c)

d)

CT-49. Great Hemisphere Amusement Park has a crisis. Government inspectors have shut down the Circle of Terror out of fear that it could collapse during an earthquake. The park has decided to rebuild the ride so that most of it is underground. The center of the circle will be one-half km underground and passengers will ride an elevator 1.5 km underground in order to board at the lowest point. As before, there will be markers visible to show how far you have traveled from your starting point and a digital read-out to tell your altitude relative to ground level. Once again, altitude is a function of distance traveled from the starting point. Make a sketch of this function and then write a formula for it.

CT-50. What central angle corresponds to a distance around the unit circle of $x = \frac{7\pi}{3}$? What other value of x takes you to the same point on the circle? Make a sketch of the unit circle showing the resulting right triangle and use what you know about special right triangle to find $\sin(\frac{7\pi}{3})$ exactly.

CT-51. Suppose you were to bend two whole sheets of $8\frac{1}{2} \times 11$ paper to form two cylinders (a tall, skinny one and a short, wide one).

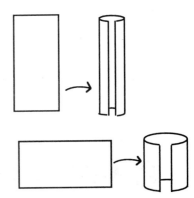

a) Do the two cylinders have the same volume? Prove your answer.

b) Is the result different if you start with $8\frac{1}{2} \times 8\frac{1}{2}$ paper?

CT-52. Here is a sequence of doodles, with some numbers to go with them:

| 180 | 120 | 90 | 72 |

a) Draw the next two, and write the numbers to go with them.

b) What number would go with the 99th doodle? With the nth doodle?

CT-53. Find the roots of each of the following quadratic functions and state the x- and y-intercepts.

a) $y = 3x^2 + 6x + 1$ b) $y = -2x^2 + 5x - 7$

CT-54. Write each of the quadratic functions in the preceding problem in graphing form. If you need help getting started, read parts (a) and (b) for some assistance.

a) In part (a) above the roots give the x-intercepts of the graph, so you can use the method of averaging the intercepts to figure out the vertex.

b) In part (b) above the roots are complex so they do not tell you where the graph crosses the x-axis; however, you can use the average of the roots to figure out the vertex. Try it, but be sure to check your answers.

CT-55.   Solve for x: $3^x + 5 = x^2 - 5$. If you do not have a graphing calculator, show your work to approximate a solution and check it in class.

CT-56.   Solve $\left(\frac{1}{8}\right)^{(2x-3)} = \left(\frac{1}{2}\right)^{(x+2)}$.

CT-57.   Dolores says that the solutions for $x^2 - x + 1 = 0$ are $\frac{1}{2} \pm \frac{i\sqrt{3}}{2}$. Is she correct? Explain your answer.

CHANGING THE LENGTH OF THE PERIOD OF THE SINE FUNCTION

CT-58.   Put your graphing calculator in radian mode. Set the domain and range of the viewing window so that you would see just one complete cycle of $y = \sin x$. What is that domain? Range?

a)   Graph **y = sin x, y = sin (0.5x),** and **y = sin (2x)** simultaneously, but make sure you know which is which. Answer these questions for each equation:

   i)   How many cycles of each graph appear on the screen?

   ii)   What is the amplitude of each graph?

   iii)   What is the period of each graph?

   iv)   Is each equation a function?

b)   Make a conjecture about the graph of $y = \sin (bx)$ with respect to each of the questions (i), (ii), (iii), and (iv) above. If you can't make a conjecture yet, try more examples.

c)   Create at least <u>three</u> of your own examples to check your conjectures. Be sure to include sketches of your graphs.

CT-59. **Without** using a graphing calculator, describe each of the following functions by stating the amplitude, period, and locator point and then sketch the graph. **After** you have completed each graph, check your sketch with the graphing calculator and correct and explain any errors.

a) $y = \sin 2(x - \frac{\pi}{6})$

b) $y = 3 + \sin (\frac{1}{3} x)$

c) $y = 3 \sin (4x)$

d) $y = \sin \frac{1}{2} (x + 1)$

e) $y = -\sin 3(x - \frac{\pi}{3})$

f) $y = -1 + \sin (2x - \frac{\pi}{2})$

CT-60. Philip was surprised! He predicted that the equation in part (e) of the previous problem would have its locator point at $(\frac{\pi}{2}, -1)$, but that was not what he saw when he graphed it. Instead, the x-coordinate of his locator was $(\frac{\pi}{4}, -1)$. Philip began to wonder if this was an exception to the pattern he had been using successfully in the other problems. Explain to him why it is not an exception, and rewrite the equation from part (e) so that it does fit the pattern of the other problems.

CT-61. Write the equation of a sine graph with period 6π, amplitude 2, and locator point $(\pi, 1)$. Use the five-point method to sketch the graph.

Take out your Parent Graph Tool Kit and revise the general equation for $y = \sin x$ to reflect what you found in the previous problems.

CT-62. Based on your explorations in class, complete the following tasks.

a) Describe what the graph of $y = 3 \sin (\frac{1}{2} x)$ will look like compared to the graph of $y = \sin x$.

b) Use the five point method to sketch both graphs on the same set of axes based on your hypothesis.

c) Explain the differences between the two graphs. How are they the same?

CT-63. What is the period of $y = \sin (2\pi x)$? Use the five point method to sketch each of the following:

a) $y = \sin (2\pi x)$

b) $y = 3 \sin (\pi x)$

c) $y = 3 \sin (2\pi x) + 1$

CT-64. Match each equation with the appropriate graph. Do this without a graphing calculator.

a) $y = \sin \left(x + \dfrac{\pi}{2}\right)$

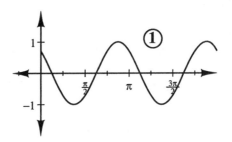

b) $y = \sin (2x)$

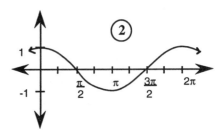

c) $y = 2 \sin \left(\dfrac{x}{2}\right)$

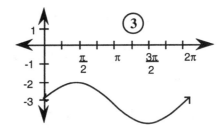

d) $y = \sin (x) - 3$

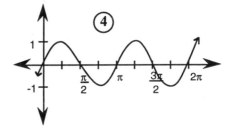

e) $y = -\sin 2\left(x - \dfrac{\pi}{8}\right)$

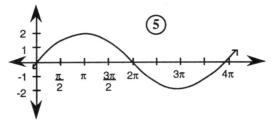

CT-65.   Ceirin's teacher had promised a quiz for the next day, so he phoned Adel to review what they had done in class.

"Suppose I have y = sin 2x," said Ceirin, "What will it look like?"

"It will be horizontally compressed by a factor of 2," replied Adel, "so the period is π."

"Okay, now suppose I want to shift it one unit to the right. Do I just subtract 1 from x, like always?"

"I think so, " said Adel, "but let's check on the graphing calculator."

They proceeded to check on their calculators, and after a few moments they both spoke at once.

"Rats," said Ceirin, "it isn't right."

"Cool," said Adel, "it works."

When they arrived at school the next morning, they compared the equations they had put in their graphing calculators while they talked on the phone. One had

$$y = \sin 2x - 1$$

while the other had

$$y = \sin 2(x - 1).$$

Which equation was right? Did they both subtract 1 from x? Explain. Describe the rule for shifting a graph one unit to the right in a way that avoids this confusion.

CT-66.   Solve each equation.

a) $\dfrac{3}{x+1} = \dfrac{4}{x}$ b) $\dfrac{3}{x+1} + \dfrac{4}{x} = 2$ c) $\dfrac{3}{x+2} + 5 = \dfrac{3}{x+2}$

d)   Explain why part (c) has no solution.

CT-67. **A Satellite's Path**

The CPM satellite (set up by students to beam solutions to problems around the world) follows an orbit in which it is over the northern hemisphere half of the time and the southern hemisphere the other half. You have been asked to help the observers on the ground locate the satellite by giving them a formula for the location at any time after the launch.

You know the following information:

- The satellite's greatest distance north of the equator is 4500 kilometers, which it reaches two hours after the launch.

- Six hours later, a bit more than half-way through its orbit, the satellite reaches its greatest distance south of the equator, which is also 4500 kilometers.

- The satellite takes twelve hours to complete an orbit.

a) Sketch a graph showing the satellite's distance from the equator over time, labeling the information you know.

b) Find an equation to model the satellite's distance from the equator over time. Be sure to tell what your variables represent so that even a NASA engineer would approve.

c) Use your model to predict the satellite's distance from the equator at:

i) 1 hour   ii) 6 hours   iii) 11 hours

d) What does your answer to (iii) imply about the location of the satellite at that time?

CT-68. Write an equation for each of the following graphs. If you have a graphing calculator use it to check your equation (be sure to set your window to match the picture). Otherwise, check when you get to class.

a)

b)

c)

d)

CT-69. Sketch a graph of:

a) $y = -2(x - 2)^2 + 3$

b) $y = (x - 1)^3 + 3$

CT-70. Write the equation of a line parallel to $3x - y = 2$. Then write the equation of a parabola that intersects your line but not the graph of $3x - y = 0$.

CT-71. Solve each of the following equations for x:

a) $171 = 3(5^x)$

b) $171y = 3(x^5)$

CT-72. A 5' x 4' x 3' box is made for the purpose of storage. What is the longest pole that can fit in the box?

CT-73. Which of these situations (if any) is best modeled by a circular function? Explain your reasoning.

a) The number of students in each year's graduating class.

b) The temperature outside your classroom window over the course of several years.

c) The high tide level at a point along the sea coast.

CT-74. What interest rate is needed to double your investment in 15 years?

CT-75. Phana's garden is 2 m wide and 5 m long. She puts a walkway of uniform width around her garden. If the area of the walkway is 30 m², what are the outer dimensions of the walkway? Drawing a diagram will be very helpful.

CT-76. Parts (c) and (d) are the Milepost problems for solving equations and inequalities involving absolute value.

a) $2(x - 1)^2 = 18$

b) $2^x + 3 = 10$

c) $2|2x + 3| = 10$

d) $-|x + 3| < 10$

SINE OF AN ANGLE

CT-77. The sine function is based on the unit circle. In radian mode, the input tells it how far around the circle to go, and the output gives the height of the corresponding point on the circle.

When you've used the sine key on your calculator in degree mode, sine meant something different: the sine *ratio*. The input represented the measure of an acute angle of a right triangle, and the output gave the ratio of the opposite leg to the hypotenuse of the triangle. Today you'll see how the sine *function* can also work in degree mode, because angle measure can also be used to specify a point on the circle.

a) Make a graph of a unit circle, using 10 units on your graph paper to represent one unit, or use the resource page. Using a protractor, draw a radius in the second quadrant which makes a 150° angle with the positive x-axis. Set your calculator to degree mode and use it to find sin (150°). What do you get? Explain the meaning of this result in terms of the sine *function*.

b) Now use your calculator to find sin (200°). Explain the meaning of this result in terms of the sine function.

c) Finally, use your calculator to find sin (-160°). What do you notice? Explain what this means in terms of the sine function.

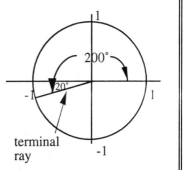

In the previous problem, sin (200°) gave the y-coordinate of a point on the unit circle in the third quadrant. In geometry you focused on angles less than 180°, but we can imagine a radius beginning at (1,0) and rotating counter-clockwise about the origin to a point in the third quadrant. If it then makes a 20° angle with the negative side of the x-axis, it makes sense to say that it rotated 200°, where each degree represents $\frac{1}{360}$ of a complete rotation. Rotations measured in this way, with the understanding that we begin at (1,0), and that counter-clockwise is the direction of positive rotation, are referred to as **ANGLES OF ROTATION IN STANDARD POSITION.** When we draw an angle in standard position, the positive x-axis is called the **INITIAL RAY**, and the radius that determines the angle is called the **TERMINAL RAY.** Add these terms to your Tool Kit.

With this understanding, the sine function has the same definition in degree mode as it does in radian mode. The input tells how far around the circle to go and the output tells the height (y-coordinate) of the corresponding point on the circle.

Use this definition to find the following **without a calculator:**

a)　sin (0°)　　　b)　sin (90°)　　　c)　sin (270°)　　　d)　sin (450°)

CT-79.　Hank wasn't happy about this latest development. "If I'm asked for the sine of an angle, how do I know if they want $\frac{\text{opposite}}{\text{hypotenuse}}$ or height on the unit circle?"

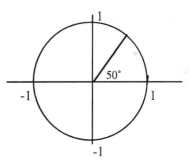

"Good question," said Paula. "At least if the angle is negative, or more than 90°, we know it means height on the unit circle. When the angle is between 0 and 90°, I'm not sure."

Paula chose to investigate the situation using a 50° angle. She drew it in standard position, as shown at right. Then she used her calculator to find sin (50°).

"Hmmm, sin (50°) is about 0.77. That looks about right to be the height of the point on the circle," she said.

"But look," replied Hank, "It's $\frac{\text{opposite}}{\text{hypotenuse}}$, too!"

Copy the circle and draw the right triangle Hank sees, and then explain why $\frac{\text{opposite}}{\text{hypotenuse}}$ is the same as the y-coordinate of the point on the circle, whenever θ is between 0° and 90°.

CT-80.   Now that we have two different modes for the sine function, representing two different ways of measuring travel around the unit circle, it is helpful to be able to switch from one to the other.

a) If you start at (1, 0) on the unit circle, and rotate 4/10 of the way around the circle, what will be the degree measure in standard position of the resulting angle?

b) Steve and Sally's rides on the Circle of Terror can be described in terms of angles in standard position. When they travel 144° around the circle, what fraction of the way around the track have they gone? Explain how to calculate how many km they've traveled along the track if you know what fraction of the circle they've covered.

c) Add this information to your Tool Kit.

MEASURING IN RADIANS

From parts (a) and (b) you can conclude that $\sin(144°) = \sin(\frac{4}{5}\pi)$. Why? (Note: When there's no degree symbol (°), we assume radian mode.) For any angle $\theta°$ in standard position there is a value of x for which traveling x units around the unit circle takes you to the same place as rotating $\theta°$. Because of this, we can use distance around the unit circle as a way to measure angles of rotation. The distance around the unit circle that corresponds to any angle of rotation is called the **RADIAN MEASURE** of the angle. Enter this in your Tool Kit. What is the radian measure of 180°?

---

d) You may have answered something like 3.14159 radians for the previous question, but it is traditional and convenient to leave that in symbolic (and exact) form as π radians. What would be the exact radian measure of each of the following angle measures? (It is very helpful to remember that $180° = \pi$ radians.)

i)   60°   ii)   90°

iii) 120°   iv)   270°

CT-81. A 70° angle is drawn for you in the unit circle at right.

a) Label the coordinates of point R.

b) How could you represent the <u>exact</u> coordinates of point R?

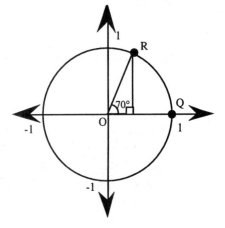

CT-82. Evaluate without a calculator:

a) sin (180°)

b) sin (360°)

c) sin (-90°)

d) sin (510°) (Use a special triangle.)

CT-83. Colleen and Jolleen are twin sisters. They have the same clothes, same hairstyles, same math class, and same calculators. When Luis asked them to find sin 30°, Colleen (who has been absent the last few days) got sin 30° = -0.9880316241 on her calculator, but Jolleen got sin 30° = 0.5 on hers. They tried it several times and got the same results. They quickly forgot about Luis and started trying to figure out what was wrong. Is one of their calculators broken, or is something else going on? Why did they get different answers?

CT-84. Convert each of the following, expressing radians in terms of π.

a) π radians to degrees b) 3π radians to degrees c) 30 degrees to radians

d) $\frac{\pi}{4}$ radians to degrees e) 225 degrees to radians f) $\frac{3\pi}{2}$ radians to degrees

CT-85. Simplify each of the following (write the expression without parentheses) and express the result with positive exponents:

a) $(x^3y^{-2})^{-4}$

b) $-3x^2(6xy - 2x^3y^2z)$

CT-86. Sketch a graph of $y = \frac{1}{2}(x + 1)^3$. Then sketch its inverse and write the equation of the inverse.

CT-87. Write the quadratic function $f(x) = 2x^2 - 16x + 34$ in graphing form.

CT-88. Six-Hundred Flags Amusement Park has decided to do the Circle of Terror one better. Their ride will consist of a circular track with a radius of one km, but the center of the circle will be 0.5 km underground, and passengers will board at the highest point, so they begin with a blood-curdling drop. As in the Circle of Terror, there will be markers visible to show how far riders have traveled from their starting point and a digital read-out to show their altitude relative to ground level. Write a formula for the function that relates these variables.

THE COSINE FUNCTION

CT-89.   You may be wondering if the cosine can also be interpreted as a circular function. The answer, of course, is "Yes."

   a)   Use your calculator to find cos (150°), cos (200°), and cos (-160°). Now look at the unit circle you made for problem CT-77, which has these angles drawn on it. What does the cosine represent on the unit circle?

   b)   Evaluate each of the following cosines without a calculator:

      i) cos (90°)   ii) cos (540°)   iii) cos (-$\frac{5\pi}{2}$)   iv) cos (8π)

   c)   As in the case of sine, the cosine of an angle between 0° and 90° can be interpreted as previously studied as a ratio of triangle sides, or in the way you discovered in part (a). Refer to problem CT-79 and explain why both interpretations lead to the same value.

   d)   Sketch a graph of the cosine function in radian mode.

   e)   Describe how the cosine graph differs from the sine.

CT-90.   Make a conjecture about what will happen to the graph of y = cos (bx) when you vary the value of b. Then test your conjecture for at least three values of b (include values both greater and less than one) and sketch your results. Does your conjecture hold? If not, revise it and test again.

CT-91.   It's time to investigate the cosine function. First, be careful when you think about the variable x. Since the cosine represents the x-coordinate of the point on the unit circle, it can be very confusing to also use x to represent the distance around the circle, which is what we are doing if we write y = cos (x). Instead, we will choose a different variable for the function. We will use θ, with the understanding that θ can be degrees or radians, depending on whether or not it has a ° on it. In general, θ is used to represent angles rather than distances, but it may be used for both purposes because the radian measure of the angle in standard position is the same as the distance around the unit circle. Investigate the function y = cos (θ). Be sure to include all the information you gave when you investigated the sine function. Add this information to your Parent Graph Tool Kit.

CT-92.   The division of the circle into 360° is ancient and somewhat arbitrary. One theory says that 360 was chosen because many numbers divide into it evenly. Mathematicians have found that radian measure is more useful.

Earlier in this unit, the Circle of Terror diagram showed an angle of one radian.

a)   Imagine a circle with a radius of 1 cm, with an angle of 1 radian drawn in standard position. As you learned in geometry, a piece of a circle is called an arc. What is the length of the arc cut off by this angle?

b)   Now imagine the circle is enlarged so that its radius is 1 inch. What is the length of the arc?

c)   Enlarge again to make the radius 1 foot. What is the length of the arc?

d)   Now suppose you have a circle whose radius is 3 feet. You are asked to draw an angle of exactly 1 radian, and you only have a tape measure. How can you do it? Explain clearly.

e)   Describe a general method for creating an angle of 1 radian.

CT-93.   There are several angles with sine and cosine values that you can figure out exactly based on your knowledge of 30°–60°–90° and 45°–45°–90° triangles.

We recommend using a whole sheet of graph or lined paper, a protractor, a ruler, and a compass for this problem so you can keep it in your Tool Kit for easy future reference.

a)   Neatly draw a set of x-y axes and a large unit-circle in the center of the paper.

b)   Use your protractor to measure a 30° angle and label it in both degrees and radians. Use your knowledge of the special right triangles to label the coordinates on the circle that are $\cos\frac{\pi}{6}$ and $\sin\frac{\pi}{6}$ as $\left(\frac{\sqrt{3}}{2}, \frac{1}{2}\right)$. Then draw and label three other angles whose cosines and sines have the same absolute values. For example, one of the other angles would be $\frac{7\pi}{6}$ (or 210°) and the coordinates for $\left(\cos\frac{7\pi}{6}, \sin\frac{7\pi}{6}\right)$ are $\left(\frac{-\sqrt{3}}{2}, -\frac{1}{2}\right)$.

c)   Follow directions similar to those in part (b) for $\frac{\pi}{4}$.

d)   Follow directions similar to those in part (b) for $\frac{\pi}{3}$.

e)   Fill in the coordinates for the cosine and sine values for multiples of $\frac{\pi}{2}$.

f)   The angle $\frac{\pi}{6}$ is called the **reference angle** for all other angles whose cosine and sine have the same absolute values. In part (a) you saw that $\frac{\pi}{6}$ was the reference angle for $\frac{5\pi}{6}, \frac{7\pi}{6}$, and $\frac{11\pi}{6}$. Name two additional angles for which $\frac{\pi}{6}$ would be the reference angle.

CT-94.

> ## REFERENCE ANGLE
>
> For every angle of rotation there is an angle in the first quadrant $0 \le \theta \le \frac{\pi}{2}$ whose cosine and sine have the same absolute values as the cosine and sine of the original. This first quadrant angle is called a **reference angle**.

What reference angle would you use to find each of the following?

a) $\sin\frac{11\pi}{6}$

b) $\cos 120°$

c) $\cos\frac{8\pi}{9}$

d) $\cos 203°$

e) $\sin 310°$

f) $\sin 113°$

CT-95.   Draw a picture of an angle that measures 6 radians.

a)   Approximately how many degrees is this?

b)   Estimate, from your picture, the sine of 6 radians.

CT-96.   Explain your method for converting degree measure to radian measure and vice-versa. Refer to problem CT-80 if you are having trouble getting started.

CT-97.   The temperature of a pizza, after it has been delivered, depends on how long it has been sitting on the family room table.

a)   Sketch a reasonable graph of this situation. Be sure to label your axes.

b)   Should your graph have an asymptote? Why?

CT-98.   Graph the following inequality: $y < \frac{1}{x+5}$

CT-99.   Using separate axes, sketch $y = \sin \theta$ and $y = \cos \theta$. Draw at least one full cycle of each. Then label the coordinates of the x-intercepts in <u>both</u> degrees <u>and</u> radians.

CT-100.   In the function $y = 4 \sin (6\theta)$, how many cycles of sine are there from 0 to 2π? How long is each cycle? (i.e., what is the period)?

Find the period and locator point and then use the five point method to sketch each of the following graphs.

a) $y = \sin \left(\frac{1}{3}\theta\right)$

b) $y = \cos 3(\theta - \frac{\pi}{2})$

c) $y = 1 + \cos 4\theta$

CT-101.   Compute each complex product.

a) $(1 + i)^2$

b) $(1 + i)^3$

MATHEMATICAL MODELING USING CIRCULAR FUNCTIONS: DAY CYCLES

CT-102.   The chart below lists the number of hours of daylight in Denver, Colorado at various dates during the year. The data was collected every 15 days.

DATE	HOURS OF DAYLIGHT	DATE	HOURS OF DAYLIGHT
Jan. 01	9.37	Jul. 01	14.98
Jan. 16	9.63	Jul. 16	14.78
Jan. 31	10.08	Jul. 31	14.32
Feb. 15	10.68	Aug. 15	13.73
Mar 02	11.23	Aug. 30	13.18
Mar 17	11.93	Sept. 14	12.47
Apr. 01	12.57	Sept. 29	11.28
Apr. 16	13.23	Oct. 14	11.17
May 01	13.83	Oct. 29	10.65
May 16	14.37	Nov. 13	9.97
May 31	14.77	Nov. 28	9.57
June 15	15.02	Dec. 13	9.35
		Dec. 28	9.38

a)   Draw a graph showing days (independent) compared to hours of daylight (dependent). Use a full sheet of graph paper and make a neat graph.

b)   What type of function could be used to model this data? Justify your choice.

c)   Would it be easier to model the data starting with a sine function or a cosine function? Explain.

CT-103.   The Day Cycles graph you just made would be a useful tool if you had an equation that approximated it. Then you could estimate, fairly accurately, the number of hours of daylight on any given day of the year.

a)   Find an equation whose graph roughly fits the data. (Pretend the minimum daylight occurs on day 0, and there are 360 days in the year.)

b)   Use your equation to approximate the number of hours of daylight on the 120th day of the year.

c)   How could you make your equation more accurate?

CT-104.   Can we use a circle with the radius not equal to 1
          to evaluate the sine and cosine functions? Yes,
          and here's how: The graph at right shows the
          point P at (-3, 4) on the circle of radius 5. Point
          P determines an angle in standard position. Call
          this angle θ.

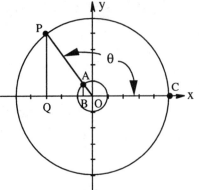

a)   Triangles PQO and ABO are similar. On the
     resource page, find the lengths of the sides
     of △PQO and write the length on each side.
     What is the ratio of the sides of △ABO to
     the sides of △PQO? If you know the length
     of a side of △PQO, what would
     you do to that number to find the length of the corresponding side of △ABO?
     Find the lengths of the sides of △ABO and label them on your resource page.

b)   What are the coordinates of point A? What are the values of
     sin (θ) and cos (θ)?

c)   Select any other point on the larger circle and label it (a, b). Draw a segment from
     that point to the origin. What are the coordinates of the point where that segment
     intersects the unit circle?

d)   Any point in the plane (other than the origin) determines an angle in standard
     position by connecting it to the origin. If a point at (x, y) is r units from the
     origin, what is the sine of the angle it determines? What is the cosine?

CT-105.   How would the graph of the number of hours of darkness (Night Cycles) compare to
          the graph of the number of hours of daylight? (Refer to problems CT-102 and CT-103.)

CT-106.   Carefully sketch one cycle each of sine and cosine on the same set of axes.

a)   Where do the two graphs intersect? Write your answers in both degrees and
     radians.

b)   Draw a unit circle or use one from a resource page. In your circle, sketch the angles
     you found in part (a). The rays you just drew should be collinear. What is the
     equation of the line formed by the two rays?

c)   Explain why the values of θ for which sin θ and cos θ intersect should be on the
     line you found in part (b).

CT-107.   Give the locator point for each of the following equations then use the five-point method
          to sketch each graph.

a) $y = 3 \sin (x + 90°)$ b) $y = -2 \sin (4x)$

CT-108.   Write a possible equation for the graph at right.

CT-109.   Convert each of the following angle measures:

a) $\frac{7\pi}{6}$ radians to degrees   b) $\frac{5\pi}{3}$ radians to degrees   c)   45 degrees to radians

d)   100° to radians   e)   810° to radians   f) $\frac{7\pi}{2}$ radians to degrees

CT-110.   Copy the following definition into your Tool Kit, then answer the questions that follow:

SINE AND COSINE FUNCTIONS

For any real number θ, the **sine of** θ, denoted sin θ, is the y-coordinate of the point on the unit circle reached by a rotation of θ radians in standard position. The **cosine of** θ, denoted cos θ, is the x-coordinate of the point on the unit circle reached by a rotation of θ radians in standard position.

Without your calculator, use the definition above to state whether each of the following values is positive, negative, or zero:

a)   sin 6   b)   cos 4   c) $\sin \frac{3\pi}{2}$ d) $\cos \frac{3\pi}{2}$

e)   Explain how to determine whether a given value of sine or cosine will be positive or negative.

CT-111. This problem is a milepost for writing and solving exponential equations.

When rabbits were first brought to Australia, they had no natural enemies. There were about 80,000 rabbits in 1866. Two years later, in 1868, the population had grown to over 2,400,000!

a) Why would an exponential equation be a better model for this situation than a linear one? Would a sine function be better or worse? Why?

b) Write an exponential equation for the number of rabbits t years after 1866.

c) How many rabbits do you predict would have been present in 1871?

d) According to your model, in what year was the first pair of rabbits introduced into Australia? Is this reasonable?

e) Is your exponential model useful for predicting how many rabbits are there now? Explain.

CT-112. Susan knew how to shift y = sin x to get the graph at right, but she wondered if it would be possible to get the same graph by shifting y = cos x.

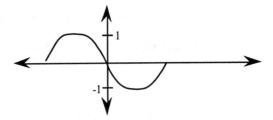

a) What do you think?

b) If you think it's possible, find the equation that does it. If you think it's impossible, explain why.

c) Adlai said, "I can get that graph **without** shifting to the right or left." What equation did he write?

CT-113. David Longshot loves playing golf after a long day of teaching mathematics. He is known for his long drives, and today he drove the ball 250 yards. He estimated that the ball reached a maximum height of 15 yards. Find a quadratic equation that would model the parabolic path of the golf ball.

MORE MODELING USING CIRCULAR FUNCTIONS

CT-114. Linda and Francis need to find an equation to fit this graph. Linda wants to use $y = \sin x$, but Francis thinks that starting with $y = \cos x$ will be easier.

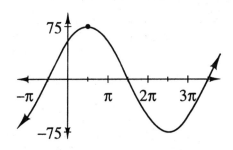

a) Which do you think is easier? Why?

b) Find equations both ways. That is, starting first with $y = \sin x$ and then with $y = \cos x$, find two different equations to fit the graph.

c) Test your ideas on your graphing calculator. Revise your equations if necessary, and make a note about what caused any error.

CT-115. Average daytime temperatures in Sidney, Australia are given below for four days during the year.

Date	January 1st	April 1st	July 1st	October 1st
Temperature	92°	70°	50°	72°

a) Sketch a graph of the temperature vs. time of year for Sidney.

b) Find an equation to approximate your graph.

CT-116. The pedal shaft on a standard bicycle is about 7 inches long and the center of the bottom bracket to which the pedal shaft is attached is about 11 inches above the ground. Sketch a graph that shows the relationship of the angle of the shaft (for one pedal) in standard position (as if the point of attachment were the origin of a set of x-y axes shifted up 11 units) to the height of one pedal above the ground as the pedal is turned.

Write an equation for a function that represents your graph.

CT-117. Solve for x: $x^2 - 5 = 2^{-x}$

CT-118. Find the x- and y-intercepts for each of the following equations.

a) $y = 2x^3 - 10x^2 - x$

b) $y + 2 = \log_3 (x - 1)$

CT-119. Too Tall Thomas has put Rodney's book bag on the pump house roof. Rodney goes to borrow a ladder from the school custodian. The tallest ladder available is 10 feet long and the roof is 9 feet from the ground. He places the ladder's tip at the edge of the roof. The ladder is unsafe if the angle it makes with the ground is more than 60°. Is this a safe situation? Explain.

CT-120. Deniz and Christina are at it again! This time Christina has broken into Deniz's computer and infected it with a virus. At first the virus will slowly erase information from Deniz's hard drive. As time goes on, the amount of information erased will increase. In t minutes after the virus starts erasing information, $5{,}000{,}000(\frac{1}{2})^t$ bytes of information remain on the hard drive.

a) Before the virus starts erasing, how many bytes of information are on Deniz's hard drive?

b) After how many minutes will there be 1,000 bytes of information left on the drive?

c) When will the hard drive be completely erased?

CT-121. Claudia graphed $y = \cos x$ and $y = \cos (x + 360°)$ on the same set of axes. She didn't see any difference in their graphs at all. Why not?

CT-122. Should $y = \sin x$ and $y = \cos x$ both be parent graphs, or is one the parent of the other? Give reasons for your decision.

CT-123. Simplify each value without using a calculator:

a) $25^{-1/2}$

b) $\left(\frac{1}{27}\right)^{-1/3}$

c) $9^{3/2}$

d) $16^{-3/4}$

THE TANGENT FUNCTION

CT-124. **Tangent Investigation**

The third trigonometric ratio you have used to solve triangles is the tangent. As you may have guessed, the tangent can also be interpreted as a circular function. The first thing you need to do is find out how it is related to the unit circle.

a) To investigate, take out a unit circle graph and draw an angle in standard position of 114° and another of 143°. The terminal rays can be extended to form lines. Use what you've learned in this unit to find the coordinates of a point where each line intersects the unit circle, and then use the coordinates of that point to write the equation of the line.

b) Next use your calculator to find tan 114° and tan 143°. What do you notice? We know that sin θ gives the y-coordinate on the unit circle at an angle of θ in standard position and cos θ gives the x-coordinate. What rule could you use to calculate tan θ ?

c) As in the case of sine and cosine, the tangent of an angle between 0° and 90° can be interpreted as a ratio of triangle sides. It can also be seen as the slope of a line through the origin. Make a unit circle sketch and explain why both interpretations lead to the same value.

CT-125. The graph of tan θ is very different from those of sine and cosine. To begin investigating, copy and complete the following table of values, using your calculator. Be sure to use the π key with your calculator in radian mode.

x	$-\frac{\pi}{2}$	$\frac{5\pi}{12}$	$\frac{\pi}{3}$	$\frac{\pi}{4}$	$-\frac{\pi}{6}$	$-\frac{\pi}{12}$	0	$\frac{\pi}{12}$	$\frac{\pi}{6}$	$\frac{\pi}{4}$	$\frac{5\pi}{12}$	$\frac{\pi}{2}$	$\frac{7\pi}{12}$	$\frac{2\pi}{3}$
tan x														

a) Why is the tangent undefined at certain values? What does this indicate about the terminal ray for those angles? Find two other values of θ (in radians) for which tan θ will be undefined.

b) Find some values of tan θ when θ is very close to $\frac{\pi}{2}$. What happens to the values of tan θ as θ gets close to $\frac{\pi}{2}$ and $-\frac{\pi}{2}$. Why? (Think about the coordinates of the point on the unit circle.)

c) Plot the points from your table of values to sketch a graph of tan θ for θ from $-\frac{\pi}{2}$ to $\frac{\pi}{2}$. (Note that the θ-values in the table are evenly spaced.) Leave room to extend the graph up to θ = $\frac{3\pi}{2}$.

>>Problem continues on the next page.>>

d) Why are the values of tan for $\theta = \frac{7\pi}{12}$ and $\frac{2\pi}{3}$ the same as for $\theta = -\frac{5\pi}{12}$ and $-\frac{\pi}{3}$?

e) What values of x in the table are the same as those for θ between π and $\frac{3\pi}{2}$? Use these values to extend your graph up to $\theta = \frac{3\pi}{2}$.

f) Is $y = \tan \theta$ periodic? Why or why not? If so, what is its period?

CT-126. Set the domain of your graphing calculator's viewing window to show $-\frac{\pi}{2} \le x \le \frac{\pi}{2}$ and the range to show $-10 \le y \le 10$. Then graph $y = \tan x$. Use radians.

a) What other function does the graph resemble?

b) Each of the sections of $y = \tan x$, separated by asymptotes, is called a branch of the function. Some people think that the branches of $\tan x$ are copies of $y = x^3$. Graph $y = x^3$ in the same window with $y = \tan x$. See if you can alter $y = x^3$ to match $y = \tan x$. What happens?

c) With the same window, graph the function $y = \frac{\sin x}{\cos x}$. What do you notice? Explain why this is so.

CT-127. Finish investigating $y = \tan x$. Be sure to include a general equation with a description of how the constants in it affect the graph. Add $\tan x$ to your Parent Graph Tool Kit.

CT-128. Make up a situation that could be accurately modeled using a circular function. Justify why you think a circular function would make a good model.

CT-129. Copy the following information into your Tool Kit, and answer the questions that follow.

> ### CONVERTING BETWEEN RADIANS AND DEGREES
>
> If an angle of rotation has radian measure R then the degree measure, D, is given
>
> by the equation: $D = \dfrac{R}{\pi}(180°)$ Likewise, R is given by the formula: $R = \dfrac{D}{180°}(\pi)$

a) Write a careful paragraph, using complete sentences, to explain why the formulas above make sense.

b) As you have seen, angles which are multiples of 30° and 45° are used very frequently in working with circular functions because their sines and cosines can be found exactly using special right triangles. For these angles there are shortcuts for applying the formulas above.

You should know that $30° = \dfrac{\pi}{6}$ radians, $45° = \dfrac{\pi}{4}$ radians, $60° = \dfrac{\pi}{3}$ radians, and

$90° = \dfrac{\pi}{2}$ radians. If you don't know them, memorize them now.

A shortcut for converting radian measures which are multiples of these values to degrees is described in problem CT-40. Look back at that problem and refresh your memory.

For angles given in degrees, divide by the largest of the numbers 30, 45, 60, or 90 that goes into it evenly. Then multiply that number by the radian equivalent of the degree value you divided by. For example, consider the first one below. Since

$210°$ is 7 x 30°, and $30° = \dfrac{\pi}{6}$ radians, the radian measure of 210° is $7 \times \dfrac{\pi}{6}$. Do the

rest of the conversions without a calculator, writing the steps as shown in the examples below.

$210° = 7\,(\,30°\,) = 7\,\left(\dfrac{\pi}{6}\right) = \dfrac{7\pi}{6}$ $\dfrac{3p}{4} = 3\,\dfrac{p}{4} = 3(45°) = 135°$

$270° =$ $\dfrac{5\pi}{3} =$

$450° =$ $\dfrac{11\pi}{3} =$

$150° =$ $\dfrac{7\pi}{2} =$

$240° =$ $\dfrac{7\pi}{4} =$

$330° =$ $\dfrac{7\pi}{3} =$

CT-130. Rip-Off Rentals charges $25 per day plus 50¢ per mile to rent a mid-sized car. Your teacher will rent you his/her family sedan and charge you only 3¢ if you drive one mile, 6¢ if you drive two miles, 12¢ if you drive three, 24¢ for four, and so on.

a) Write a rule that will give you the cost to rent each car.

b) If you plan to rent the car for a two-day road-trip, which is the better deal if you drive: 10 miles? 20 miles? 100 miles?

CT-131. Solve for x: $|x + 5| = |x| - 5$. To find all solutions you will probably need to graph two functions.

CT-132. Eddie was solving the equation

$$\cos(4x) = (\cos x) + 1.$$

His solution is shown at right.

a) Check his answer in both degrees and radians. Is he right?

b) If he is wrong, find his mistake and explain how you would solve his equation. You do not actually have to solve it—just explain how you would do it.

$$\cos(4x) = (\cos x) + 1$$

$$\frac{\cos(4x)}{\cos} = \frac{\cos x}{\cos} + 1$$

$$4x = x + 1$$

$$3x = 1$$

$$x = \frac{1}{3}$$

CT-133. Solve for x: $\log_2 x = 2^x$.

CT-134. Sketch a graph of $x^2 + y^2 = 100$.

a) Is it a function?

b) What are its range and domain?

c) In your circle, make a central angle that measures $\frac{2\pi}{3}$ radians. If you remove this wedge of the circle, what is the left-over area?

CT-135. Daniel sketched these graphs for $y = \sin x$ and $y = \cos x$.

Unfortunately, he forgot to label which is which, and now he can't remember. Help him out. Explain how he can tell (and remember!) which graph is sine and which is cosine.

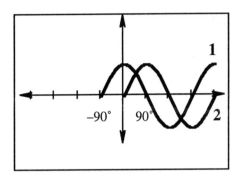

CT-136. Make sure that your parent graph Tool Kit accurately contains the following information. Then answer the questions below.

The **GENERAL EQUATION FOR THE SINE FUNCTION** is

$$y = a \sin b(x - h) + k$$

This function has amplitude = a, period $= \dfrac{2\pi}{b}$, and locator point (h, k).

The **GENERAL EQUATION FOR THE COSINE FUNCTION** is

$$y = a \cos b(x - h) + k$$

This function has amplitude = a, period $= \dfrac{2\pi}{b}$, and locator point (h, k + 1).

A circular function has a "peak" at (2, 3). (The technical name for such a point where a function changes direction is a **relative maximum.**) From that point it decreases to a low point, or **relative minimum**, at (5, -11).

a) Find the amplitude of the function.

b) Find the period of the function.

c) Write the formula for this graph using a cosine function .

MODELING AND TRANSFORMATIONS WITH THE TANGENT FUNCTION

time	meters
0	0
0.3	200
0.7	400
1.3	600
2.5	800
5.3	1000
16.8	1200
24.7	1250
34.1	1300
46.0	1400
52.9	1600
54.9	1800
55.9	2000
56.5	2200
56.8	2400
57.1	2600
57.3	2800

CT-137. Eoin (pronounced like Owen) lives near the seashore, and ever since he was little, he has been mesmerized by watching the beam of light from the lighthouse move along the shore as the light rotates. There is a straight sidewalk at the base of the seawall that runs along the beach. When Eoin was younger he would run along the sidewalk and try to race the beam as it moved across the wall along side him. He found that he could win the race for a while, but then the beam would move faster and faster and leave him behind. He realized that when the light first appeared on the wall far down the shore it moved very fast, then it slowed down as it came toward him and sped up again as it moved off into the distance.

As he grew older, he found ways to collect data so he could understand how the beam behaved. There were openings in the wall where the streets intersected the sidewalk. He determined that they were 200 meters apart. He realized that he could use the wall as a number line. He chose one of the openings in the wall near where the beam first became visible each time around and wrote 0 in chalk on the wall there. Then he rode his bike along the sidewalk from that point, writing chalk numbers at each opening in the wall to make his number line. Finally he was ready. He borrowed a stopwatch, started it when the light hit the 0 mark, and recorded how long the beam took to reach points along the wall. Some of the data he collected is listed in the table above right.

a) Enter the data that Eoin collected into your graphing calculator and using time as the independent variable, graph it. Estimate the locator point. What do you think could be the parent graph? Why does it make sense to use a periodic function?

b) Eoin realized he had more information. He noticed that the light made one full revolution in exactly 2 minutes (120 seconds) and that it only pointed toward the shore for half that time. How does this apply to the function that will best fit Eoin's data?

c) Help Eoin out. Find a function to fit his data. Check it on your graphing calculator.

CT-138.　Graph the function g(x) = cos 4x - sin 2x.

a)　Why does it make sense that this function is periodic? What is its period? How many cycles does cos 4x complete in that interval? How many cycles does sin 2x complete?

b)　Combinations of trigonometric functions are used to represent more complicated cycles. Consider the following graph of an average person's blood pressure over time:

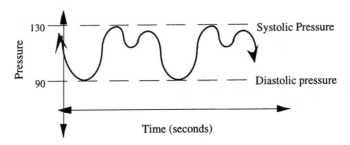

This represents blood pressure of 130 over 90 (130 systolic, 90 diastolic). Think of g(x) as the parent graph for the graph above and adjust the function g(x) above to make it fit the graph shown.

CT-139.　Compare the graphs of y = - sin x and y = sin (-x). What do you notice? Use the Circle of Terror to explain why.

CT-140.　Give the locator point for each of the following functions then use the five-point method to sketch each graph.

a)　y = sin (0.5(x - π))

b)　y = 10 sin(3x) - 2

c)　y = 5 cos (x + $\frac{\pi}{4}$)

d)　y = cos (2(x - $\frac{\pi}{4}$))

CT-141.　Sketch a unit circle. In your circle, sketch in an angle that has:

a)　a positive cosine and a negative sine.

b)　a sine of -1.

c)　a negative cosine and a negative sine.

d)　a cosine of about -0.9 and a sine of about 0.3.

e)　Could an angle have a sine equal to 0.9 and cosine equal to 0.8? Give an angle or explain why not.

CT-142.   For the system of equations at right, $x^2 + y^2 = 25$
                                                      $y = x^2 + 36$

find the intersection of the graphs.   To find the algebraic solution of the system you need
to solve for x and y. In this case which variable is easier to solve for first: x or y? Do
it. Now try to solve for the other variable first. What caused you to get stuck?

CT-143.   Sketch a graph of $y = -x^2(x - 2)^2(x + 2)^2$.

CT-144.   Inverse functions

Find the equation for the inverse of the following function: $y = 2\sqrt{3(x-1)} + 5$. Sketch
the graph of both the original and the inverse.

REVIEW AND SUMMARY

CT-145.   Last week Tim was sitting in his math class
playing with an ant (what else?) instead of
working on circular functions with his team. He
was trying to force the helpless ant to scurry in a
perfect square. Luckily for the ant, Tim's
teammates stopped him. Tim apologized, and to
show him there were no hard feelings, the team
let him help with one of their math problems.
"OK, Tim," they said. "Look at the diagram.
Here's a sketch of that poor ant you were
pestering. It's walking along that square, on
which we have conveniently put a set of axes.
The ant starts at (1, 0) and walks
counterclockwise."

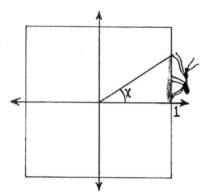

Consider a function (or non-function) where the input is the angle the
ant makes with the positive x-axis and the output is the ant's <u>distance
from the y-axis</u>. With your team, **investigate this function or
non-function**. Be sure to include the usual information: intercepts,
domain, asymptotes, etc.

CT-146. In problem CT-141, part (e) you found that it is not possible for an angle to have a sine equal to 0.9 and cosine equal to 0.8. In fact, the sine and cosine are so closely linked that once you know the sine of an angle you can calculate the absolute value of the cosine, and vice versa. Look at the unit circle graph at right.

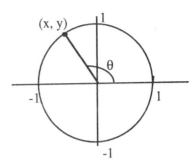

a) What equation must x and y satisfy if they are coordinates of a point on the unit circle?

b) What do you know about the relationship between x and θ? Between y and θ?

c) You now have three equations in three variables, one from part (a) and two from part (b). Use substitution to eliminate x and y and create an equation in terms of only θ.

d) This important equation is called the **Pythagorean Identity**. Use it to answer the following question: If the cosine of an angle is 0.8, what are the possible values of the sine of that angle?

CT-147. Given the points O(0, 0) and R(-5, -12), we will find the measure of the angle formed by $\overline{OR}$ in standard position.

a) What is the sine of the angle formed by $\overline{OR}$ in standard position?

b) Use your calculator (in degree mode) to find the measure of an angle whose sine is the number you found in part (a). Is this the angle formed by $\overline{OR}$ in standard position?

c) How many angles in standard position are there which have a sine equal to the number you found in part (a)?

d) Can the calculator know which is the one you're looking for? Which one do you think it gives you? How can you use that answer to find the angle formed by $\overline{OR}$?

CT-148. In problem CT-139 you found that sin (-x) = -sin x by comparing the graphs of y = sin (-x) and y = -sin x. Is a similar relation true for cos (-x)? What does cos (-x) equal? Why?

CT-149. Trigonometry means measurement of triangles and refers to the use of sine, cosine, and tangent to find unknown sides or angles of triangles. The study of circular functions is also referred to as trigonometry. What is the relationship between coordinates on the unit circle and the familiar opposite-adjacent-hypotenuse ratios of right triangle trigonometry?

CT-150. **UNIT 8 SUMMARY ASSIGNMENT**

a) What are circular functions? Give a definition as you understand it. Then summarize the important new ideas of this unit, including an example for each one, along with a complete solution. In selecting examples, you should create at least three original problems that represent important concepts developed in the unit and show their solutions.

b) What topics of trigonometry/circular functions do you have questions about and what do you think you understand well?

c) Since the start of this course you have been learning about mathematics as a tool for modeling. Tell what you know about mathematical modeling so far. What is it? W̷ would someone want to do this? What functions might someone use for modeling? Describe types of situations that fit each of the functions we have studied so far.

CT-151. Add the following information to your Tool Kit and answer the question below:

THE TANGENT FUNCTION

For any real number θ, the **TANGENT of** θ, denoted tan θ, is the slope of the ray which represents a rotation of θ radians in standard position. It is also equal to the ratio $\frac{y}{x}$, where (x, y) is the point reached by a rotation of θ radians on the unit circle. In addition, $\tan x = \frac{\sin x}{\cos x}$. The general equation for the tangent function is

$$y = a \tan b(x - h) + k$$

This function has period $= \frac{\pi}{b}$, vertical asymptotes at $\frac{\pi}{2b} + h \pm \frac{n\pi}{b}$ for n = 1, 2, . . ., and locator point (h, k).

Without a calculator, sketch the graph of $y = \tan \frac{1}{3}(x - \pi) - 2$. Show at least 2 cycles and be sure to show the asymptotes.

CT-152. Add the following information to your Tool Kit, and answer the question below.

THE PYTHAGOREAN IDENTITY

For any value of x, $\sin^2 x + \cos^2 x = 1$

(Note that $\sin^2 x$ is an abbreviated way to write $(\sin x)^2$.)

If $\sin x = \frac{1}{3}$, find the values for cos x.

CT-153. Consider the system of equations at right. Can the system be solved by substitution? By the addition/subtraction method? By graphing? $y = \cos x$
$y = -1$

    a)   If x is measured in degrees, list at least five solutions

    b)   Write several solutions if x is measured in radians.

    c)   Consider the lists of solutions you wrote in parts (a) and (b) as sequences and write a rule for each sequence of solutions as a way to represent ALL possible solutions.

CT-154. Write the equation of a circular function that has an amplitude of 7 and a period of 8π. Sketch its graph.

CT-155. Sketch a graph of $y = x^3(x - 2)(x + 2)^2$.

CT-156. Find the solutions, real or complex, of the system at right: $y = x^2 + 2x + 5$
$y = 2x^2 + 4x + 7$

CT-157. **TOOL KIT CHECK-UP**

Your Tool Kit contains reference tools for algebra. Return to your Tool Kit entries. You may need to revise or add entries.

Be sure that your Tool Kit contains entries for all of the items listed below. Add any topics that are missing to your Tool Kit NOW, as well as any other items that will help you in your study of algebra.

REGULAR TOOL KIT

- Five-Point Method for Graphing Periodic Functions
- Angles of Rotation
- The Sine and Cosine Functions
- The Tangent Function

- Radian Mode
- Radian Measure
- Converting between Radians and Degrees
- The Pythagorean Identity

PARENT GRAPH TOOL KIT should include complete entries for:

- Sin x
- Tan x

- Cos x

CT-158.   **PORTFOLIO: GROWTH OVER TIME - PROBLEM #2**

On a separate piece of paper (so you can hand it in separately or add it to your portfolio) explain **everything** that you now know about the function below. Be sure to add everything that you have learned since the last time you did this problem and do not leave out anything that you included in your earlier attempts.

$$f(x) = 2^x - 3.$$

CT-159.   **Growth Over Time Reflection** Look at your three responses to the growth-over-time problem above. Write an evaluation of your growth based your responses. Consider each of the following while writing your answer.

a)   What new concepts did you include the second time you did the problem? In what ways was your response better than your first attempt?

b)   How was your final version different from the first two? What new ideas did you include?

c)   Did you omit anything in the final version that you used in one of the earlier problems? Why did you omit it?

d)   Rate your three attempts by making three bars like those below and shading each bar to represent how much you knew on each attempt.

First Attempt:
Second Attempt:
Final Attempt:

e)   Is there anything you would add to your most recent version? If so, what is it?

UNIT 9

The Search for Sunken Treasure
MORE TRIANGLES AND TRIGONOMETRY

Unit 9 Objectives

The Search for Sunken Treasure: MORE TRIANGLES AND TRIGONOMETRY

This unit uses what you have learned about trigonometry and circular functions to develop further the trigonometry of triangles. You will also learn more about trigonometric functions and their inverses.

In this unit you will have the opportunity to:

- develop the Law of Sines, which will allow you to determine missing parts of some triangles.

- develop the Law of Cosines, which, with the Law of Sines, will allow you to determine missing parts of any triangle.

- investigate inverse functions for trigonometric functions.

The following problem is the theme problem for this unit, but there is not enough information given for you to solve it now. To solve it you will need to use the Laws of Sines and Cosines.

ST-0. **THE SEARCH FOR SUNKEN TREASURE** Sandy Salvage has heard that a ship loaded with gold just sank off the coast of Florida in international waters. This means whoever gets there first can claim the gold. Getting there first is not a problem since Sandy has two of the best and fastest ships in the world, the Goldrush and the Goldfish.

Sandy's problem is that Blackbeard also wants the treasure. Blackbeard's ship, the Surging Skurge, is an old wreck. The only way Blackbeard will get his hands on the treasure is to let Sandy get the treasure aboard and then attack Sandy's ship. Sandy has decided that if he sends a decoy ship he will have a 50% chance of getting away with the treasure.

Your team has been captured by Blackbeard. You must determine which of Sandy's ships is the treasure ship. If your team finds the treasure ship Blackbeard will spare your lives. If you pick the wrong ship, you walk the plank!

The only information that Blackbeard gives you is a note from one of his spies with an angle of descent of 2.18° from the seaport to the location of the treasure.

PROBLEM SOLVING

REPRESENTATION/MODELING

FUNCTIONS/GRAPHING

INTERSECTIONS/SYSTEMS

ALGORITHMS

REASONING/COMMUNICATION

Unit 9
The Search for Sunken Treasure: MORE TRIANGLES AND TRIGONOMETRY

THE LAW OF SINES

ST-1.   Think back to your knowledge of right triangle trigonometry. For the triangle at right, answer the following questions.

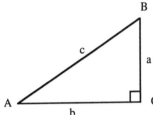

a)   What is the ratio for sin A?

b)   What is the ratio for cos A?

c)   What is the ratio for tan A?

ST-2.   For the triangle at right with side lengths a, b, and c:

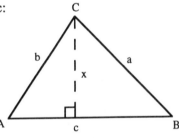

a)   Solve for x in terms of a and ∠B.

b)   Solve for x in terms of b and ∠A.

c)   What can we conclude?

d)   Show how your answer to part (c) leads to the formula: $\frac{\sin A}{a} = \frac{\sin B}{b}$.

e)   What do you think is probably true of $\frac{\sin C}{c}$? Explain how you could show it.

f)   Add the information the box below to your Tool Kit.

>>Problem continues on the next page.>>

In parts (a) through (e) above, you derived the **LAW OF SINES**.

For <u>any</u> ΔABC, it is always true that:

$$\frac{\sin A}{a} = \frac{\sin B}{b} = \frac{\sin C}{c}$$

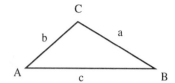

This law is powerful because it allows you to use the sine function to solve for measures of angles and lengths of sides for <u>any</u> triangle, not just right triangles.

For example, if ∠A = 53°, a = 18', and ∠B = 39°, you can solve for b by substituting the values and solving the equation. Remember that the sine values represent <u>numbers</u> in the equation.

$\frac{\sin 53°}{18} = \frac{\sin 39°}{b}$	substitute
$b(\sin 53°) = 18(\sin 39°)$	fraction busters
$b = \frac{18(\sin 39°)}{\sin 53°}$	solving for b
$b \approx 14.18'$	calculations

Note that you can use your calculator to convert the sine values into decimal approximations at any time during the solution, but it is most efficient to wait until the end of the problem.

ST-3. Michelle pointed out to Jodi that the ratios $\frac{\sin A}{a} = \frac{\sin B}{b} = \frac{\sin C}{c}$ could also be written $\frac{a}{\sin A} = \frac{b}{\sin B} = \frac{c}{\sin C}$. Is Michelle correct? Why or why not?

ST-4. Nathan lives 200 ft. down the river from Tong. Both live across the river from Amy. Nathan views the other two houses at a 100° angle while Tong sees them at 38°.

a) Find the distance between Nathan's and Amy's house.

b) Find the distance between Tong's and Amy's house.

ST-5.   Use the Law of Sines to find x and y. Be sure to
         show how you set up the equation.

ST-6.   ΔPQR is an isosceles triangle with base angles of 46° and equal sides of length 26 cm.
         Draw a diagram and use the Law of Sines to complete parts (a) through (c).

         a)   Find the length of its base.   b)   Find the length of its perimeter.

         c)   Find its area.

ST-7.   Sketch the graphs of each of the following on separate axes.

         i) $y = (x + 3)^2 - 6$ ii) $y = |(x + 3)^2 - 6|$ iii) $y < (x + 3)^2 - 6$

         a)   What are the domain and range for the graph in part (i)?

         b)   What are the domain and range for the graph in part (ii)?

         c)   How is the graph in part (iii) different from the other two parts?

ST-8.   Without graphing on a graphing calculator, find where the graph $y = 5 \cdot 2^x$ crosses

         the line $y = 6$? Show your method.

ST-9.   Calculate the product $(3 + i)(1 + 2i)$. Illustrate with a sketch of the complex plane
         showing both factors and the product.

ST-10.   The points (0, 6), (0, 0) and (4, 6) are connected with straight lines to enclose a region.
         Imagine spinning this region about the y-axis.

         a)   Describe the shape of the solid you get. Make a sketch.

         b)   Compute the volume of the figure.

ST-11. The Lincoln's new business is doing very well. The first week they took in $1000, the second week $1100, the third week $1200, and each week thereafter $100 more than the week before.

   a) Decide what they started with and find an equation that describes the amount of money taken in for any week.

   b) How much did they take in during the 20th week?

ST-12. Use elimination or matrix multiplication to solve this system of equations:

$$\begin{aligned} x + y - z &= 12 \\ 3x + 2y + z &= 6 \\ 2x + 5y - z &= 10 \end{aligned}$$

ST-13. Jeanne Marie bought a sweater originally priced at $50 for 35% off. How much did she pay for the sweater?

AREA FROM THE LAW OF SINES

ST-14. How do you find the area of a triangle? List as many ways as you can with examples.

   a) Suppose in the triangle at right you knew the length of the base but not the length of the altitude. What could you do to find the area?

   b) Could you find the area if you knew neither the base nor the altitude?

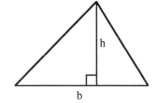

ST-15. Explain completely how the Law of Sines could help you find the area of the triangle at right.

ST-16. Given any ΔABC with altitude x (an example is shown below right):

   a) draw a diagram and label it in the same way as the one at right, then represent the area of the triangle.

   b) what is the ratio for sin A? Solve this expression for x.

   c) substitute this expression for x into your area equation in part (a).

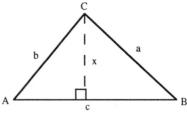

ST-17. Using the triangle from the previous problem:

a) Represent the area of the triangle algebraically.

b) What is the ratio for sin B? Solve this expression for x.

c) Substitute this expression for x into your area equation (in part (a)) to get another formula for the area of ΔABC.

ST-18. Based on the same triangle you used in the last two problems, discuss with your team how to write an area formula that uses sin C. Based on your discussion, write a step-by-step explanation of how to find the area of a triangle when given the lengths of two sides and the measure of the angle between them. You may want to put this new way to find the area of a triangle in your Tool Kit.

ST-19. An isosceles triangle has a perimeter of 42 inches. A base angle measures 62°. What is the area of the triangle?

ST-20. Compute the area of these triangles using the information given:

a) <u>Given:</u>

m∠B = 37°
a = 14
c = 23

b) <u>Given:</u>

m∠A = 42°
c = 12
b = 30

ST-21. Have you ever wondered why the TV weather-person reports the temperature and the humidity at the same time? When it is hot and very humid, you feel hotter. When it is not very humid, you feel cooler. Suppose the temperature reaches its daily maximum at 3 p.m., and the humidity level reaches its daily maximum at 9 p.m.

a) Sketch a graph of the temperature over a three-day period. You can assume daily cycles of highs and lows and use the five-point method to outline your graph.

b) Sketch a graph of the humidity level over a three-day period.

c) Imagine combining these two graphs into one which would represent "the discomfort level." When do you think is the most uncomfortable time of the day for most people?

ST-22. Solve the system at right for x and h: $x^2 + h^2 = 25$

$(7 - x)^2 + h^2 = 36$

ST-23. A seven foot board is cut into two pieces. If one piece is x feet long, how long is the other piece?

ST-24. Graph $y = x^{3/2}$. You can find enough points using a regular scientific calculator.

a) Graph the inverse.

b) State the domain and range for each function.

c) How many point(s) of intersection are there for the two equations? What are they?

ST-25. A function, f(x), is shown at right.

a) If this is a complete graph, what are the domain and range of f(x)?

b) Make a sketch of what f(x + 3) would look like.

c) Make a sketch of what 3·f(x) would look like.

ST-26. Solve for x.

a) $2x^3 = 75$

b) $2(3)^x = 75$

APPLICATIONS OF AREA AND LAW OF SINES

ST-27. The towns of Lake Forest and Greenville are 12 miles apart. The angles of elevation to a balloon directly between the towns are 12° and 33° respectively.

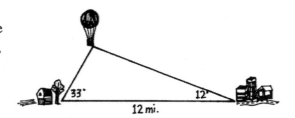

a) Find the altitude of the balloon.

b) How far would you have to drive from Greenville to the balloon if there were no wind and the balloon came straight down?

ST-28.   Kaun Kreit, the cement contractor, has a job to pour cement for a patio that already has a sidewalk down the middle. The measurements that Kaun got from the owner were from a picture like the one at right. In the picture all of the lengths are in inches.

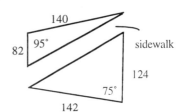

a)   Find the area of the top surface of each piece of patio in square feet.

b)   If the concrete is to be 4 inches thick, find the volume of concrete needed for the job.

c)   If concrete costs $60 per cubic yard, how much will Kaun have to pay for the load of concrete?

ST-29.   Mathematicians invent symbols and abbreviations, called notation, to represent mathematical concepts. Sometimes the notation is more difficult to understand than the concepts! Consider the functions $y = \sin^{-1} x$ and $y = \dfrac{1}{\sin x}$.

a)   Use your graphing calculator to graph the equation $y = \sin^{-1} x$ (use the $\sin^{-1}$ button) and sketch the graph.

b)   Use your graphing calculator to graph the equation $y = \dfrac{1}{\sin x}$ and sketch the graph.

c)   Are these graphs the same? Now graph the equation $y = (\sin x)^{-1}$. Which two graphs are the same? Why does this make sense?

ST-30.   Consider this sequence of triangles.

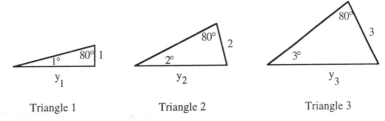

Triangle 1   Triangle 2   Triangle 3

a)   What would the nth triangle look like?

b)   Write a general equation for the length of y_n.

c)   Suppose a function is defined as follows: using the pattern generated above, the input is the triangle number and the output is y for that triangle. Write a formula for this function. What are the domain and range for this function?

d)   If you have a graphing calculator, use it and make a sketch of the graph.

ST-31.   Find the area of the shaded figure if $\angle BAC = 30°$
and $r = 5$.

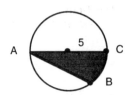

ST-32.   A fire is spotted by two lookout stations
that are 10 miles apart. The Smoky
Ridge station measures an angle of 78°
between the fire and the Firesight station.
Firesight measures an angle of 43°
between the fire and Smoky Ridge.

a)   How far is the fire from Firesight
Station?

b)   How far is the fire from Smoky Ridge?

ST-33.   On January 1st, the student population at Awl R. Smart High School, a year-round
school, was 1368 students. Three months later, on April 1st, the population seems to
have declined exponentially, and is 1124 students.

a)   Assuming that the population is declining exponentially, write an equation which
will give the student population at time x in months.

b)   Will the population ever reach zero?

c)   The school board will shut the school down if the student population drops below 100
students. When will this happen?

ST-34.   Write $(a^{-1} + b^{-1})^{-1}$ as a single fraction with positive exponents.

ST-35.   Solve each quadratic equation and then graph the solutions in the complex plane.

a) $x^2 + 4x + 5 = 0$ b) $x^2 - 6x + 13 = 0$

ST-36.   Here is another funny rule: If $A ¤ B ¤ C$ means $\dfrac{A^{(B-C)}}{A^{(C-B)}}$. What is:

a) $2 ¤ 3 ¤ 4$?   b) $4 ¤ 3 ¤ 2$?   c) $A ¤ A ¤ A$?

ST-37.   If a 4-cm cube is first painted red and then cut into sixty-four 1-cm cubes, what is the
          probability that a cube chosen at random will be painted on:

          a)   0 sides?   b)   1 side?   c)   2 sides?

          d)   3 sides?   e)   4 sides?   f)   all 6 sides?

ST-38.   Solve each of the following for x and/or y.

          a) $5 \cdot 4^x = 12$ b) $x^2 + y^2 = 16$
                                                            $y = x^2 - 4$

ST-39.   Draw examples of:

          a)   a regular polygon.   b)   a regular pyramid.

          c)   a right cylinder.   d)   a cone.

SOLVING TRIANGLES GIVEN THREE SIDES

ST-40.   The lengths of the sides of a triangle are 3, 4, and 5.

          a)   Is this triangle a right triangle? Justify your answer.

          b)   Sketch a picture of this triangle.

          c)   Find the measures of the other parts (i.e. the three angles) to the nearest hundredth
                of a degree.

ST-41.   Suppose that you want to find the measures of the angles in a triangle with sides
          measuring 5, 6, and 7.

          a)   Is this a right triangle? Justify your answer.

          b)   Explain what happens if you try to find the measures of the other parts, the three
                angles, by using the Law of Sines.

ST-42. Since the Law of Sines doesn't seem to help us in cases like the one in the preceding problem, we need to develop another method to find the measures of the angles.

a) In the picture at right, if the length of $\overline{AP}$ is x, what expression represents the length of $\overline{PB}$?

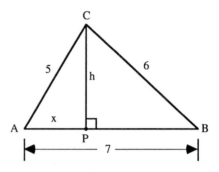

b) Use the Pythagorean Theorem to write a system of two equations: one using 5, x and h and the other using the length of $\overline{PB}$, h, and 6.

c) Solve your system of two equations for x and h.

ST-43. Now that you have found the lengths of the sides of the smaller **right** triangles, you can find the measures of the angles. What are the measures of the angles to the nearest tenth?

ST-44. Find the measures of each of the angles in a triangle with sides of length:

a) 5, 7, and 9.

b) 6, 8, and 10.

ST-45. In this problem use the same steps (using the Pythagorean Theorem) as you used to solve the previous problems. This time you will use only variables.

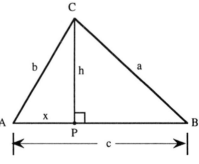

a) Write two appropriate equations using the smaller right triangles.

b) Solve the system for x. Your solution should contain a, b, and c.

c) Use your result in part (b) as a substitute for x and solve for h. The result should contain a, b, and c and will look very messy.

ST-46. Solve the following equations for x. Round answers to the nearest 0.1°

a) $8 = 5 + 2 \tan x$
b) $4^2 = 5^2 - 2(4) \tan x$
c) $6 - 2 \tan x = 4 + 5 \tan x$

ST-47. Macario just completed part (a) of the previous problem. After writing the original statement, his first step was to write $8 = 7 \tan x$ and then he divided by 7 to get $1.143 = \tan x$. Is there anything wrong with the method that he is using? Explain.

ST-48. Shawn was working on simplifying an answer that he got to a physics problem. His original solution was:

$$a = \sqrt{70^2 + 25^2 - 2(70)(25)(\cos 50°)}$$

$$a = \sqrt{4900 + 625 - 3500(\cos 50°)}$$

$$a = \sqrt{2025(\cos 50°)}$$

$$a = \sqrt{2025(0.642788)}$$

$$a = \sqrt{1301.6}$$

$$a \approx 36.1$$

What is wrong with this solution? What is the correct value of a?

ST-49. Consider the sequence where 87 is the initial value:

$$87 \qquad 71 \quad 55 \quad 39 \quad \cdots$$

a) What are the next three terms?

b) Write a formula for the nth term after the initial value.

ST-50. A population of bacteria cells grows at the rate shown in the table below.

a) How many cells are there after six hours?

b) Write a formula which will give the number of cells at hour n.

Hours	Cells (in thousands)
0	5
1	15
2	45

ST-51. Where do these three planes intersect?

$$3x + 4y = 19$$
$$2y + 3z = 8$$
$$4x - 5z = 7$$

ST-52.   As grain is being unloaded from a freight car, the rising pile forms the shape of a cone. The pile grows as more and more grain is unloaded, but the cones at different stages are always similar. After ten minutes the height of the cone is five feet and the radius of the base is nine feet. After thirty minutes, the height is twelve feet. How much area, on the ground, does the pile cover at this point?

ST-53.   Compute each complex product.

a) $\left(1+i\sqrt{3}\right)^2$ b) $\left(1+i\sqrt{3}\right)^3$

THE LAW OF COSINES

ST-54.   Recall from yesterday the problem where we wanted to find the angles in a triangle with side lengths 5, 6, and 7. In order to solve that problem it was necessary to solve a system of quadratic equations. Although you were able to solve this problem, it involved many subproblems. We would like to turn this long series of subproblems into a shorter method by developing a general rule or formula.

Consider the figure at right:

a)   Find e in terms of c and d.

b)   Split the figure into **two right triangles** and make clearly labeled sketches of the new triangles.

c)   Use the Pythagorean Theorem with each **right triangle** to find two equations (one for b^2 and one for a^2), but don't use e. Use what you found in part (a) as a substitution for e.

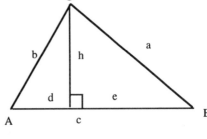

ST-55.   Using the **smaller right triangle** above, what is the ratio for cos A?

ST-56. Our goal is to create an equation, similar to the Pythagorean Theorem, which tells how the lengths of the sides of the original triangle are related even when the triangle is not a right triangle. The lengths we are interested in are a, b, and c.

a) Look at the equations you found in problem ST-54 part (c). To find the formula we seek, which variables need to be eliminated?

b) Using the techniques you have learned for solving systems of equations, eliminate h from this system (i.e., combine the two equations to make one equation in which the h^2 term no longer appears).

c) Solve the resulting equation for a^2. Simplify the result by expressing it without parentheses and combining similar terms.

d) What does this expression remind you of?

e) What do you think is the significance of the term -2cd?

f) Solve the equation in problem ST-55 for d, then substitute for d in your answer to part (c) above.

g) Explain why it makes sense that, in order to find a^2, you need to know angle A, as well as lengths b and c.

In the previous problem you derived one version of **LAW OF COSINES**.

For <u>any</u> $\triangle ABC$, it is always true that: $\mathbf{a^2 = b^2 + c^2 - 2bc \cos A}$.

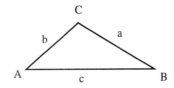

This law is very useful because it allows you to use the cosine function to solve for measures of angles and lengths of sides for <u>any</u> triangle, not just right triangles.

ST-57. The Law of Cosines can be thought of as the Pythagorean Theorem with a correction term for non-right triangles. To investigate, suppose b = 3 and c = 4.

a) What is the value of a when $m\angle A = 90°$?

b) Find 'a' when $m\angle A = 40°$. How does this value compare to the 'a' in part (a)?

c) Find 'a' when $m\angle A = 110°$. How does this value compare to the 'a' in part (a)?

d) What relationship do you notice between the size of $\angle A$ and the "correction term"?

ST-58. Rewrite the Law of Cosines in the form "cos A = "; that is, solve for cos A.

ST-59. You are a surveyor who needs to lay out a triangular lot at the corner of an intersection. The two streets bounding the lot make an angle of 70°. The lengths of the two sides of the lot on these streets are 140 feet and 112 feet.

a) Decide whether or not there is exactly one lot which can have the required properties and explain why you made this decision.

b) Find the length of the third side of the lot.

c) Find the other two angles of the lot.

ST-60. Suppose that the city of Eau Claire passes an ordinance that corner lots cannot be larger than 7200 square feet in area. Would the lot in the preceding problem be approved in Eau Claire? Justify your answer.

ST-61. Substitute the known sides and angle into the Law of Cosines to find the missing side x to the nearest hundredth.

a)

b)

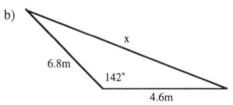

ST-62. The Law of Cosines can be used to solve for missing angles as well. Refer to your result in problem ST-58, then solve each of the following problems for z:

a)

b)

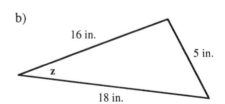

ST-63. Let $f(x) = (x + 3)^3(x^2 - 4x)$. Find the roots of $f(x)$ and make a rough sketch of the graph.

ST-64.   Refer to the Quadratic Formula for solving $ax^2 + bx + c = 0$. Under what conditions will
          the equation have:

          a)   one real solution?   b)   two real solutions?   c)   no real solutions?

ST-65.   Write each of the following as a single fraction:

          a) $\dfrac{2}{x} + \dfrac{4}{y}$ b) $\dfrac{1}{x-2} - \dfrac{1}{x+2}$

          c)   Justify each of the steps you took in part (b).

ST-66.   McGumper is locked in a
          shrinking room. The initial
          dimensions are 10 feet by 10
          feet by 10 feet. After one
          minute the room is 9.5 feet
          long, 9.5 feet wide and 9 feet
          high.

          a)   What is the initial
                volume of the room?

          b)   What is the volume after
                one minute?

          c)   If the dimensions of the
                room continue to change
          at this constant rate, what is the volume of the room after n minutes?

          d)   Sketch a graph to show how the volume changes as time passes.

          e)   McGumper needs a minimum of 100 cubic feet of space and 6 minutes to escape.
                Will McGumper make it out safely?

ST-67. To find the height h of a small mountain in the California Coast Range, two angle measurements were taken 1200 feet apart along a direct line toward the mountain. With this information, find the height of the mountain.

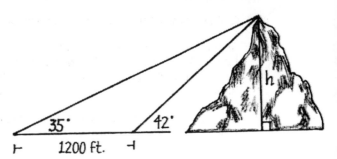

ST-68. Triangle ABC has m∠A = 65°, m∠C = 45° and BC = 10 cm. Find the length(s) of $\overline{AC}$. Hint: draw a diagram!

ST-69. In a major league baseball diamond, which is in fact a square, the bases are 90 feet apart, and the pitcher's mound is exactly 60 feet 6 inches from home plate.

a) Draw a diagram of the baseball diamond.

b) Find the distance between the pitcher's mound and third base.

ST-70. An isosceles triangle has an area of 60 square centimeters and a base of 10 centimeters. Draw a sketch of such a triangle.

a) Draw the line segment from the midpoint of the base to the opposite vertex to get two smaller triangles. List everything you know about these smaller triangles.

b) Find the lengths of the two congruent sides of the isosceles triangle.

c) List the subproblems that you had to solve to answer part (b).

ST-71. Tuan Nguyen noticed that during the winter, even with his heater running, the temperature in his house would rise and fall throughout a 24 hour period. Here are some temperatures he recorded at different times.

time	Midnight	4:00 a.m.	8:00 a.m.	Noon	4:00 p.m.	8:00 p.m.
temperature	63°	59°	63°	71°	75°	71°

Using Tuan's recorded amounts:

a) graph the data.

b) write an equation which could model this data.

ST-72.   In geometry, we had several methods for showing that two triangles are congruent. (For example, we could use the **SSS** congruence property.)

a)   List as many methods as you can remember.

b)   Suppose you know three sides of a triangle (**SSS**). Would you want to use the Law of Sines, the Law of Cosines, or some other techniques from trigonometry to compute the three angles of the triangle? Creating an example might help you to think about this.

c)   Use whatever technique you decided on in part (b) to compute the angles of a triangle with sides 3, 6 and 7.

ST-73.   Al needs to drill a water well for his new home in the hills. Becky, who lives in the valley below said that she had to drill 84 feet before she struck water. The distance straight up the hill to Al's cabin is 3150 feet. If the angle of inclination for the hill averages 15°, how far down will Al have to drill assuming the water is at the same level as it was for Becky? Do you think this situation is, in reality, likely to occur?

ST-74.   Hue was making $6.50 an hour working at Burger Delite and looking to move up.

a)   When she was made night manager, her salary went up 40%. How much was she making then?

b)   Hue figured she was on easy street and began arriving late for work, so she was demoted and had her salary reduced by 40%. What does she make now?

c)   Forty per cent was added then taken off. Why is Hue's new salary lower than her original salary?

ST-75.   Solve for x if $x^3 + 4x = 0$.

ST-76.   Let $z = \dfrac{(a^3 b^{-2})^{-3}}{ab^3}$.

a)   Write z as a fraction using only positive exponents.

b)   Write z as a fraction using only negative exponents.

ST-77.   The junior class at Pohatsa High School decided it would be more cost effective to buy CD's and tapes for their school dances than to hire a DJ. Danielle found that six CD's cost the same as ten cassette tapes while Kris found that 12 CD's and 15 tapes cost $272.73. Find the cost per CD and the cost per tape.

ST-78.   Plot the following eight values of the polynomial function f(x) given below on one set of axes. This function has at least how many roots?

$$f(-5) = -1 \qquad f(-3) = 3 \qquad f(-1) = 6 \qquad f(5) = 0$$

$$f(0) = 5 \qquad f(1) = -1 \qquad f(3) = -4 \qquad f(9) = 8$$

ST-79.   Simplify each of the following expressions:

a) $2^x \cdot 2^x$ b) $\dfrac{2^x}{2}$

ST-80.   Factor: $2^x + 2$.

ST-81.   John thinks that $\log (A^n) = \log (A) + n$ and here is his proof. Examine each step and if it correct, tell why. If it incorrect, change it so that it is correct.

Let $x = \log A$.

That means that $A = 10^x$.

Then it is true that $(A)^n = (10^x)^n = 10^{x+n}$

If $(A)^n = 10^{x+n}$, then $\log (A)^n = \log 10^{x+n} = x + n$

So finally $\log (A)^n = x + n = \log (A) + n$

ST-82. Consider ΔABC at right:

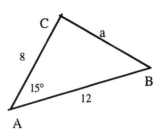

a) Why is this a well-defined triangle? What theorem ensures that all triangles with this given information will be congruent?

b) Find the length of the missing side a.

c) Use the Law of Sines to find m∠C. Then use subtraction to find m∠B. Record your answers.

d) Now use the Law of Sines to find ∠B first and then use subtraction to find ∠C. Record your answers.

e) Which triangle is correct? Explain how you can tell.

ST-83. What happened in the previous problem? Does the order in which we find the angles really matter? On a Unit Circle resource page, draw ∠C (the correct ∠C!) from problem ST-82 in standard position. What type of angle is this?

a) Find the sine of ∠C. Record that value on your paper and show it on the unit circle.

b) You know how to use the sin⁻¹ key to find the measure of an angle when you know its sine. What would you expect to get if you find sin⁻¹ of your answer to part (a)? Do it. What do you actually get? Does it look familiar? Record this angle on your paper and draw it on the same unit circle.

c) What relationship do these two angles have? Why do they have the same sine?

d) Make a conjecture about your findings.

ST-84. **USE SIN⁻¹ WITH CAUTION!**

a) What kind of angle is 110°? Find the sine of 110° and record this value. Using the sin⁻¹ key, find sin⁻¹ of the value you just recorded. What angle did you get? What is the relationship between these two angles?

b) When you find sin⁻¹(0.9397) on your calculator, you are essentially asking "What is **the** angle whose sine is 0.9397?" But there isn't just one such angle, and the calculator can only give you one answer. In general, which answer does it give you?

c) Every time you use the Law of Sines to find the measure of an angle, you must consider the possibility that the angle you are looking for is not the one the calculator gives you! What must you do to make sure that your answer is correct?

d) Record your answer to part (c) in your Tool Kit.

ST-85.   Sometimes you can't tell whether the missing angle is acute or obtuse. This happens when the triangle is not uniquely defined by the information given. Consider a triangle, ABC, with $\angle A = 30°$ and side c = 10. Using the Law of Sines, and each value of 'a' given below, determine the measure of $\angle C$.

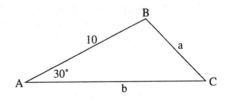

a)   a = 5   b)   a = 3   c)   a = 7

d)   Sketch a picture to illustrate your answer to part (a). Use it to explain your answer to part (b).

e)   Did you get two answers in part (c)? Perhaps you assumed that b is the longest side, so $\angle C$ must be acute, but the drawing is deceptive; we don't know the length of side b. Draw another version of the triangle, with $m\angle A$ still 30°, c = 10 and a = 7, but with $\angle C$ the largest angle. It helps to imagine side 'a' hinged at vertex B, since $\angle B$, $\angle C$, and side b are all unknown. Label this drawing with the correct measures of its angles.

ST-86.   We could describe problem ST-85 as an example of SSA: finding the missing parts of the triangle when given two sides and an angle other than the one between the known sides.

a)   For each of the following SSA cases, draw as many different triangles fitting the data as you can. The sides and angles are listed in order as you go around the triangle:

i)   40°, 5, 7   ii)   40°, 7, 5   iii)   30°, 10, 5

b)   SSA should not be one of the congruence theorems you listed in problem ST-72. Explain why SSA is not a congruence theorem.

ST-87.   Write out several sentences explaining how to use the Law of Sines to find all possible solutions to a triangle for which you know two sides and an angle that is not included between them (SSA). Make sure your answer applies to all three examples in problem ST-86 (a).

ST-88.   Investigate the SSA case of 30°, 11, 5. Make a sketch, and use the Law of Sines to find one of the missing angles. Explain the result.

ST-89.   Are there any other combinations of three angles and/or sides that could be given to mislead you into thinking there was a triangle when there wasn't? If so, what are they?

ST-90.   For each of the congruence methods you listed in part (a) of problem ST-72, decide whether you can find the other three parts of the triangle using only the Law of Sines, only the Law of Cosines, or if you will need to use both?

ST-91.   A trapezoid has an altitude of 6 cm and bases of length 20 cm and 8 cm.

    a)   Find its area.

    b)   The original trapezoid is cut by a line parallel to and halfway between its parallel edges to make two new trapezoids. Find the area of each.

ST-92.   A circle of radius 10 cm cut out of cardboard weighs 120 gm.

    a)   How much would a 60° sector weigh?

    b)   How much would a circle of radius 15 cm cut out of the same cardboard weigh? *Think carefully! This is not as simple as it may appear!*

ST-93.   Write each of the following expressions as a single fraction:

    a) $\dfrac{2}{5} + \dfrac{4}{x}$ b) $\dfrac{x^2}{x+1} - \dfrac{2}{x}$

ST-94.   In the figure at right, solve for x.

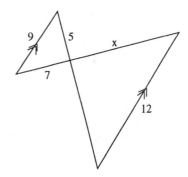

ST-95.   Consider the triangle below right.

    a)   Using the given information, could you draw a non-congruent triangle? What congruence property justifies your answer?

    b)   Find the lengths of the unknown sides and the measure of the missing angle.

THE SEARCH FOR SUNKEN TREASURE!

ST-96.   It was another lazy day in southern
Florida. Sandy Salvage, the
famous underwater explorer (he's
the only diver ever to have gone to
a depth of 1 kilometer in just scuba
gear) and treasure hunter of The
Golden Mind Company, has heard
that a ship loaded with gold just
sank off the coast of Florida in
international waters. All Sandy has
to do is be the first company to get
to the wreck site and he can claim
the underwater treasure. Getting
there first is, of course, not a

problem since Sandy has two of the best and fastest ships in the world, the Goldrush
and the Goldfish.

Sandy's problem is that Blackbeard, the famous pirate of the high seas, also wants the
treasure. Blackbeard's ship, the Surging Skurge, is an old wreck herself, and the only
way Blackbeard will get his grimy hands on the treasure is to wait until Sandy gets the
treasure aboard, then attack Sandy's ship. Sandy has decided that if he sends a decoy
ship, he will have a 50% chance of not having to fight off the villain.

Your team, which has been captured by Blackbeard (because of your mathematical
power), must determine which of Sandy's ships has been chosen to be the treasure ship.
You must help Blackbeard get the treasure. If your team finds the correct ship Blackbeard
has promised to spare your lives. If you pick the wrong ship, you walk the plank!

The only information that Blackbeard could give you was a note from one of his spies
with the angle of descent of 2.18° from the seaport to the actual location of the treasure.

Be sure to read each part of the following three problems carefully and refer back to this
introduction if necessary.

ST-97.   The Goldrush left port on a due east heading for 15
km then turned toward the north 55° from east for 27
km. The Goldrush dropped anchor there, but sent a
mini submarine in the same direction as a line going
directly from the port <u>through</u> the Goldrush. The sub
descended at a 48° angle for 2 kilometers.

a)   How far from port was the Goldrush when it
dropped anchor?

b)   How far was it from the shore to the final
location of the sub?

c)   What was the angle of descent from the shore to the final location of the sub?

ST-98.   The Goldfish left the port at the same time and headed 15° south of due east for 20 kilometers. From that heading the crew turned toward the north 80° for 38 kilometers. At that point the Goldfish dropped anchor and the diver-down flag went up. The treasure appeared to be directly beneath the ship.

   a)   What is the distance between port and the Goldfish when it dropped anchor?

   b)   What is the depth of the water if this is where the treasure is located?

   c)   How far is it from the shore to the possible location of the treasure?

ST-99.   Well, you scurvy barnacles, make your decision! Are you spared, or do you walk the plank? Which ship do you send Blackbeard after, the Goldrush or the Goldfish? Explain your reasoning.

ST-100.   A quadrilateral has its vertices at A(0, 0), B(8, 1), C(6, 7), and D(-1, 9).

   a)   Sketch the figure on graph paper.   b)   Find the length of the longer diagonal.

   c)   Explain in a sentence or two how you could find the measure of angle A. (Don't do it—just tell _how_ you would do it.)

ST-101.   Find the acute angle formed by the intersection of the lines $y = -\frac{1}{5}x + 4$ and $y = -\frac{4}{5}x + 1$. Starting with a precise graph might be helpful.

ST-102.   In a Modoc High School production, the stage crew must build a model of the Leaning Tower of Pisa. The model will be 15 feet long, but when they stand it up it will not reach that altitude since it will be leaning 10° from the vertical. A wire which will hold the tower in place is attached to the floor 20 feet from the bottom of the Leaning Tower model. How long must the wire be to reach the top of the Leaning Tower of Pisa?

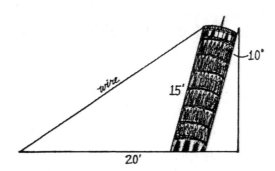

ST-103.   Plot the points (0, 2), (3, 4) and (6, 9).

   a)   Find the equation of the line that best fits these points.

   b)   Find the equation of the parabola which best fits these points.

   c)   Find the equation of the exponential function which best fits these points.

ST-104. Find the angles in the triangle formed by the points A(-2, 6), B(4, 3), and C(4, -3).

ST-105. Make a sketch of the graph of each of the equations below. On the same set of axes, sketch the inverse. Then algebraically find the equation of the inverse.

a) $y = x^3 + 5$

b) $y = 4 \cdot 2^x$

ST-106. Of the inverses you found in the previous problem, which are functions? Justify your answer.

ST-107. Solve each of the following for x:

a) $\log_2 \left(\frac{3x}{x + 1} \right) = -1$

b) $\log_3 \left(\frac{2x + 28}{x} \right) = 2$

ST-108. Solve the following system for x and y:

$$2x - y = 7$$
$$x + 2y = 9$$

ST-109. Find the value of $(3y - 5)^2$ if $2y + 2 = 16$.

INVERSE TRIGONOMETRIC FUNCTIONS

ST-110. Take out two full, clean sheets of graph paper. On each page, set up x- and y-axes, centered on the page. Let the units on your x-axis be in radians. On one graph, make a neat and accurate graph of $y = \sin x$ and on the other a graph of $y = \cos x$. Do them in thick, heavy pencil and include two full cycles, one on each side of the origin. Use the technique of folding the page along the line $y = x$ to make a graph of the <u>inverse</u> of each of these functions. What is the formula for each of these graph? Label each graph with its formula.

ST-111. Investigate the two inverses.

ST-112. Using your graphing calculator, try to find an equation which, when graphed, will give the inverses you have on the graph paper. Why do you get only a portion of the graph of the inverse? Explain completely.

ST-113. You have been using the function $y = \text{Sin}^{-1} x$ on your calculator for some time, but as you saw in the previous problem this function is not precisely the inverse of $y = \sin x$, since that inverse is not function. Instead, $y = \text{Sin}^{-1} x$ is the inverse of a part of the sine function; to see which part, graph the inverse of $y = \text{Sin}^{-1} x$. In this piece of the sine function (or restricted sine function, because x has been restricted to certain values), each value in the range appears exactly once, so that when you take the inverse of *this* function it will be a function; for each x between -1 and 1 inclusive, there will be exactly one angle y whose sine is x. That angle is referred to as the **principal angle whose sine is x**, and this function in addition to being called the **Inverse Sine of x**, denoted $y = \text{Sin}^{-1} x$, is also called the **Arcsine of x**, denoted $y = \text{Arcsin x}$. (Warning: what in this case looks like an exponent of -1 **does not** mean $\frac{1}{\sin x}$. See problem ST-29.) Refer to the graphs of $x = \sin y$ and $y = \text{Sin}^{-1} x$ from problems ST-110 and ST-112. You may also use the Circle of Terror diagram.

a) Find four solutions to the equation $\sin y = 0.5$. Which of these is $\text{Sin}^{-1} 0.5$?

b) Find four solutions to the equation $\sin y = -0.5$. Which of these is $\text{Sin}^{-1} -0.5$?

c) Of all the values of y for which $\sin y = x$ for a given x, which is the *principal* value of y whose sine is x? (i.e., which one is $\text{Sin}^{-1} x$?) How is this related to the restricted sine function?

d) What is the domain of $y = \text{Sin}^{-1} x$? Why?

ST-114. The situation for the inverse of the cosine is similar, but not identical, to that for sine. The **Inverse Cosine of x**, denoted $y = \text{Cos}^{-1} x$, is also called the **Arccosine of x**, or $y = \text{Arccos x}$, and the output it gives is the **principal angle whose cosine is x**.

a) $Y = \text{Cos}^{-1} x$ is the inverse of part of $y = \cos x$, but which part? Make a graph of the inverse of $y = \text{Cos}^{-1} x$ (this is the restricted cosine function). What is the domain of this graph? Is it the same as the domain of the inverse of $y = \text{Sin}^{-1} x$? Explain.

b) Find four solutions to the equation $\cos y = 0.5$. Which of these is $\text{Cos}^{-1} 0.5$?

c) Find four solutions to the equation $\cos y = -0.5$. Which of these is $\text{Cos}^{-1} -0.5$?

d) Of all the values of y for which $\cos y = x$ for a given x, which is the *principal* value of y whose cosine is x? (i.e., which one is $\text{Cos}^{-1} x$?)

ST-115. In each of the following equations, x is in **radians**. Solve for x. Each equation has infinitely many possible solutions; your teacher will tell you which of them to list.

a) $3 + 2 \sin x = 2$

b) $(\cos x + 1)(3 \cos x - 1) = 0$

c) $(\sin x - 2)(5 \sin x - 3) = 0$

The Search for Sunken Treasure: More Triangles and Trigonometry

ST-116. Graph $y = \tan x$ and $y = \text{Tan}^{-1} x$ (also known as **Arctan x**) on your graphing calculator. Make a sketch of what you see.

a) $Y = \text{Tan}^{-1} x$ is the inverse of which part of $y = \tan x$? This is the restricted tangent function; what is its domain?

b) Of all the values of y which solve $\tan y = x$ for a given value of x, which one is the principal angle whose tangent is x?

ST-117. For what value(s) of k does the quadratic equation $x^2 - 4x + k = 0$ have:

a) one solution?   b) two real solutions?

c) no real solutions?

ST-118. For what value(s) of m does $x^2 + 2mx + 9 = 0$ have:

a) one real solution?   b) two real solutions? This may require some careful thinking.

ST-119. Sketch the graph of each of the following equations without using a graphing calculator:

a) $y = -2 + \sin (x - \frac{\pi}{4})$ b) $y = 3 - 4 \cos (x + \frac{\pi}{3})$

ST-120. All three sides are given in the triangle at right. Calculate the measures of all the angles.

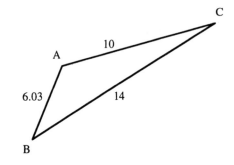

ST-121. A newly planted tree is supported by guy-wires attached to its trunk at a point 14 feet above the ground. There are three wires, each making a 60° angle with the ground. The stakes that attach them to the ground are at the vertices of an equilateral triangle. Find the sides of this triangle and the length of each guy-wire. (Draw a picture.)

ST-122. Convert each of the following angles from radians to degrees.

a) $\frac{\pi}{5}$ b) $\frac{-2\pi}{3}$ c) $\frac{13\pi}{12}$

ST-123. Why is the domain of Arcsin the same as the domain of Arccos? Why is the domain of Arctan different ?

ST-124. Add the following information to your Tool Kit:

INVERSE CIRCULAR FUNCTIONS

Y = ARCSIN X is the name for the Inverse Sine Function. It means the same as $\text{Sin}^{-1} x$ or "find the principal angle whose sine is x." In other words, it gives the angle of rotation between $-\frac{\pi}{2}$ and $\frac{\pi}{2}$ radians or between -90° and 90° that has x as its sine.

Y = ARCCOS X is the name for the Inverse Cosine Function. It means the same as $\text{Cos}^{-1} x$ or "find the principal angle whose cosine is x." In other words, it gives the angle of rotation between 0 and π radians or between 0° and 180° that has x as its cosine.

Y = ARCTAN X is the name for the Inverse Tangent Function. It means the same as Tan^{-1} or "find the principal angle whose tangent is x." In other words, it gives the angle of rotation between $-\frac{\pi}{2}$ and $\frac{\pi}{2}$ radians or between -90° and 90° that has x as its tangent.

ST-125. Graph the functions $y = \tan^2 x + 1$ and $y = \frac{1}{\cos^2 x}$ on your calculator. What do you notice? Explain. You'll need another way to express tan x and the Pythagorean Identity. Use your Tool Kit!

ST-126. Find three values of x (in radians) such that $x = \tan x$.

ST-127. **UNIT 9 SUMMARY ASSIGNMENT**

Now that you have learned a little bit more trigonometry, we want you to answer a question again: what <u>is</u> trigonometry? Give a definition as you understand it now. Then summarize the important new ideas of this unit, including an example for each, along with a complete solution. In your examples, you should give at least two original problems of your own creation that represent important concepts developed in this unit and show their solutions. Finally, on what topics do you still have questions? What do you think you understand well?

ST-128.   Find all the missing parts for each of the following triangles:

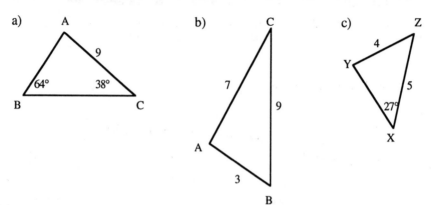

a)   A

9

64°   38°

B   C

b)   C

7

9

A

3

B

c)   Z

4

Y

5

27°

X

ST-129.   Solve the following system for x, y, and z.

$$x + 2y + 3z = 1$$
$$2x - y - 3z = 11$$
$$y + z = -1$$

ST-130.   A rectangle has an area of 240 cm² and its length is 3 times its width. Compute the length of its diagonal.

ST-131.   Solve for y if $3^{(y^2 - 4y)} = 1$.

ST-132.   Use the Pythagorean Identity to simplify $\frac{\sin x}{\cos x} + \frac{\cos x}{\sin x}$.

ST-133.   Solve each equation.

a) $\frac{1}{x} + \frac{1}{3x} = 6$

b) $\frac{1}{x} + \frac{1}{x+1} = 3$

ST-134.   Solve exactly for x if $\left(x + 2\right)\left(x - \frac{3}{x}\right) = \left(x - 2\right)\left(x + \frac{3}{x}\right)$.

ST-135.   Simplify the following: $\log_2 (4^{10} \div 8^3)$.

ST-136. Sketch the graph of each of the following.

a) $y = \log_2 (x + 2)$ 　　 b) $y = 2 + \log_2 x$ 　　 c) $y = |\log_2 x|$

ST-137. Solve the following problems for x.

a)

b)

c)

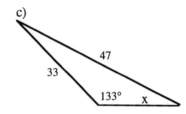

ST-138. Solve each equation. Give answers in **degrees**.

a) $\tan^2 x - 3 = 0$ 　　 b) $2 \cos x \cdot \sin x + \cos x = 0$ 　 c) $3 \sin^2 x + 4 \sin x + 1 = 0$

ST-139. **TOOL KIT CLEAN-UP**

Tool Kits often need to be reorganized to continue to be useful. Your Tool Kit contains entries from units 1 through 9.

Examine the list of Tool Kit entries from this unit. Add any that you are missing.

Identify the concepts that you understand.

Choose entries to create a Unit 1 - 9 Tool Kit that is shorter, clear, and useful.

- Area of SAS Triangles
- Law of Cosines

- Use Sin⁻¹ with Caution
- Inverse Circular Functions

ST-140. **COURSE SUMMARY ASSIGNMENT**

Since the start of this course you have been learning about mathematics as a tool for solving many problems. Tell what you think are the five or six most important concepts in mathematics you have learned this year. How have you used these concepts this year? Give specific problems with solutions to illustrate your choices.

UNIT 10

Policy Making
PROBABILITY

Unit 10 Objectives
Policy Making: PROBABILITY

In this unit you will learn about probability through two visual representations: tree diagrams and area models. These representations make conditional probability understandable and lead to the consideration of decision making in relation to some important policy issues such as mandatory testing for drugs and diseases.

In this unit, you will have the opportunity to:

- use tree and area diagrams to represent multiplication, particularly the multiplication of probabilities expressed as fractions, decimals, and percents.

- use tree and area diagrams to model problems of conditional probability.

- compute expected values and determine whether games are fair.

- apply matrices to probabilities.

- learn about some ways in which a knowledge of probability can provide valuable information in relation to important policy decisions.

An understanding of probability is valuable in relation to important policy issues that are often decided for political reasons. As the issues get more complicated, a knowledge of probability and statistics could make a big difference in the decisions each of us will help to make. The following hypothetical problem is one example. Read through the problem now. We will complete it later in the unit.

PM-0. **AIDS TESTING AND MULTIPLICATION:** With the growth of the number of AIDS cases, some people have called for mandatory testing for the HIV virus with public disclosure of the results. Others argue that mandatory testing would jeopardize the lives and livelihood of many people who do not have the disease and is therefore an unwarranted and unjust invasion of their privacy. Furthermore, they argue that if testing is not mandatory, more people who are at risk will volunteer for testing, increasing the likelihood of identifying and helping people who have the disease.

If the test for HIV is 99% accurate on the population to be tested (suppose that in this case doctors, dentists and other health practitioners would be tested) and 100 out of 100,000 people in that group actually are HIV positive, what percentage of those who are tested will be false-positive? In other words, what is the probability that a health practitioner would be identified as having the AIDS virus who actually did not?

PROBLEM SOLVING
REPRESENTATION/MODELING
FUNCTIONS/GRAPHING
INTERSECTIONS/SYSTEMS
ALGORITHMS
REASONING/COMMUNICATION

Unit 10
Policy Making: PROBABILITY

PM-1. When you first learned to add you probably did addition by counting. You could combine a set of four buttons with a set of three buttons and count seven buttons. A **discrete** model looked something like:

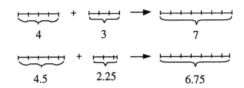

Later on you learned to measure and learned number names for parts of a whole number, so you could use a **continuous** model:

Then you mastered multiplication. For example, to compute 4 x 3, you at first used discrete arrangements of four groups of three:

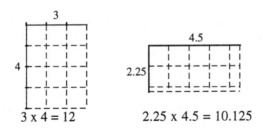

Later you may have used a continuous model related to area.

$$3 \times 4 = 12 \qquad 2.25 \times 4.5 = 10.125$$

Area is a useful way to think about multiplying fractions.

One day when Alfred and Fritz were mowing neighboring lawns to earn money, Al yelled over to Fritz, "Let's take a break. How much have you done?" Fritz yelled back, "Oh, about three-quarters of a half." "Huh?" said Alfred.

Use an area model to explain to Alfred what Fritz meant when he said he had finished mowing $\frac{3}{4}$ of $\frac{1}{2}$ of his rectangular lawn. Then explain how this model relates to the product $\frac{3}{4} \cdot \frac{1}{2}$.

PM-2. There is another way to visualize four groups of three. Think of branches of a tree: start with four branches, then add three branches on each of those four. (Read the model at right from bottom to top.)

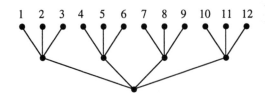

An advantage of this model is that it is easy to extend to multiply three or more numbers. For example, 4 x 2 x 3 starts with four branches, then expands with two branches on each of those four, then extends three branches on each of the eight from the 4 x 2 part. (We can draw our trees sideways or upside down.) There should be 24 endpoints in the figure at right.

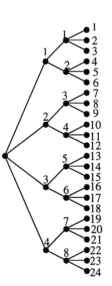

Think about the following situation:

Maryanne said she was late to class on Monday because she couldn't decide what outfit to wear. On Sunday, her birthday, she received two new pairs of jeans: one white, the other faded blue; three tops: one plain, one striped, and one print; and two jackets: one lightweight and one heavier. On Monday morning she realized everything color-coordinated with everything else.

a) Draw a multiplication tree to represent all the possible outfits she could wear: jeans, tops, and jackets.

b) How many different completely new outfits did she have to choose from?

c) If she chose randomly, what is the probability she chose the print top and the white jeans?

d) What is the probability that the striped top was part of her outfit.

e) In what other ways could you have organized the information in this problem?

Both the AREA and TREE models for multiplication should be useful as you work on the problems in this unit.

PM-3. You will need to work in a team of four. Have one person act as recorder while the other three act as players.

    a) List the names of the people in your team alphabetically. The first person on the list is player A, the next is player B, the third is C, and the fourth is the recorder. Write down who has each role.

    b) Play "Rock - Paper - Scissors" at least 20 times. Each time all three players match, player A gets one point. Each time two of the three players match, player B gets a point. If none of the players match, then player C gets a point. Record the players' points.

    c) If you could choose to be any player, A, B, or C, which would you choose? As a team, prepare a justification for your choice. A tree model might help, or you may just want to make a well-organized list.

    d) What is the probability that A will win? B? C?

    e) What can you do to make the game fair, that is, so that each person has an equally likely chance of winning? Write up your plan and justify it.

PM-4. Use the averaging method to find the vertex of each parabola.

    a) $y = x^2 + 8x + 12$ b) $y = x^2 - 2x + 3$

PM-5. Use what you know about locator points to find the vertex of each parabola:

    a) $y = (x + 4)^2 - 4$ b) $y = (x - 1)^2 + 2$

    c) Compare your answers in this problem with the previous one. They should be the same even though the problems look different. Show why both parts (a) should give the same answer.

PM-6. Complete the square to convert to graphing form. Give the vertex and sketch the graph.

    a) $f(x) = x^2 + 6x + 7$ b) $f(x) = x^2 - 10x$

PM-7. Complete the square twice to convert the equation $x^2 + 8x + y^2 - 12y = 12$ to graphing form, then describe the graph.

PM-8.   Spud has a problem. He knows the solutions for a quadratic equation are
         x = 3 + 4i and x = 3 - 4i but in order to get credit for the problem he was supposed to
         have written down the equation. Unfortunately he lost the paper with the original
         equation on it. His friends are full of advice.

   a)   Alexia says, "Look, just remember when we did polynomials. If you wanted 7 and
         4 to be the answers, you just used (x - 7)(x - 4). So you just do x minus the first
         one times x minus the other."

   b)   Hugo says, "No, no, no. You can do it that way, but that's too complicated. I think
         you just start with x = 3 + 4i and work backwards. So x - 3 = 4i, then, hmmm.
         Yeah, that'll work."

         Help Spud figure out the original equation. You may want to use the advice of either or
         both friends.

PM-9.   **Without a calculator**, solve each equation below for $0 \le x \le 2\pi$.
         (Some parts have two answers!)

   a) $\sin x = -1$ b) $2 \cos x - 1 = 0$

   c) $\tan x = 1$ d) $2 \sin x = 4 \sin x + 1$

PM-10.   Solve each of the following equations:

   a) $\dfrac{x}{x + 1} = \dfrac{5}{7}$ b) $\dfrac{2}{y} = \dfrac{3}{y + 5}$

   c) $\dfrac{x}{x + 1} + \dfrac{2}{x - 1} = \dfrac{8}{x^2 - 1}$ d) $\dfrac{2}{y + 5} - \dfrac{3}{y} = \dfrac{3}{y + 5}$

PM-11. **PENCILS AND ERASERS**

Penny Ante's teacher has a box
with pencils and erasers in it.
There are currently three yellow,
one blue, and two red pencils in it
along with one yellow and two
red erasers. She has just bet her
friend a dime to his dollar that she could walk by the teacher's desk and, without looking,
grab a blue pencil and a red eraser from the box. Should her friend accept this challenge?

Your task is to determine the probability that Penny will walk away with a blue pencil and
a red eraser. There are several ways to organize this problem.

Gerri suggests making a list of all the possible
color combinations, pencil first then eraser.

RY	BY	YY
RR	BR	YR

"So," says Gerri, "the answer is $\frac{1}{6}$."

"That doesn't seem quite right," Says Marty. "There are more yellow pencils in there
than blue ones. I don't think the chance of getting a yellow pencil and a red eraser should
be the same as getting a blue pencil and a red eraser. Maybe we need to account for all
three yellow pencils with Y_1, Y_2, Y_3."

a) Make a tree diagram or a well-organized complete list of all the possibilities, using
subscripts to account for the colors for which there is more than one pencil or eraser.

b) Use the tree or list to find the probability of Penny snatching the blue-red
combination.

c) Should Penny's friend take the bet? Why or why not?

PM-12. From your tree diagram or list in the preceding problem it should now be easy to find the
probability for each of the six color combinations of a pencil and eraser that Marty named.

Make a list of the correct probabilities for Gerri. For example, $P(BR) = \frac{1}{9}$.

PM-13. What are the outcomes of rolling two dice, one red and
one white? So far we have used tree diagrams to organize
our thinking about sample spaces or possible outcomes.

a) Think about what would be involved in drawing a
tree to show the outcomes, then go on to part (b).

b) In part (a) we said "think about" for a good reason.
Most of the people who try to draw a tree diagram
for this problem end up with a mess on their paper
because they didn't anticipate the amount of space it
would take. Sometimes an area diagram is easier to
draw and at least as useful. In the area diagram at
right the **X** indicates that the red die shows a 2 and
the white die a 5. What does square **A** represent?

c) In the diagram, what does **B** represent?

d) What does **C** represent?

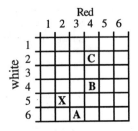

PM-14. Use graph paper and make diagrams similar to the one above. For each of the following
situations shade the appropriate squares and give the probability of the specified outcome
of rolling a red die and a white die.

a) Shade in the squares that show the red die is a 3. Find the probability that the red die
comes up three.

b) Shade in the squares that show either the red or white die is a 3. Find the probability
that at least one of the dice comes up three.

c) Shade in the squares that show the red and white dice came up the same number.
Find the probability of getting the same number on both dice.

d) Shade in the squares that show the sum of the numbers on the red and white dice is
8. Find the probability of the sum being 8.

PM-15. Look at the diagram for problem PM-13.

a) What do the 36 different squares in the diagram represent? Explain why there must
be 36.

b) If you rolled two identical dice, would you still get 36 possible outcomes?

362   UNIT 10

PM-16.   Suppose you roll two dice.

    a)   What is the probability that exactly one of them shows a 2?

    b)   What is the probability that both of them show a 2?

    c)   What is the probability of at least one 2?

    d)   What is the probability of no 2's?

PM-17.   Suppose you roll two dice but one of them has two 6's and no 1's.

    a)   Draw an area diagram of the possible outcomes.

    b)   Find the probability that the sum of the numbers on the two dice is 8.

PM-18.   Suppose you have the two ordinary dice. For each integer $n = 2, 3, 4, ..., 12$, calculate $p(n)$, the probability that the sum on the two dice is n points. For example, since there are two ways to make 3 points, $p(3) = \frac{2}{36}$. Did you use a tree or an area diagram?

PM-19.   Solve the following equations.

    a) $\frac{3}{x} + \frac{5}{x - 7} = -2$ b) $\frac{2x + 3}{4} - \frac{x - 7}{6} = \frac{2x - 3}{12}$

PM-20.   Solve these systems of equations.

    a) $x - 2y = 7$ b) $\frac{x + 4y}{3} - \frac{6y - x}{4} = -3$
          $2x + y = 3$ $\frac{x}{10} + 5y = 2$

PM-21.   Solve for x and y if:

    a) $2x + y = 12$ b) $2x + y = 12$
          $xy = 16$ $xy = 20$

    c)   Explain how the graphs of (a) and (b) relate to the solutions of each system of equations.

PM-22.   At McDugal's Golden Parabola, Ramona bought four hamburgers and two milkshakes for $4.10. Inez bought three hamburgers and one milkshake and spent $2.80. What is the cost of a hamburger? A milkshake?

PM-23.   The line $y = 3x - 4$ is perpendicular to another line which goes through the origin. What is the relationship between the slopes of perpendicular lines? If you do not remember, sketch a careful graph of a line with slope 3, and a line perpendicular to it to see what the slope must be. Find the equation of the perpendicular line through the origin.

PM-24.   Calculate the total surface area and volume of the prism at right.

8 cm

9 cm

10 cm

PM-25.   Solve the equations below for x. Show and justify all steps leading to your solution. Answers will contain a, b, and/or c.

a) $cx - a = b$

b) $\dfrac{x}{a} - b = c$

c) $(x - a)(x - b) = 0$

d) $ax^2 - acx = 0$

e) $\dfrac{x}{a + b} = \dfrac{1}{c}$

f) $\dfrac{1}{x} + a = b$

MORE TREES AND AREA MODELS

PM-26.   **PENCILS AND ERASERS AGAIN**

There are still two red, one blue, and three yellow pencils and one yellow and two red erasers in the box. Show and explain how you could use this area diagram to figure out the probabilities for all the pencil-eraser color pairs. What is the probability of getting the yellow pencil and red eraser combination?

erasers

	R₁	R₂	Y₁
Y₁	$\frac{1}{18}$		
Y₂			
Y₃			
R₁			
R₂			
B			

pencils

PM-27.   The area diagram at right could be used to represent the probabilities in the pencil/eraser problem. Explain how it is related to the one in the preceding problem.

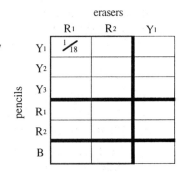

$p(R) = \frac{2}{3}$ $p(Y) = \frac{1}{3}$

$p(Y) = \frac{1}{2}$ $\frac{1}{3}$

$p(R) = \frac{1}{3}$

$p(B) = \frac{1}{6}$

PM-28. Another way to organize the pencil and eraser problem is to draw a simpler tree diagram based on the probabilities:

a) Copy and complete the probability tree shown at right.

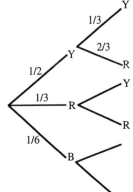

Y P(Y, Y) = 1/2 of 1/3 which equals 1/6

1/3

2/3

R P(Y, R) = 1/2 of 2/3 which equals 1/3

b) Describe what you did to find the probabilities for the color combinations.

c) Explain how the second tree is a shortcut for the tree or list you made in problem PM-11.

INDEPENDENT EVENTS

In the pencils and erasers problem, you saw that the probability of drawing a blue pencil and a red eraser equaled the product of the pencil probability and the eraser probability   P(blue pencil and red eraser) = P(blue pencil) x P(red eraser)

$$\frac{1}{9} = \frac{1}{6} \times \frac{2}{3}$$

When the probability of two events happening equals the product of their probabilities the events are said to be **independent**.

PM-29. How are the tree diagram in problem PM-28 and the area diagram in problem PM-27 related? Which method of diagramming did you like best for solving the pencil-erasers problem? Explain your reasons.

PM-30. A Nevada roulette wheel has 38 slots numbered 00, 0, 1, 2, 3, ..., 36. Eighteen of the numbers 1, 2, ..., 36 are red and 18 are black; 0 and 00 are green.

a) What is the probability of landing on red?

b) What is the probability of not landing on red?

c) The bettor put his money on red twice in a row. Use an area or a tree diagram to show how to find the probability that he won both bets.

PM-31. Harold had several jars of specially sorted jelly beans. They were specially sorted because he likes the purple ones best and the black ones next best so these were both in one jar. His next favorites were yellow, orange, and white, in that order, and these were in another jar. The rest were in the garbage. Harold allowed himself only one jelly bean from each jar per day. He also wore a blindfold when he selected his jelly beans so as not to eat all of the best ones first.

What is the probability that Harold gets his favorite jelly bean from each jar if jar #1 has 60% purple and 40% black, and jar #2 is 30% yellow, 50% orange, and 20% white? Be sure to show and explain your solution.

PM-32. Use the method of completing the square to reorganize these equations for easy graphing. State the locator point and sketch the graph.

a) $f(x) = x^2 + 4x + 6$

b) $x^2 + 6x + y^2 - 8y = 0$

PM-33. Betty's Quick Stop makes 15% profit on its lunches and 22% profit on its dinners. If Betty took in $2,700 on Tuesday and made $513.01 profit, how much was spent at lunch? Write one or two equations, then solve.

PM-34. Solve each of the following ratio problems for x.

a)   Forty-two percent of x is 112.

b)   Forty-two is x percent of 112.

c)   Twenty-seven is x percent of 100.

d)   Twenty-seven percent of 500 is x.

PM-35. The Flat family's roof is 32 feet wide and 60 feet long. Their TV antenna rises 25 feet above the center of the roof and the wires are attached to the top of the antenna. Guy wires are attached at each corner of the roof and at the midpoint of each edge. What is the total length of wire needed (without counting any extra needed for attaching it)?

PM-36. In the previous problem, suppose that the height of the antenna is x feet. Represent the total length of the guy wires in terms of x.

PM-37. In the original antenna problem, find the angle that the guy wires to the corners make with the roof.

PM-38. Solve $\sqrt{x^2 + 6} = x + 2$.

PM-39. Find the inverse of $g(x) = (x + 1)^2 - 3$ with the domain $x \geq -1$. Sketch both graphs and te the domain and range of the inverse function.

CONDITIONAL PROBABILITY

PM-40. Suppose you roll two dice, one red and one blue, and get a sum of 10.

a) List the different ways this can occur.

b) Sketch an area diagram and shade these possibilities.

c) What is the probability of getting a sum of 10?

d) Suppose you know the sum is 10 but not what is on each die. Explain why the probability that you rolled two 5's would be $\frac{1}{3}$.

PM-41. Suppose you roll two dice and the sum is more than 8.

a) Shade the squares on an area diagram where this outcome could occur.

b) What is the probability that both dice show the same number?

c) What is the probability that exactly one 6 is showing?

d) What is the probability that at least one 5 is showing?

e) In part (d) you calculated the conditional probability that a five will show given that the sum on the dice is greater than eight. Here is another way to think of the problem.

> Event A is sums that contain at last one 5
> Event B is sums greater than 8
> Event AB is the intersection of events A and B, that is sums that contain at least one five and are greater than 8.

Then we can compute P(A/B), the **conditional probability** that at least one five was showing given that the sum was greater than 8, by using the probabilities P(AB) and P(B)

$$P(A/B) = \frac{P(AB)}{P(B)}$$

Complete this calculation and compare this method and result with part (d).

PM-42. A spinner comes up blue, red, and green with a probability of $\frac{1}{3}$ for each color.

a) Sketch an area diagram for spinning twice.

b) Shade the region on your area diagram that corresponds to getting the same color twice.

c) What is the probability that both spins give the same color?

d) If you know that you got the same color twice, what is the probability the color was blue?

PM-43. A spinner comes up red 25% of the time and green 25% of the time. The rest of the time it lands on blue.

  a) Draw an area diagram for spinning twice, and shade the region on your area diagram corresponding to getting the same color twice. A neat and accurate diagram on this problem will help in understanding the next several problems. What are the dimensions of the whole diagram?

  b) What is the probability that both spins give the same color?

  c) If you know that you got the same color twice, what is the probability the color was blue?

PM-44. Guess what? Another spinner. This time the spinner lands on red half of the time and on green one-third of the time. The rest of the time it lands on blue.

  a) Draw an area diagram for spinning twice, and shade the region that corresponds to getting the same color on both spins.

  b) Suppose you know that the spinner landed on the same color twice. What is the probability that color was green?

If you have difficulty with problems PM-45 or 46, the first thing to do is go back and think about what you did in problems PM-42, 43, and 44.

PM-45. A spinner has just two colors, red and blue. The probability the spinner will land on blue is x.

  a) What is the probability it will land on red?

  b) Sketch an area diagram for spinning twice.

  c) When it is spun twice, what is the probability it will land on the same color both times?

  d) Given that it lands on the same color twice, what is the probability that it landed on blue both times?

PM-46. On a spinner with blue, red, and green sectors, blue occurs a fraction x of the time and red occurs the same fraction.

  a) Write an expression to represent the fraction of time green occurs.

  b) Sketch an area diagram of spinning twice.

  c) Shade the region on your area diagram corresponding to getting the same color twice.

  d) What is the probability that both spins give the same color?

  e) If you know that you got the same color twice, what is the probability the color was blue?

PM-47. Solve each of the following for x. What are the three methods used for finding unknown parts of triangles? Refer to your Tool Kit if necessary

a)

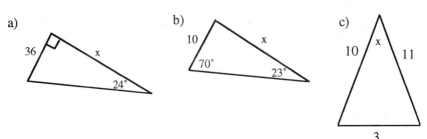

b)

c)

PM-48. For what values of n does the equation $2x^2 + nx + 9 = 0$ have exactly one root?

PM-49. Sketch the graph of $y = (x + 2)^3 + 4$.

a) Rewrite the equation $y = (x + 2)^3 + 4$ without parentheses. Remember order of operations.

b) How would the graph in part (a) differ from the graph of the original equation?

c) What is the parent of $y = (x + 2)^3 + 4$? Of $y = x^3 + 6x^2 + 12x + 12$?

PM-50. Julio runs $\frac{3}{10}$ mile in $1\frac{1}{2}$ minutes. If he keeps running at that rate, how long will it take him to run 2 miles? **m** miles?

PM-51. Where do these graphs intersect? You should be able to do these without a graphing calculator.

a) $2x + y = 10$
        $x + y = 25$

b) $2x + y = 10$
        $x^2 + y^2 = 25$

PM-52. We can add, subtract and multiply complex numbers by essentially treating **i** as a variable and using standard rules of algebra, but dividing is trickier. Suppose we want to divide $5 + 6i$ by $3 + 4i$ or, in other words, simplify this fraction: $\frac{5 + 6i}{3 + 4i}$. What we mean here is: what number times $3 + 4i$ equals $5 + 6i$? The direct way to solve this is to write the equation $(3 + 4i)(a + bi) = 5 + 6i$.

a) Multiply out the left side of this equation. This will result in both real and imaginary terms. The real terms must equal 5, and the imaginary must equal **6i**. This results in two equations that can be solved for a and b. Do this, and state the answer to the division problem.

b) The process in part (a) is important in understanding complex division, but there is an easier way. See what happens when you multiply the numerator and denominator of the fraction by the conjugate of $3 + 4i$.

c) How does the result for part (b) compare to your answer to part (a)? What do you need to do to show they are the same?

PM-53. Divide the following complex numbers by multiplying the numerator and denominator by the conjugate of the denominator. Write the answer in the form $a + bi$.

a) $\dfrac{5}{3 - 4i}$

b) $\dfrac{4 + 2i}{1 - i}$

c) $\dfrac{2 - 3i}{1 + 2i}$

PM-54. If $A = \begin{bmatrix} 3 & 2 \\ -1 & 0 \\ 1 & -3 \end{bmatrix}$ and $B = \begin{bmatrix} 2 & -1 \\ 3 & 0 \end{bmatrix}$ compute the following if possible.

a) AB

b) BA

c) B^2

PM-55. Using a graph of $y = \sin x$ for reference, graph $y = |\sin x|$.

MORE CONDITIONAL PROBABILITY

PM-56. On the midway at the County Fair there are many popular games to play. One of them is Flip-to-Spin-or-Roll. You start by flipping a coin. If heads comes up, you get to spin the big wheel, which has ten equal sectors: three red, three blue, and four yellow. If the coin shows tails, you get to roll a cube with three red sides, two yellow sides, and one blue side. If your spin lands on blue or the blue side of the cube comes up, you win a stuffed animal.

a) Draw **both** an area diagram and a tree diagram to represent Flip-to-Spin-or-Roll.

b) Which diagram was easiest to make? From which diagram is it easiest to tell what result is most likely?

c) What is the probability of winning a stuffed animal?

d) Tyler won a stuffed animal. What is the probability that he started off with heads? From which diagram was it easiest to find this?

e) About how many times would you expect to have to play this game in order to win a stuffed animal?

f) If it cost a dollar to play the game, and the stuffed animal could be purchased at the Bob's Bargain Basement for $3.50, was it worth it? Explain.

PM-57. In the children's game, Build-a-Farm, each player first spins a spinner. Half of the time the spinner comes up red. Half of the time the spinner comes up blue. If the spinner is red, you reach into the red box. If the spinner is blue, you reach into the blue box. The red box has 10 chicken counters, 10 pig counters, and 10 cow counters, while the blue box has 5 chicken counters, 4 pig counters and 1 cow counter.

   a) Sketch an area diagram for the situation where a child spins and then draws. Note that the parts corresponding to the two boxes of animal markers will be quite different.

   b) Shade the parts of the diagram corresponding to getting a pig counter. What is P(pig)?

   c) Find the probability of getting a cow counter.

   d) Find the probability that if you got a cow counter you also spun red.

   e) Find the probability that if you got a cow counter you also spun blue.

   f) Would this have been easier with a tree model? Try it and decide.

   g)
┌───┐
│ **CONDITIONAL PROBABILITY**   │
│   │
│ The probabilities you computed in parts (c) and (d) are **conditional probabilities**. In part (c) you calculated the probability that you spun red given that you got a cow counter. P(R/C) is short for P(Red/Cow), "probability of red given cow." │
│   │
│ One way to compute the probability is to write P(Red/Cow) = P(Red cow)/P(cow) │
│   │
│ $$P(R/C) = \frac{P(RC)}{P(C)} = \frac{\frac{1}{6}}{\frac{13}{60}} = \frac{1}{6} \times \frac{60}{13} = \frac{10}{13}$$ │
└───┘

   Use the above method to calculate P(B/C) and compare your result with your answer to part (e).

PM-58. If Letitia studies for her math test tonight, she has an 80% chance of getting an "**A**." If she does not study, she has a 10% chance. Whether she can study or not depends on whether or not she has to work at her parents' store. Earlier in the day Frank, who usually works weekdays, said he was feeling sick and there is only a 50% chance he will be there tonight.

   a) Draw a tree diagram of the situation.

   b) Draw an area diagram of the situation.

   c) Shade the parts of the area diagram corresponding to Letitia getting an "**A**."

   d) Find the probability Letitia gets an "**A**."

   e) If Letitia got an "**A**," what are the chances she studied?

PM-59. La Troy has been studying very hard for his English test. He thinks that given any question he has a 99% chance of getting it right.

    a)   What is the probability that he gets the first three questions right?

    b)   If the test has fifty questions, what is the probability he gets them all correct?

    c)   Suppose La Troy wanted a 90% chance he would get every question on the test. What would his chances have to be of getting each question correct?

    d)   If you didn't already, write an equation to represent part (c) and solve it.

PM-60. Two similar triangles are cut out of the same piece of sheet metal. The smaller weighs 250 g and the larger weighs 400 g. If the shortest side of the smaller triangle is 26 mm, how long is the shortest side of the larger triangle?

PM-61. Find the volume of the trapezoidal prism at right. Show all subproblems.

PM-62. Find the equation of the line that is perpendicular to $y = \frac{1}{2}x - 3$ and passes through (10, 14).

PM-63. For $y = 5x^2 + 4x + 20$:

    a)   find the roots.

    b)   find the vertex and rewrite the equation in graphing form.

PM-64. A sequence starts 24, 12, . . .

If it is <u>arithmetic</u>:

    a)   Find t(3) = ?   t(n) = ?

    b)   What shape is the graph?

    c)   What term is -624?

If it is <u>geometric</u>:

    d)   Find t(3) = ?   t(n) = ?

    e)   What shape is the graph?

    f)   What term is $\frac{3}{128}$?

PM-65. Solve each of the following equations for x.

    a) $1234x + 23456 = 987654$

    b) $\frac{10}{x} + \frac{20}{x} = 5$

    c) $5x^2 - 6x + 1 = 0$

    d) $x^3 - 3x^2 + 2x = 0$

PM-66. Solve each equation for $0° \leq \theta \leq 360°$. You may need your calculator but remember that your calculator only gives ONE answer. Most (all?) of these have more than one answer. Think about the quadrants.

a) $\sin \theta = 0.5$

b) $\cos \theta = -0.5$

c) $4 \tan \theta - 4 = 0$

d) $3 \sin^2 \theta = 1$

PM-67. Factor each expression and simplify it.

a) $\dfrac{x^2 - 4}{x^2 + 4x + 4}$

b) $\dfrac{2x^2 - 5x - 3}{4x^2 + 4x + 1}$

c) Justify each step in simplifying the expression in part (a).

EXPECTED VALUE

PM-68. Add a brief explanation of **expected value** to your Tool Kit, then complete parts (a) through (d) below.

> To calculate the **EXPECTED VALUE** of an event, multiply the probability of each possible outcome by the value of that outcome, and add the results together.
>
> For example, suppose a game show contestant rolls one die to determine her grand prize. If she rolls a 6, she wins $10,000 and if she rolls anything else she wins $1000. Her expected value is :
>
> (the probability of a six)($10,000) + (the probability of not rolling a six)($1000)
>
> $= \dfrac{1}{6} (\$10,000) + \dfrac{5}{6} (\$1000) = \$2,500.$
>
> In a **FAIR GAME** with several people, the expected values are equal. If you pay to play a game, then it is fair if the cost to play equals the expected value.

Double Spin is a new twist on the Wheel of Few Bucks. You get to spin the spinner twice, and you have to match the amounts to win. The $100 sector is $\dfrac{1}{8}$ of the circle.

a) What is the probability of winning $100?

b) What is the probability of winning anything at all?

c) What is the expected value for a winner of this game? You'll need to solve four subproblems to answer this.

d) If it costs $3.00 to play this game, is it worth playing?

PM-69.   **BASKETBALL: SHOOTING ONE-AND-ONE FREE THROWS**

Rimshot McGee has a 70% free throw
average. Rimshot is at the foul line in a
one-and-one situation with seconds left in
the game. The opposing team is ahead by
one point.

a)   What do you think is the most likely
outcome for Rimshot: zero points,
one point, or two points? Discuss
this with your team and see what
people think before you proceed.

b)   The majority of people, when asked
the question in part (a), say one point,
but if you set up a model you may
change their minds. Use an area
model or a tree diagram to argue
which outcome is most likely.

c)   What is Rimshot's expected value in
terms of points? Could this answer
be the cause of confusion or the
reason most people would think
one point was most likely? Explain your answer.

d)   What is the difference between "most likely" and "expected value?"

PM-70.   Dunkin' Delilah Jones has a 60% free throw average.

a)   What would be the most likely result when she shoots one-and-one?

b)   Try at least three other possible free throw percentages, and make a note of the most
likely outcome.

c)   Is there some free throw percentage that would make two-points and zero-points
equally likely outcomes? Find it.

d)   If you did not already do so, draw an area or tree diagram for part (c) using x as the
percentage and write an equation to represent the problem. Write the solution of the
equation in simplest radical form.

e)   The result in part (d) is a well known number. Ask your teacher to explain other
circumstances in which it appears.

PM-71.   Find all values of 'a' for which the equation $ax^2 + 5x + 6 = 0$ has a solution that is a
real number. Express 'a' in terms of one or more inequalities.

PM-72.   On a spinner, blue occurs a fraction x of the time while red and green are equal. There
          are no other colors.

          a)   Represent the probability that the spinner will land on green.

          b)   Sketch an area diagram for spinning twice.

          c)   Shade the region on your area diagram corresponding to getting the same color twice.

          d)   What is the probability that both spins give the same color?

          e)   If you know that you got the same color twice, what is the probability the color was
               blue?

PM-73.   Where do $x^2 - y = 4$ and $y = 2x - 1$ intersect?

PM-74.   If $\log_b 5 = 3$, compute $\log_b 2$.

PM-75.   Using a graph of $y = \cos x$ for reference, graph $y = |\cos x|$.

PM-76.   Find the measures of the angles that the graph of $y = \frac{3}{5}x + 11$ makes with the x-axis
          (to the nearest 0.01).

PM-77.   Multiply and simplify:

          a) $(3 + 2i)(4 + i)$ b) $(2 + 3i)(2 - 3i)$

          c) $(5 - 2i)(5 + 2i)$ d) $(a + bi)(a - bi)$

PM-78.   Change each of the following complex fractions into a single fraction.

          a) $\dfrac{1 + \frac{1}{x}}{x}$ b) $\dfrac{\frac{1}{2}}{1 - \frac{1}{x}}$

          c)   Justify each step you used in part (b).

PM-79.   When he was in first grade, Harvey used to love
games with spinners. One game he especially liked
had two spinners and several markers that you
moved around a board. You were only allowed to
move if your color came up on BOTH spinners.
Harvey always chose purple because that was his
favorite color and, after all, he was only six years old.

a)   What was the probability that Harvey could move his marker?

b)   What was the probability for the better choice of color?

c)   How often did no one get to move?

d)   There are at least two ways to figure out part (c). Discuss your method of solution
with your team and show a second way to solve part (c).

PM-80.   Sometimes it is easier to figure out the probability that something will
not happen than the probability that it **will**. Show two ways to do
this problem and decide which is easier.

Crystal is spinning this spinner and claims she has a good chance of
having the spinner land on red at least once in three tries. What is the
probability that the spinner will land on red at least once in three tries.

PM-81.

The set of all possible outcomes of an event is called the **SAMPLE SPACE**.

a)   If you flipped three coins, would a tree diagram or an
area model be better for determining the sample
space?

b)   How many outcomes are there?

c)   What is the probability of flipping:

(i)   three heads?   (ii)   at least two heads?

(iii)   one head and two tails?   (iv)   at least one tail?

(v)   exactly two tails?   (vi)   at least one head and one tail?

(vii) Which is more likely, flipping at least two heads or at least two tails? Explain.

PM-82.   Eddie told Alfred, "I'll bet if I flip three coins I can get exactly two heads." Alfred
          replied, "I'll bet I can get exactly two heads if I flip four coins!" Eddie scoffed, "Well, so
          what? That's easier." Alfred argued, "No, it's not. It's harder." Who is right? Show
          all your work and be prepared to defend your conclusion.

PM-83.   One way to win in a game with two dice is to throw a sum of six before getting a sum of
          seven. (Anything else that happens—sums of 2, 3, 4, 5, 8, 9, 10, 11, or 12—is
          ignored.)

          a)   How many ways are there to get a sum of six?

          b)   How many ways are there to get seven?

          c)   How many possible outcomes are important in this problem?

          d)   What is the probability of getting a six before a seven?

PM-84.   Use the five-point method to graph at least one full cycle of each graph.
          a) $y = 2 \sin x$ b) $y = \cos (2x)$

          c) $y = -1 + 2 \cos x$ d) $y = -1 + 2 \sin (x + \frac{\pi}{2})$

PM-85.   Show how to solve these exponential problems <u>without</u> using your calculator. You will
          have radicals or logarithms in your answers.

          a) $3^x = 17$ b) $x^3 = 17$

PM-86.   Write a brief explanation of how you would divide one complex number by another and
          give at least two examples. You may want to refer to problem PM-52.

PM-87.   Consider the function $y = x^2 + 5x + 7$.

          a)   Complete the square to find the vertex.

          b)   Find the y-intercept.

          c)   Use the vertex, the y-intercept, and the symmetry of parabolas to find a third point
                and sketch the graph.

PM-88.   If Emily bought three pounds of oranges and four pounds of bananas for $2.67 and Beth
          bought four pounds of oranges and two pounds of bananas for $2.46, how much should
          Jenel expect to pay for nine pounds of oranges and seven pounds of bananas?

PM-89. Sam says, "log (AB) = log A + log B. Joe says, "log (AB) = (log A)(log B) and I can prove it." Examine Joe's proof and determine if he is correct or if there is something wrong. Explain completely. Is either person correct?

First: If $x = \log A$, then $10^x = A$ and if $y = \log B$, then $10^y = B$.

Second: $AB = 10^x 10^y = 10^{xy}$ so $\log (AB) = xy$.

Finally: $\log (AB) = xy = (\log A)(\log B)$.

PM-90. Suppose three people were solving a geometry problem involving similar right triangles. One got an answer of $\sqrt{48}$, another got $4\sqrt{3}$, and the third got $\frac{12}{\sqrt{3}}$. Would they realize that all three answers are equal? To make it easier to compare answers, it is useful to write square roots in "simplest form." "Simplest" means:

(1) getting the square root part as small as possible by taking out square factors and

(2) only dividing by integers.

For example:

$$\sqrt{48} = \sqrt{16} \cdot \sqrt{3} = 4\sqrt{3}$$

$$\frac{12}{\sqrt{3}} = \frac{12}{\sqrt{3}} \cdot \frac{\sqrt{3}}{\sqrt{3}} = \frac{12\sqrt{3}}{3} = 4\sqrt{3}$$

Simplify what you can, then perform the indicated operations:

a) $\sqrt{3}(\sqrt{18} + \sqrt{32})$

b) $\sqrt{98} + \sqrt{27} + \sqrt{147} + \sqrt{18}$

c) $\frac{\sqrt{5}}{\sqrt{10}}$

PM-91. The congruent sides of an isosceles triangle are labeled $2x + 5$ and $3x - 8$ units, respectively. Find the length of each of the congruent sides.

Both of the following problems would be good to put into your portfolio.

PM-92. An understanding of probability is valuable in relation to important policy issues that are often decided for political reasons. As the issues get more complicated, a knowledge of probability and statistics could make a big difference in the decisions each of us will help to make. For example, with the growing number of AIDS cases, some people have called for mandatory testing for the HIV virus with public disclosure of the results. Others argue that mandatory testing jeopardizes the lives and livelihood of many people who do not have the disease and is therefore an unwarranted and unjust invasion of their privacy. Furthermore, they argue if testing is not mandatory, more people who are at risk will volunteer for testing, increasing the likelihood of identifying and helping people who do have the disease.

In order to explore these issues further we will consider a hypothetical situation. Suppose that the currently used test for HIV is 99% accurate (current tests are not this accurate), and suppose that in the population to be tested (in this case it is doctors, dentists, and other health practitioners) 100 out of 100,000 people actually are HIV positive. The question is: what is the probability that a health practitioner would be identified as having the AIDS virus who actually did not?

a) Make a diagram for this situation.

b) How does the number of people who are HIV positive compare with the number of people who will be told they are HIV positive but really are not?

c) If a randomly tested health practitioner's test comes back positive, what is the probability that he is **not** actually HIV positive? In other words, if you are told that you are sick, what is the probability that you are not sick?

d) Write up your conclusions. In other words, what would you do if you were in a position to decide about mandatory testing of health practitioners and why? What about mandatory testing for other groups?

PM-93.   LUNCH WITH A CALCULATING SWINGER

George is in a zebrawood tree deep in an
Amazon rain forest. He spies a bunch of
bananas in a tree below. At the same time he
notices movement on the jungle floor. He is
12 meters above the ground, holding onto a
vine. If he jumps, his distance from the
ground will get smaller, then larger. He
figures that a quadratic function is a
reasonable mathematical model. But the
movement he saw was Praether the local
panther who, if he times it well, could leap
to a height of three meters to snag George at
the bottom of his swing. One second after
he jumps, he will be 8.5 meters above the
ground, and 3 seconds after he jumps he
will be 4.5 meters above the ground.
Should George go for the bananas?

a)   Define independent and dependent
      variables and name three points that would be on the graph.

b)   Find an equation for this function.

c)   What is the minimum height of his swing? Knowing the vertex will give the
      answer to this question. To be able to see the vertex in the equation, first multiply
      $y = 0.5x^2 - 4x + 12$ by 2 to get $2y = x^2 - 8x + 24$. Then complete the square.
      When you are done, multiply both sides by $\frac{1}{2}$.

d)   Sketch the graph of this function, and advise George regarding lunch.

PM-94.   If $f(x) = x^2 + 7x$, calculate:

a) $f(2)$ b) $f(-3)$ c) $f(i)$ d) $f(-3.5 + 1.5i)$

e)   solve $f(x) = 0$

PM-95.   Make a sketch of a graph $f(x)$ which has the indicated number and type of roots.

a)   5 real roots.   b)   3 real and 2 complex.

c)   4 complex.   d)   4 complex and 2 real.

PM-96. Draw a circle and a line tangent to it at any point x on the circle. Now draw a line from the center of the circle through point x.

a) What do we know about these two lines?

b) What do we know about their slopes?

PM-97. Write the equation of the line tangent to the graph of $(x - 7)^2 + (y - 2)^2 = 169$ at the point (12, 14). (A diagram will certainly help in organizing this problem.)

PM-98. Without graphing, find where each of the following curves crosses the x-axis. (Find the **exact** points!)

a) $f(x) = x^2 - x - 12$

b) $f(x) = 2x^2 - 3x - 9$

c) $f(x) = 2x^2 + x - 7$

d) $f(x) = 3x^2 - 2x + 7$

e) $f(x) = 3x^3 + 2x^2 - 8x$

f) $f(x) = 2x^3 + 2x^2 + 13x$

APPLYING MATRICES TO PROBABILITY

PM-99. **HOME OWNERS AND RENTERS IN MINIOPOLIS**

Every year some families who have been renting manage to purchase a home or condominium. Conversely, some families (frequently older ones) sell their homes and move into rental properties. A recent study has found that in Miniopolis each year 40% of the renters become homeowners, while 10% of homeowners become renters. Of course, that also means that 60% of renters continue to rent, and 90% of homeowners remain owners.

Currently there are 140,000 renters and 160,000 homeowners in the city. City planners want to know how these numbers will change over the next 20 years and they will pay top dollar to find out. Can you help?

a) How many homeowners will there be in Miniopolis next year, assuming that the percentages stated above remain true?

b) How many renters will there be next year?

c) How many homeowners and renters will there be after one more year?

PM-100. It's easy to see that a shortcut will be helpful if we want to find the numbers after 20 years. You may already see the pattern, but we'll use some variables to make it clear. Let $H(n)$ = the number of homeowners after n years, and let $R(n)$ = the number of renters after n years. Suppose you don't know the initial numbers of homeowners and renters. Write expressions for $H(1)$ and $R(1)$ in terms of $H(0)$ and $R(0)$.

PM-101. Does problem PM-100 remind you of matrix multiplication? It should! Make three matrices: T, C, and N, so that C contains the current numbers of homeowners and renters, N contains next year's numbers of homeowners and renters, and $N = CT$. It may be helpful to review how you express a system of linear equations as an equivalent matrix equation. The matrix T is called the transition matrix.

PM-102. Since each number of homeowners and renters will become the basis for calculating the next year's numbers, we will let D_n represent the matrix of homeowners and renters after n years. The matrix equation becomes $D_{n+1} = D_n T$ (we call D_n a distribution matrix). Find D_5, and explain its meaning.

PM-103. To find D_5 did you also have to find D_4, D_3, D_2, and D_1? Perhaps you found the shortcut. Think back to your work on sequences in Unit 1.

a) What is the generator for this sequence of matrices?

b) Which type of sequence is this?

c) If you have the sequence 3, 15, 45, . . ., how can you represent and find $t(100)$ without finding all the terms up to that one?

d) Apply that same reasoning to find D_5.

e) Did you get the same answer? Now find D_{10} and D_{20}. What appears to be happening? What will you tell the city planners about what to expect over the long term?

PM-104. In the Miniopolis situation there were only two categories (homeowner and renter), and the probability of proceeding from one category to another depended only on the former condition. The matrix method we used for modeling this situation is called a **MARKOV CHAIN** because it was developed by the Russian mathematician, Andrei Andrevich Markov (1856 - 1922). Here's a more complex example:

In Bigg City there are estimated to be 120,000 homeowners, 200,000 renters, and 5,000 homeless families. Studies have shown that from one year to the next, among homeowners, 10% will become renters and the rest remain owners. Among renters, 20% will become homeowners, 1% will fall on hard times and become homeless, and the rest remain renters. And among the homeless, 50% become renters and the others remain homeless.

a) Find the number of owners, renters, and homeless families after one year.

b) Create a transition matrix T so that $D_n = D_0 T^n$, where D_n contains the number of residents in each category after n years.

c) Write and label the Initial Distribution matrix for this situation.

d) Investigate what will happen over the long term.

PM-105. Let T_n be the sum of the first n counting numbers.

a) To the right are diagrams of $T_1 = 1$, $T_2 = 1 + 2 = 3$, $T_3 = 1 + 2 + 3 = 6$, $T_4 = 1 + 2 + 3 + 4 = 10$. The letter T is used because these are called **triangular numbers**. Why?

n=1   n=2   n=3   n=4

b) $T_n = an^2 + bn + c$ is a quadratic function of n. Use the first three triangular numbers to write three equations in a, b, and c.

c) Write a matrix equation you could use to solve for a, b, and c. Explain how to solve it.

PM-106. Sunshine Hospital has four categories for the status of its patients: well (W) (about to be discharged), good (G), critical (C), and deceased (D). Sunshine's patients move from one category to another each day according to the probabilities shown below.

$$\begin{array}{c c c c c} & W & G & C & D \\ W & \begin{bmatrix} 1 \\ 0.5 \\ 0.1 \\ 0 \end{bmatrix} & \begin{matrix} 0 \\ 0.3 \\ 0.2 \\ 0 \end{matrix} & \begin{matrix} 0 \\ 0.1 \\ 0.6 \\ 0 \end{matrix} & \begin{matrix} 0 \\ 0.1 \\ 0.1 \\ 1 \end{matrix} \end{bmatrix} \\ G \\ C \\ D \end{array}$$

a) Explain the meaning of each of the numbers in the second row.

b) The numbers in the distribution matrices can also be seen as probabilities. If Maura enters Sunshine Hospital in critical condition, her "initial distribution" matrix is [0 0 1 0]. Multiply this matrix by T, the transition matrix above, and explain the meaning of the answer in terms of probabilities.

c) How can Maura find the probability that she will be well after three days? How can you find the probability that another patient will get well eventually? If you have a graphing calculator, find those probabilities.

d) What happens to the probability of "G" or "C" in the long run?

e) This Markov Chain has two states called **absorbing states**. What are the two absorbing states, and what does this term mean?

f) In light of your answers to parts (c) and (d), how do you account for the fact that there are always plenty of people in critical condition in Sunshine Hospital?

PM-107. For the function $f(x) = \dfrac{\sqrt{x + 4}}{2} - 1$:

a) sketch the graph and the inverse.

b) find the equation of the inverse function.

c) determine the domain and range of the inverse.

d) compute $f^{-1}(f(2))$.

PM-108. Compute the volume of the solid at right.

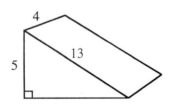

PM-109. A bowl contains three candies, two red ones and a green one. Work with a partner and decide who is player A and who is player B. Then take turns choosing a candy from the bowl without looking. Player A takes one and keeps it, then player B takes one. If the colors match, player A gets a point; if they differ, player B gets a point. Is this a fair game? First try the game experimentally, then show your analysis of the probabilities.

PM-110. Now put four candies in the bowl, three of one color and one of another. Will this game be fair? Again, check experimentally then give your analysis using probabilities.

PM-111. Are there other ways to put different numbers of two colors of candy in the bowl that would lead to a fair game while keeping the rest of the rules the same as in previous two problems? Try a number of different possibilities, analyze each one using probability, make some hypotheses, and report any conclusions or generalizations that you can justify mathematically.

Evaluation:

Problem PM-111 is, of course, the most important part of this investigation. Your report will be evaluated based on:

- The number and variety of cases you investigate and analyze.
- Your organization of the data, your analyses, and your general conclusions.
- The extent to which you can mathematically justify any generalizations you make.

PM-112.   **THE PROBABILITY OF WINNING A CASINO DICE GAME**

To play this game you roll two dice. If your total is 7
or 11 points, you win. If your total is 2, 3, or 12
points, you lose. For any other number (4, 5, 6, 8,
9, or 10), that number becomes your point. You
continue to roll until your point comes up again or a 7
comes up. If your point comes up first, you win. If
7 comes up first, you lose.

a)   As a team, play the game ten times. Record how
many wins and losses your team has. Combine
your information with that of the class. Are the
results fairly even or were there many more wins
or losses?

b)   List the number of ways to get each sum 2, 3, ..., 12. (Do they total 36?)

For the remaining parts of the dice game, leave answers in fraction form.

c)   Find the probability you win on the first throw?

d)   Find the probability you lose on the first throw?

e)   Find the probability the game ends on the first throw?

PM-113.   Besides getting a 7 or 11, another way to win is to roll a 4 (your point) then another 4
before you roll a 7.

a)   Find the probability of a 4.

b)   Find the probability of a 4 before a 7.

c)   Find the probability of rolling a 4 and then rolling another 4 before a 7. Check your
answer before going on.

d)   Find the probability of a 5.

e)   Find the probability of a 5 before a 7.

f)   Find the probability of a 5 and another 5 before a 7.

g)   Find the probabilities for winning with the sums 6, 8, 9, and 10. Look for
symmetry.

PM-114.   List the ways to win the dice game. This is a fairly long list but it will be helpful for the
next question.

a)   What is the probability of winning? Look for symmetry as you do this.

b)   If you won the game, what is the probability that you won by throwing 7 or 11 on
the first throw?

c)   What is the probability of losing this game?

PM-115. Solve each equation.

a) $2^{(x-1)} = 64$

b) $9^3 = 27^{(2x-1)}$

c) $x^6 = 29$

d) $6^x = 29$

PM-116. In a certain county, weather service records based on the last 120 years show that if it rains or snows on a given day, there is a 70% chance that it will do so the next day as well. If it does not rain or snow on a given day, there is a 20% chance that it will rain or snow the following day.

a) Make a transition matrix to represent the information above. Label the rows and columns.

b) Suppose it rains today. The distribution matrix that represents this beginning state is $D_0 = [\ 0\ \ 1\ ]$ or $D_0 = [\ 1\ \ 0\ ]$, depending on how you arranged your transition matrix. Which of these fits yours?

c) Find the product $D_1 = D_0\ T$, and explain what the entries mean.

d) If it is clear on Monday, show how to find the probability that it will rain on Friday.

PM-117. Sally's mother has two bags of candy but she says that Sally can only have one piece. Bag #1 has 70% orange candies and 30% red ones. Bag #2 has 10% orange, 50% white, and 40% green candies. She closes her eyes, randomly chooses one bag, and pulls out one candy.

a) Draw a diagram.

b) Find the probability of getting a red candy.

c) Find the probability of getting an orange candy.

d) If Sally got an orange candy, what is the probability that she chose bag #1?

PM-118. Solve for x.

a)

b)

PM-119. In the summer of 1994, a couple were going through their attic and found a $1000 bond issued by the State of Nevada in 1865. It read "Pay to the Bearer" (whoever has possession.) States issue bonds when they need to borrow money. In 1865, Nevada was a new state and in great need of cash so it issued this bond at an interest rate of 24%.

   a) Why do you think that the Supreme Court of the State of Nevada refused to authorize payment of the bond?

   b) If $1000 were invested at 24% from 1865 until 1994, how much would it be worth? If you didn't have an answer to part (a) before, do you now?

   c) What is the place value of the first digit in the answer to part (b)?

PM-120. In tennis, a player is allowed two serves. If the first one is in, the ball is played until someone wins the point. If the first serve is out, the player serves again. If the second serve is out, the player serving loses the point. If the second serve is in, the ball is played until someone wins the point. Joe Racquet gets his first serve in about 70% of the time. When this happens, he wins the point about 80% of the time. If he misses his first serve, his second serve goes in about 97% of the time. When this happens he wins the point about 40% of the time.

   a) Find the probability that Joe wins a point when he is serving. Show clearly how you found it.

   b) If you know Joe won a point while serving, what is the probability his first serve went in?

   c) Which type of diagram did you use to answer (a) and (b)? Why?

PM-121. **TOOL KIT CHECK-UP**

Your Tool Kit contains reference tools for algebra. Return to your Tool Kit entries. You may need to revise or add entries.

Be sure that your Tool Kit contains entries for all of the items listed below. Add any topics that are missing to your Tool Kit NOW, as well as any other items that will help you in your study of algebra.

- Tree and Area Diagrams
- Expected Value
- Independent Events

- Fair Game
- Sample Space
- Conditional Probability

UNIT 10 SUMMARY PROBLEM

Choose two problems that represent the important concepts of this unit. Copy each problem (or a restatement of it) and show how to do each problem in more than one way. Your explanations should be clear enough so that someone who is not in this class can understand them.

UNIT 11

The Ice Cream Shoppe
COUNTING AND SAMPLING

Unit 11 Objectives
The Ice Cream Shoppe: COUNTING AND SAMPLING

In this unit we will consider questions that involve many numbers. For example, phone number is made up of an area code and is followed by seven digits. Each town or area of a city usually has the same first three digits. Have you ever thought about whether there are enough phone numbers for everyone in your city or town? If a city has a population of 75,000, would there be enough phone numbers for everyone using six prefixes? The fact that the phone company has been splitting area codes in many metropolitan areas is evidence that they do run out of numbers.

Problems such as the phone number situation described above are known as counting problems, because we need to **count** how many different phone numbers are available. Counting problems arise in all sorts of situations and applications. In this unit you will have the opportunity to:

- Learn some general techniques for counting as well as develop formulas for permutations and combinations.

- Use these counting techniques to solve a variety of probability problems.

- Improve your problem solving skills to help you solve any counting problem whether or not you know a technique or a formula.

- Learn how to use what you know about counting to write the result of raising a binomial to an integral power.

Read the following problem and think about the different ways you can request three scoops of ice cream, keeping in mind that it can be on a cone or in a bowl. Then go on to problem IC-1.

IC-0. **THE ICE CREAM SHOPPE** On the eighth day of temperatures above 100°, Millie Zmelt's Easy Ice Cream Shoppe had only five flavors left. As usual, some customers ordered their ice cream in cones and some in a dish, but everyone ordered three scoops, the maximum Millie was allowing that day to ensure that her inventory would last. Millie had also considered allowing no more than one scoop of a particular flavor per customer in order to keep a balanced variety on hand. The number of choices available to customers would depend on whether they chose a cone or a dish and on the decision of the MZE Shoppe's management as to whether to allow more than one scoop of the same kind of ice cream. There are four counting problems here (at least). For each possible situation, how many choices does the customer have?

PROBLEM SOLVING
REPRESENTATION/MODELING
FUNCTIONS/GRAPHING
INTERSECTIONS/SYSTEMS
ALGORITHMS
REASONING/COMMUNICATION

Unit 11

The Ice Cream Shoppe: COUNTING AND SAMPLING

SAMPLE SPACES AND BRANCHING DIAGRAMS

IC-1.   Suppose that you were going to flip three coins: a penny, a nickel, and a dime.

    a)   Make an organized list that shows all the possible outcomes. This list of all the possible outcomes is known as the **sample space** for this experiment.

    b)   How many outcomes are there?

    c)   What is the probability of flipping:

        i)   three heads?   ii) at least two heads?

        iii) one head and two tails?   iv) at least one tail?

        v)   exactly two tails?   vi) at least one head and one tail?

    d)   Which is more likely: flipping at least 2 heads or at least 2 tails? Explain your answer.

    e)   Remember that one way to create an organized list to represent this sample space is to make a **tree diagram**. The first coin, the penny, can either come up heads or tails. From there, we show the possible outcomes as **branches**. If you did not do so already, represent this sample space as a tree diagram.

IC-2.   You have decided to take a vacation. You want to go from Los Angeles to San Francisco and then to Hawaii, and you have all summer for your trip. To get from Los Angeles to San Francisco you can choose to drive, fly, take a bus, or take the train. From San Francisco to Hawaii you can fly, cruise, or sail.

    a)   Make a tree diagram to represent the possible choices in this problem.

    b)   How many choices do you have for the first leg of your trip? How many for the second?

    c)   In how many different ways can you travel from Los Angeles to Hawaii?

    d)   If you randomly choose your means of transportation, what is the probability of flying both times?

IC-3.   While playing Scrabble®, you need to make a word out of the letters A N P S.

a)   How many arrangements of these letters are possible?

b)   Of those arrangements, how many are words? What are they?

c)   What is the probability of a two-year-old randomly making a word using the four letters?

IC-4.   A typical counting problem might read: "How many four-digit numbers can be made using the digits 1, 2, 3, 4, 5, 6, 7 if it is okay to repeat a digit in a number?" In order to solve this problem, you could take a variety of approaches.

a)   Try to make a list (sample space) of the possibilities. What is the difficulty here in trying to create a sample space?

Try to make a tree diagram for this problem. What is the difficulty here in trying to make a tree diagram?

b)   A better method for organizing this problem is to condense it into a **decision chart**. Start by asking, "How many decisions (or choices) do I need to make in this problem?" In this case, the problem asks for four-digit numbers so there are **four** decisions. You can set up a chart for the four decisions as follows:

_____	_____	_____	_____
1st digit	2nd digit	3rd digit	4th digit

c)   How many choices do you have for the first digit?

d)   The problem states that it is okay to repeat digits. What does that imply?

e)   How many choices do you have for the second digit? the third? the fourth? Visualize a tree diagram.

f)   Explain how to find the answer to the original question. Justify your reasoning.

IC-5.   Refer back to the Scrabble® problem (IC-3). Make a tree diagram **and** a decision chart for that problem.

a)   Discuss with your team the similarities between the tree diagram and the decision chart.

b)   Explain how you can determine the number of arrangements by looking at the tree diagram.

c)   How do you get the same answer from the decision chart?

IC-6.   Make a decision chart to help you answer the following question:

"How many four-digit numbers could you make with the digits 1, 2, 3, 4, 5, 6, 7 if you could not repeat the use of any digit?"

IC-7.   Use decision charts to answer parts (a) and (b) then explain the similarities and differences in the two situations.

a)   A child's game contains nine discs, each with one of the numbers 1, 2, 3, ..., 9 on it. How many different 3-digit numbers could be formed by choosing any three discs?

b)   A new lotto game called Quick Spin has three wheels, each with the numbers 1, 2, 3, ..., 9 equally spaced around the rim. Each wheel is spun once and the number the arrow points to is recorded. How many three digit numbers are possible?

IC-8.   Rondal High School had a student enrollment of 1245 in 1997, 1328 in 1998, and 1413 in 1999. School officials predicted that the 2000 enrollment would be 1505. The capacity of the school is 1800 students. Based on this information, when do you predict that the school will reach its capacity?

a)   Graph this data. Determine the line of best fit and write a possible equation for that line.

b)   What do the slope and y-intercept of the line represent?

c)   According to your graph and data, estimate the enrollment of Rondal High in 1992.

d)   When do you think that Rondal High was built? Explain your thinking.

IC-9.   What is the probability that $x^2 + 7x + k$ will factor if $0 \le k \le 20$ and k is an integer?

IC-10. Earthquake magnitudes are measured by the amount of energy that is released. Since the amount of energy released from a large earthquake can be millions of times greater than the energy released by a small quake, a scale was created (the Richter scale) to give magnitudes in numbers that are easy to use. An earthquake measuring 3.4 on the Richter scale, for example, has an energy release of $10^{3.4}$ kilo joules.

a) How many times more energy is released by an earthquake that measures 5.5 on the Richter scale than one that measures 4.5?

b) How many times more energy is released by an earthquake that measures 4.1 than one that measures 3.9? Give your answer as a power of 10 and as a decimal.

c) What would the magnitude be of an earthquake that released half as much energy as a quake measuring 8.6 on the Richter scale?

IC-11. Represent the integer that is:

a) one less than n.

b) one more than n.

c) one less than n - 1.

d) one less than n - 4.

IC-12. Verify algebraically that $g(x) = \dfrac{2x - 3}{5}$ is the inverse function of $f(x) = \dfrac{5x + 3}{2}$.

IC-13. Solve this system for y and z:

$$\frac{z + y}{4} + \frac{z - y}{2} = 1 \quad \text{and} \quad \frac{3z - y}{4} + \frac{4z + 2y}{11} = 3$$

IC-14. Convert the following measurements in degrees to radians.

a) 45°

b) 75°

c) -15°

d) 450°

C-15.   Arissa's sample is disappearing! Originally she had 59,049 elements in her sample, but at the end of each hour that passes only one-third of the previous amount remains.

   a)   Write a formula to represent the number of elements in her sample space after t hours.

   b)   After ten hours, she hopes to use her sample space in an experiment. How many elements remain after ten hours?

C-16.   Write a quadratic equation with roots $x = 3 \pm 5i$.

FROM BRANCHES TO FACTORIALS

C-17.   Marcos is selecting classes for next year. He plans to take English, Physics, Government, Pre-calculus, Spanish and Journalism. His school has a six-period day. In how many different ways might the school arrange his day?

   a)   Make a decision chart for this problem.

   b)   What is the probability that Marcos will get first period Pre-calculus?

   c)   What is the probability that Marcos will get both first period Pre-calculus <u>and</u> second period Physics?

C-18.   On your calculator, see if you can find a button like $\boxed{n!}$.

   This is the **factorial** function button.

   a)   Find the values of 8 factorial (written 8!, then 7!, then 6!, . . ., 1!

   b)   Which one of these is the same as the number of Marcos' possible schedules?

IC-19.

> **FACTORIAL** is a shorthand for multiplication of a list of consecutive, descending whole numbers: n! = n(n - 1)(n - 2) $\cdots$ (3)(2)(1).
>
> For example, 4 factorial = 4 • 3 • 2 • 1 = 24 and 6! = 6 • 5 • 4 • 3 • 2 • 1 = 720.

    a)   Explain why 6! gives the correct solution to the possible number of ways to arrang Marcos' schedule.

    b)   Explain why 4! gives the correct solution to the possible number of ways to arrang the letters **M   A   T   H.**

IC-20.   How many distinguishable batting orders can be made from the nine starting players on baseball team?

IC-21.   How many distinct rearrangements of the letters in the word FRACTIONS are there?

IC-22.   Five students are running for Junior Class President. They must give speeches before t election committee. In how many different orders could they give their speeches?

IC-23.   Remembering what n! means can help you do some messy calculations quickly, as well as help you do problems that might be too large for your calculator. For instance, if we wanted to calculate

$$\frac{9!}{6!}$$

we could use the n! button on our calculator and find that 9! = 362880, and 6! = 720, s

$$\frac{9!}{6!} = \frac{362880}{720} = 504.$$

But, if we remember that 9! = 9 • 8 • 7 • 6 • 5 • 4 • 3 • 2 • 1 and 6! = 6 • 5 • 4 • 3 • 2 • 1 the we can write

$$\frac{9 \cdot 8 \cdot 7 \cdot \cancel{6} \cdot \cancel{5} \cdot \cancel{4} \cdot \cancel{3} \cdot \cancel{2} \cdot \cancel{1}}{\cancel{6} \cdot \cancel{5} \cdot \cancel{4} \cdot \cancel{3} \cdot \cancel{2} \cdot \cancel{1}} = 9 \cdot 8 \cdot 7 = 504$$

Use this idea to simplify each of the following problems before computing the result.

    a) $\dfrac{10!}{8!}$ b) $\dfrac{20!}{18!2!}$ c) $\dfrac{7!}{4!3!}$ d) $\dfrac{75!}{73!}$

UNIT

IC-24.   If $f(n) = n!$, evaluate each of the following:

a) $\dfrac{f(5)}{f(3)}$ b) $\dfrac{f(6)}{f(4)}$ c) $\dfrac{f(9)}{f(7) \cdot f(2)}$

IC-25.   What is the probability that $x^2 + kx + 12$ will factor if $0 \le k \le 8$ and k is an integer? Make an organized list (sample space) to help you determine the probability.

IC-26.   Consider the following situation:

You must park in a parking garage that charges $3.00 for the first hour and $1.00 for each hour (or any part of that hour) after that.

a)   How much will it cost to park your car for 90 minutes?

b)   How much will it cost to park your car for 118 minutes? 119 minutes?

c)   How much will it cost to park your car for 120 minutes? 121 minutes?

d)   Graph the cost in relation to the length of time your car is parked.

e)   Is this function continuous?

C-27.   Victoria is playing with her balance scale and balances 3 blue blocks and 2 red blocks on one side with 5 blue blocks and a red block on the other. Later, her brother balances 2 red blocks and a blue block with 40 g. How much does each block weigh?

C-28.   Factor and reduce to simplify: $\dfrac{5x + 10}{x^2 + 6x + 8}$. Justify each step.

C-29.   Use an idea from the previous problem to simplify and add these fractions. Justify each step.
$$\frac{x - 2}{x + 2} + \frac{2x - 6}{x^2 - x - 6}$$

C-30.   Change the angles that are given in radians to degrees and the angles that are given in degrees to radians.

a) $108°$ b) $320°$ c) $\dfrac{7\pi}{9}$

d) $\dfrac{19\pi}{12}$ e) $\dfrac{17\pi}{2}$ f) $260°$

IC-31. How many solutions are there to the system of equations at right. Justify your response.

$$y = x^2 - 2x + 2$$

$$y = 2x - 2$$

IC-32. Graph each inequality and find the area of the enclosed region:

$$y \geq |x - 2| \quad \text{and} \quad y \leq 4 - |x|$$

IC-33. A conveyor belt carries grain to the top of a barn, where it drops the grain allowing it to fall in a pile on the ground. The pile is in the shape of a cone.

Recall that $V = \frac{1}{3}\pi r^2 h$ is the volume for a cone.

a) Find the volume when the height is ten feet and the radius of the base is four feet.

b) The cone-shaped piles at each stage are all similar. If the radius of the base is four feet when the height is ten feet, what is the radius of the base when the height is 15 feet?

c) Consider the angle the side of the cone-shaped pile makes with the ground. Is this angle changing? Justify your answer. If not, what is the measure of the angle?

FACTORIALS TO PERMUTATIONS

IC-34. Jasper finally managed to hold on to some money long enough to open a savings account at the credit union. When he went in to open the account, the accounts manager told him that he needed to select a 4-digit **pin** (**p**ersonal **i**dentification **n**umber). She also said that he could not repeat a digit but that he could use any of the digits 0, 1, 2,..., 9 for any place in his 4-digit code.

a) Make a decision chart for this problem.

b) How many digits does he have to choose from for the first place?

c) Once he chooses a digit to use for the first place, how many does he have to choose from for the second? the third? the fourth?

Notice that the decision chart looks like the beginning of 10! but it doesn't go all of the way down to one. We can use factorials to represent this problem, but we must compensate for the factors that we do not need.

d) Reduce, and leave in factored form: $\frac{10!}{6!}$.

e) How does the solution to part (d) relate to the decision chart in part (a)?

C-35.   Twenty-five art students submitted sculptures to be judged at the county fair. Awards are going to be given for the six best sculptures. You have been asked to be the judge. You must **choose and arrange in order** the best six sculptures.

a)   Make a decision chart for this problem.

b)   How many sculptures do you have to choose from for the first place award?

c)   Once you have chosen a sculpture for first place, how many do you have to choose from for second place? the third? the fourth?

d)   Show the numerical simplification of $\frac{25!}{19!}$.

e)   Explain how the solution to part (d) relates to the original problem and the decision chart in part (a).

f)   Where did the 19 come from? How could you get 19 from the numbers in the original problem? Why did 19! in the denominator become an important step in coming up with an answer to the problem? Discuss this with your team.

C-36.   With your team, discuss how you could use factorials to express each of the following solutions:

a)   Fifty-two contestants are vying for the Miss Teen pageant crown. In how many different ways can the judges pick the next Miss Teen and her three runners-up?

b)   The volleyball team is sponsoring a mixed-doubles sand court volleyball tournament and sixteen pairs have signed up for the chance to win one of the seven trophies and cash prizes. In how many different ways can the teams be chosen and arranged for the top seven slots?

c)   Carmen is getting a new locker at school and the first thing she must do is decide on a new combination. The three number combination can be picked from the numbers 0-35. How many different locker combinations could she make up if none of the numbers can be repeated?

IC-37.

Problems about batting orders and questions about how many numbers you could make without repeating any digits are called **PERMUTATIONS**. The following lists give some more examples and some non-examples.

Permutations:

- All the arrangements of the letters ABC.

- The possible 4-digit numbers you could make if you had square tiles, one with each number 2, 3, 4, 5, 6, 7, 8.

- From a group of 8 candidates, one will become president, one vice president, and one secretary of the school senate.

Not-permutations:

- All the possible license plate letter triples that could be made using A, B, C.

- The possible 4-digit numbers you could make if you could choose any digit from 2, 3, 4, 5, 6, 7, 8.

- From a group of 8 candidates, three will be selected to be on the executive committee.

a) List some possible license plate letter triples using A's or B's or C's that would not be in the list of arrangements of the cards lettered A, B, and C.

b) Compare the two lists of 8 candidates. How do they differ?

c) What are the important characteristics that a counting problem has to have in order to classify it as a permutations problem?

d) Discuss with your team a general method for solving the examples on the left above, and write a description for your general method that would work for any problem that could be identified as a permutations problem.

IC-38.

PERMUTATIONS, A SPECIAL NOTATION

Problem: Eight people are running a race. In how many different ways can they come in first, second, and third?

This is a problem of counting **permutations**, and the result can be represented $_8P_3$, which means the number of ways to **choose and arrange** three things from a set of eight.

$$_8P_3 = 8 \cdot 7 \cdot 6 = 336$$

A more complicated but more compact way to write this is:

$$_8P_3 = 8 \cdot 7 \cdot 6 = \frac{8 \cdot 7 \cdot 6 \cdot 5 \cdot 4 \cdot 3 \cdot 2 \cdot 1}{5 \cdot 4 \cdot 3 \cdot 2 \cdot 1} = \frac{8!}{5!} = \frac{8!}{(8-3)!}$$

In general, $_nP_r = \frac{n!}{(n-r)!}$ for n items chosen r at a time. Record this notation and what it stands for in your Tool Kit.

C-39. The basketball cheerleaders printed large letters on cards that spell out your school's mascot. Each card has one letter on it and each cheerleader is supposed to hold up one card. At the end of the first quarter, they realize that someone has mixed up the cards.

a) How many ways are there to arrange the cards?

b) If they hadn't noticed the mix up, what would the probability be that the cards would have correctly spelled out the mascot?

C-40. Mr. Dobson is planning to give a quiz to his class tomorrow. Unfortunately for his students, Mr. Dobson is notorious for writing quizzes that seem to have no relevance to the subject whatsoever. With this in mind, his students know that their efforts will be purely guesswork. If the quiz contains ten questions that the students will have to match with ten given answers, what is the probability that Randy Random will get all ten questions matched correctly?

C-41. The first four factors of 7! are 7, 6, 5, 4 or 7, (7 - 1), (7 - 2), (7 - 3):

a) What are the first four factors of 12! ?

b) What are the first six factors of n! ?

c) What are the first five factors of (n - 3)! ?

d) What are the first five factors of (n + 2)! ?

C-42. A state is chosen at random from the 50 states. Find the probability that it:

a) is on the east coast.

b) has at least one representative in the house of representatives.

c) has three U.S. senators.

d) does not border an ocean or the gulf of Mexico.

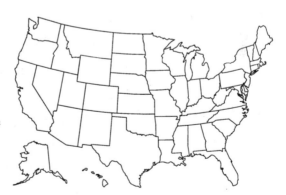

C-43. Which is bigger: (5 - 2)! or (5 - 3)! ? Justify your answer.

C-44. Find the value of each permutation:

a) $_5P_3 = ?$ b) $_7P_4 = ?$ c) $_8P_2 = ?$

IC-45.   What do you think 0! will equal?

a)   Try it on your calculator to see what you get.

b)   What does $_8P_8$ mean? What *should* $_8P_8$ be equal to? Write $_8P_8$ using the factorial formula. Why is it necessary to have $0! = 1$?

c)   Remember how we showed that $2^0 = 1$? One way was to go down the sequence of powers of 2: $\frac{2^4}{2} = 2^3$, $\frac{2^3}{2} = 2^2$, $\frac{2^2}{2} = 2^1$, $\frac{2^1}{2} = 2^0$, but $\frac{2^1}{2} = 1$, so $2^0 = 1$. We can use a similar argument for 0!. Explain why $\frac{5!}{5} = 4!$. Use that pattern to construct an argument for why 0! should equal 1.

IC-46.   Compute the quotient $(4 - 7i) \div (8 - 9i)$. Refer to problem PM-52 if you need help.

IC-47.   The Postal Service requires 33 cents postage on a first class letter weighing less than but not equal to 1 ounce. An additional 22 cents is added for each ounce or part of an ounce above that. Graph the relationship between price and weight for first class mail.

IC-48.   How many of the following are in a standard deck of cards? This is information you will need to know in order to solve some future problems.

a)   cards   b)   diamonds

c)   twos   d)   face cards

IC-49.   Graph $y = \sqrt{4 - x^2}$. Imagine revolving this around the x-axis, faster and faster, so that i appears to form a three dimensional figure.

a)   Make a sketch of the three dimensional figure. What is it called?

b)   Use $V = \frac{4}{3}\pi r^3$ to find the volume of the three dimensional figure.

> The following problem is a good example to keep for future reference and you may want to add it to your portfolio.

C-50.   Five members of the Spirit Club have volunteered for the club governing board. These members are: Al, Betty, Carl, Darla, and Eugene. The club members will select three of the five as board members for the next year. One way to do this would be to elect a governing committee of three in which all members would have the same title. A second way would be to select a president, vice-president, and secretary.

a)   How many different slates of officers are possible? (This means a president, vice-president, and a secretary are chosen. Al as president, Betty as vice-president, and Carl as secretary is considered a different slate from Al as president, Betty as secretary, and Carl as vice-president.)

b)   How many different governing committees are possible? Don't try to calculate this; just make a list of all the possibilities.

c)   The Spirit Club expects many more members will join during the second semester and there will be more volunteers for the governing board. The club members have voted to have a governing committee (all three members have the same title), and they'd like a way to calculate how many different committees of three are possible from any number of volunteers. They know that listing all the possibilities will take a long time.

Jaime, another member of the club, was assigned to answer the question. He decided to start with his favorite problem-solving strategy: solving a smaller problem. He began by finding how many committees of two could be formed from four volunteers and he started by making a list of all the possibilities.

Ngan was looking over Jaime's shoulder and asked, "Why not make a decision chart? There are four choices for the first member, and three choices for the second, so there should be 12 possible committees. Fred showed her his list which only had 6 committees and asked, "Where are the others?"

Make your own list and see if you can find more than 6 committees. If not explain why Ngan's method gave too many. It may help to make a tree diagram for her method.

d)   Jaime and Ngan figured out what was wrong with Ngan's method, but they didn't have any other ideas for calculating an answer without a list or a tree, so they decided to see if they could find a way to adapt Ngan's method to make it work.

Ngan said, "My method gave 12 committees, but there were only 6, so let's just do it my way, and then divide by 2."

Jaime was more cautious. "Let's try that on another example, say, committees of three people chosen from four volunteers."

"Okay," said Ngan, "My way gives 24."

"I made a list, and there are only four possibilities. I'm sure I got them all," Jaime replied.

Show how Ngan got 24, and explain why her method gives <u>six</u> times the actual number here, but only gave twice the correct number in the previous example.

>>Problem continues on the next page.>>

e) Finally they felt ready to tackle the big problem: suppose you had n volunteers from whom r people would be chosen for the governing committee. They started with Ngan's method, which they realized was the same as finding how many ways they could make a slate of officers (president, vice-president, secretary, etc.).

Use permutation notation to express this number, and explain what they must divide by to get the number of committees.

Create a formula using permutation notation and factorials and test it on the original question from part (b).

f) Add the following information to your Tool Kit.

In selecting committees, we care about who is selected but we do **not** care about the **order** of selection or any **arrangement** of the groups. Selections of committees, or of subsets of items from a larger set without regard to the order of the group selected, are called **COMBINATIONS**.

Lists in which the order of selection is important, but selections cannot be repeated are called **PERMUTATIONS**.

IC-51. In the California state lottery there are 51 numbers to choose from. How many ways are there to choose 6 of the 51 numbers? How many **combinations** of 6 numbers can be chosen from the list of 51?

As in the committee problem, order is not important. We can start with factorials, find the number of permutations $_{51}P_6$ and then divide by the number of arrangements of each group, 6!.

Our numerator represents the total number of ways to arrange six numbers (out of 51 numbers) where the order matters. Each group of the same six numbers is counted $6! = 720$ times. Since they are the same and grouped together, we need to divide to find out how many combinations there are without regard to order.

a) Find the number of possible combinations for the California Lottery.

b) What is the probability of selecting the six winning numbers?

IC-52. Five cards are drawn from a standard deck of 52 cards.

a) Show a decision chart for the number of choices for the first card, second card, and forth up to the fifth card, and write the total number of arrangements of the cards th you found using permutation notation.

b) How many ways can you arrange the five cards selected? Write your answer both as a number and using a factorial.

c) Since order generally does not matter when playing cards, we need to divide out the number of repetitions of the same set of five cards. Calculate the number of five card hands that can be selected from a deck of 52 cards.

IC-53. "This is strange," said Nora. "First we learned factorials, which count the number of ways to arrange a group of objects in order. Then we learned permutations, which count ways to *choose* **and** *arrange* a subgroup from a larger group. Now we're learning combinations, which count ways to just choose a subgroup from a larger group. Why didn't we learn how to choose before we learned how to choose-and-arrange?"

"I see!" said José. "The permutation formula was based on a decision chart: how many ways to pick the first object, times how many ways to pick the second, etc. So we were choosing and arranging at the same time. We didn't choose, then arrange."

"But why **can't** we choose, then arrange?" said Nora. "It should be a simple decision chart:

$$\frac{{}_nP_r}{\text{Number of ways to choose and arrange}} = \frac{}{\text{number of ways to choose}} \bullet \frac{}{\text{number of ways to arrange what was chosen}}$$

Fill in the blanks in Nora's decision chart.

COMBINATIONS: A SPECIAL NOTATION

Let's see how Nora's idea fits in with what you've learned so far. Consider the following problem.

Problem: Ten people are running for the prom committee. In how many different ways can a committee of 4 be chosen?

To begin, this is a problem of counting **combinations**. Since the order does not matter, it will help to have a notation for combinations. We use ${}_{10}C_4$ to represent the number of ways to **choose** four things from a set of ten. (This is often read as "10 choose 4.")

Rewrite Nora's decision chart equation for the prom committee problem, using our notations for permutations, combinations, and arrangements.

Solve the equation for ${}_{10}C_4$.

Explain why the equation above can also be written as ${}_{10}C_4 = \frac{10!}{(6!)(4!)}$.

Finally, write a general formula, in two different versions, for ${}_nC_r$, the number of ways to choose r things from a total of n. Remember, Nora was right:

(number of ways to choose)(number of ways to arrange) =
                           (number of ways to choose and arrange)

therefore:

(number of ways to choose) = $\dfrac{\text{(number of ways to choose and arrange)}}{\text{(number of ways to arrange)}}$.

$$ {}_nC_r = \frac{{}_nP_r}{r!} = \frac{n!}{(n-r)!\,r!} $$

IC-54.   There are twelve people signed up to play darts during lunch. How many ways can a three-person dart team be chosen?

IC-55.   Find the value of each of the following:

   a) $_{10}C_8 = ?$ b) $_{12}C_7 = ?$ c) $_7C_1 = ?$

IC-56.   On the 6-person bowling team only four players bowl at one time. How many different four-person teams can be made?

IC-57.   How many different bowling line ups can be made in the previous problem?

IC-58.   What is 0! ?

   a)   How many ways are there to choose all five items from a group of five items? What happens when you substitute into the factorial formula to compute $_5C_5$? Since you know (logically) what the result has to be, use this fact to explain why mathematicians decided that 0! equals 1.

   b)   On the other hand, how many ways are there to choose **nothing** from a group of fi items? And what happens when you try to use the factorial formula to compute $_5C$

   c)   In order to extend the use of the formula for combinations to the examples describe in parts (a) and (b) mathematicians agreed that 0! must equal 1.

Definition: 0! = 1

Some would argue that there is logic to this if you think of selecting zero items from a list. There is just **one** way to do this, which is to leave them all unselected.

IC-59.   Two cards are dealt from a randomly shuffled deck (a regular deck of 52 cards). To establish the sample space for this problem you need to think of choosing two from a set of 52.

   a)   How many ways are there to do this?

   b)   How many diamonds are there? How many ways to choose two diamonds out of the diamonds in the deck? What is the probability of dealing two diamonds from th whole deck of 52 cards?

   c)   If you did not already do so, express your solution to part (b) in the form $\frac{_aC_b}{_dC_e}$.

   d)   What is the probability of dealing two face cards?

   e)   If you did not already do so, express your solution to part (d) in the form $\frac{_aC_b}{_dC_e}$.

IC-60.   Given seven points in a plane, no three of which are collinear:

a)   how many different lines are determined by these points?

b)   how many distinct triangles can be formed?

c)   how many distinct quadrilaterals can be formed?

IC-61.   Explain why the answers to parts (b) and (c) of the preceding problem are the same.

IC-62.   Graph: $y = 1 + \tan (x - \frac{\pi}{4})$

IC-63.   If $n > 3$, how could you write $n \cdot (n - 1) \cdot (n - 2) \cdot (n - 3)!$ more efficiently?

IC-64.   Simplify:

a) $3^{-2} \cdot 3^4$ b) $3^{-4} \cdot 3^4$ c) $(3^{-1} + 3^{-3}) \cdot 3^4$

IC-65.   You can use part (c) of the previous problem to get the answer to this problem or you can use other methods, but be careful about the order in which you do the operations.

$$\frac{3^{-2} - 3^{-1}}{3^{-3} + 3^{-4}}$$

IC-66.   Consider the following two sequences. The initial value is underlined in each sequence:

Sequence 1: 52, 54, 56, 58, . . .

Sequence 2: 1, 2, 4, 8, 16, . . .

a)   Which sequence is arithmetic and which is geometric? Justify your answer.

b)   Write a formula for the nth term of each sequence.

c)   Do these sequences have any terms in common? If so, what are they (and prove it)? If not, why not?

IC-67.   Compute:

a) $\left(\frac{\sqrt{2}}{2} + \frac{i\sqrt{2}}{2}\right)^2$ b) $\left(\frac{-\sqrt{2}}{2} - \frac{i\sqrt{2}}{2}\right)^2$

c)   Use the results from parts (a) and (b) above to solve $x^2 = i$ (the square   roots of **i**.)

OTHER COUNTING TECHNIQUES

> Permutations? No! Combinations? No! Then what? What other kinds of counting problems are there?

IC-68. Andrea has just purchased a 5-digit combination lock (mathematicians might call some of these locks permutation locks), and it allows her to set up her own combination. She can use the numbers 0 - 9 for her combination and she must have five of them.

a) How many 5-digit combinations can she make so that no digit is repeated?

b) How many 5-digit combinations are possible if she **can** repeat the digits?

IC-69. Joaquin is getting a new locker at school and the first thing he must do is decide on a new combination. The three number combination can be picked from the numbers 0 through 21.

a) How many different locker combinations can Joaquin choose if none of the numbers can be repeated?

b) If he can let the numbers repeat, how many locker combinations can he choose from?

IC-70. Another school nightmare: Monday morning brings a surprise quiz with nine true or false questions. Fortunately the teacher writes a bonus problem on the board: How many different true-false answer patterns could there be for the nine questions on the quiz?

IC-71. How many different ways can you have your quarter pound hamburger prepared if you can have it prepared with or without mustard, ketchup, mayonnaise, lettuce, tomatoes, pickles, cheese, and onions?

IC-72. What has been different about the last four problems? Did you solve them with permutations? With combinations? What method did you use to solve them?

IC-73.   Yesterday in chemistry class Alberto took a four question quiz. The four questions were true/false and he had forgotten to study, so he had to guess. Using **'W'** for wrong and **'R'** for right:

a)   Create a sample space for the sequences of wrong and right solutions that are possible for this quiz.

b)   Create a tree diagram for this problem.

c)   What is the probability that Alberto will get:

i)   4 right?   ii)   3 right?   iii)   2 right?

iv)   1 right?   v)   0 right?

d)   What score should Alberto expect to get on his quiz?

IC-74.   The Colorado Rookies and the Tampa Bay Demons have made it into the World Championship. After four games, the Rookies are leading the series three to one. The Series is a "best of seven" situation (the first team with four wins, wins). Assume that each team is equally likely to win an individual game.

a)   What is the probability that the Rookies will win the World Championship?

b)   What is the probability that the Demons will win the World Championship?

IC-75.   A member of the U.S. Public Health Service came up with a list of words from which impressive sounding 3-word phrases can be formed if you choose one word at random from each of these three columns.

integrated	management	options
total	organizational	flexibility
systematized	monitored	capability
parallel	reciprocal	mobility
functional	digital	programming
responsive	logistical	concept
optional	transitional	time-phase
synchronized	incremental	projection
compatible	third-generation	hardware
balanced	policy	contingency

a)   How many different three-word phrases can be constructed from the list?

b)   How many different three-word phrases can be constructed if each column had only four words in it?

c)   How many different 3-words phrases can be constructed if each column has fourteen words?

d)   Try it out. Write a sentence containing one of the three-word phrases.

IC-76.   Sai Chiam and one of his friends were chosen to be captains of the A and B soccer teams during PE. Their PE teacher asked each of them to pick a number from 1 to 10. What is the probability that:

a)   Sai Chiam's number is greater than his friend's number?

b)   His number is equal to his friend's number?

c)   His number is less than his friend's number?

d)   Be prepared to explain your method for figuring out these probabilities.

IC-77.   A biologist wanted to find out how many trout were in a lake. He caught 250 trout, tagged them and returned them to the lake. If he later came back and caught 200 trout and 5 of them had tags, how many trout can the biologist expect the lake to contain.

IC-78.   Simplify:

a) $\dfrac{n!}{(n-1)!}$

b) $\dfrac{(n+2)!}{n!}$

IC-79.   Use your knowledge of how to solve $2y^2 + 5y - 3 = 0$ in order to solve for x:

$$2 \sin^2 x + 5 \sin x - 3 = 0.$$

IC-80.   Josephina thinks that she has discovered a new pattern.

$$\frac{x-1}{x-1} = 1 \Rightarrow \frac{x^2-1}{x-1} = x+1 \Rightarrow \frac{x^3-1}{x-1} = x^2+x+1 \Rightarrow \frac{x^4-1}{x-1} = x^3+x^2+x+1$$

a)   Check her equations above by multiplying. Does her pattern work?

b)   Based on her pattern, what does $\dfrac{x^5-1}{x-1}$ equal? Is it true? Justify your answer.

c)   Make a conjecture about how to represent the result for $\dfrac{x^n-1}{x-1}$. You will probabl[y] need ", . . .," in the middle of your expression.

IC-81.   Water boils at 100°C or 212°F. Water freezes at 0°C or 32°F. Write a linear equation to calculate the temperature of water in Fahrenheit if you know the temperature in Celsius.

THE ICE CREAM SHOPPE

> This problem is definitely one you should keep as an example for later reference. It would also be a good problem for your portfolio.

IC-82. After seven days of temperatures above 100°, Millie Zmelt's Easy Ice Cream Shoppe had only five flavors left: chocolate fudge, French vanilla, maple-nut, lemon custard, and blueberry delight. On the eighth day of the heat wave, some customers ordered their ice cream in cones and some in a dish, but everyone ordered three scoops, the maximum Millie was allowing that day to ensure that her inventory would last. Millie had also considered allowing no more than one scoop of a particular flavor per customer in order to keep a balanced variety on hand. The number of choices available to customers would depend on whether they chose a cone or a dish and on the decision of the MZE Shoppe's management as to whether to allow more than one scoop of the same kind of ice cream. For a cone the order in which the scoops are served makes a difference; for a dish the order does not matter. There are four counting problems here (at least). For each possible situation, how many possibilities does the customer get to choose from?

IC-83. Make a chart organizing and describing types of counting problems you solved in the previous problem along with their solutions. One of the problems is a set of permutations, another is combinations, the remaining two have no particular names, but for one of them there is an easy way to write a formula for its solution. For which ones can you give a formula for counting? It would be a good idea to make a neat, organized copy of your conclusions to keep for future reference in your Tool Kit.

IC-84. Millie Zmelt decided it was okay to serve cones with multiple scoops of the same flavor and you sent your friend Randy Random to get a cone for you.

    a) What is the probability he would bring you a cone with **all** three scoops the same? (Assume he made a random selection).

    b) What is the probability he would get all three different?

IC-85. With your team, find another situation where four types of counting problems could be involved. Write a short paragraph describing such a problem.

IC-86. A pizza parlor has 12 toppings other than cheese. How many different pizzas can they create with five **or fewer** toppings?

IC-87. John has to graph a set of parabolas of the form $y = x^2 - 4x + 2^n$ where n is an integer and $0 \le n \le 6$. What is the probability that one of these parabolas, chosen at random, will have:

a)   one x-intercept?   b)   two x-intercepts?

c)   no x-intercepts?

IC-88. Another pizza parlor is having a lunch special. They have a rack of individual pizzas each with three different toppings. The price is really low because they forgot to indicate on the boxes what toppings were on the pizza. If they only have ten ingredients, and if each pizza has a different combination of three ingredients, and all three-combinations were used:

a)   how many pizzas are on the rack?

b)   how many have Canadian bacon, pineapple, and one other ingredient?

c)   what is the probability of getting a pizza that has mushrooms on it?

IC-89. Write an explanation of the difference between a combination and a permutation so your friend, who is taking Pre-calculus and doesn't understand counting techniques, can understand.

IC-90. Without using a graphing calculator, graph $y = \sin x$ and $y = \cos x$ on the same set of axe Use $0 \le x \le 2\pi$. On the same axes and in a different color, graph $y = \sin x + \cos x$ by mentally adding the two approximate y-values for a sufficient number of x-values.

IC-91. Simplify:

a) $\dfrac{(n - 3)!}{(n - 5)!}$ b) $\dfrac{n!}{(n - 2)!}$

IC-92. Solve for x.

$$\frac{x}{2x + 1} - \frac{1 - x}{2x - 1} = \frac{2x + 7}{4x^2 - 1}$$

IC-93.   Solve for x in the figure at right.

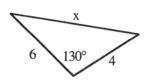

IC-94.   Joanne was making repairs to her deck and needed to buy some supplies. She purchased 2 posts, 3 boards and 4 piers for $52. Needing more materials she went back to the lumber yard and bought one post and 5 boards for $13. Realizing she did not need the piers she made a third trip where she bought 3 more boards, returned the 4 piers and ended up with a refund of $34. What was the cost of each item?

IC-95.   A tree casts a 12 m shadow when the angle of elevation of the sun is 42°. How tall is the tree?

TWISTS ON PERMUTATIONS AND COMBINATIONS

IC-96.   For some counting problems, it is important to do some thinking before you start. For example, in the problem below, the number must be less than 500, so you need to use what you know about the hundreds digit first. Don't forget to count two digit and one digit numbers as well.

a)   How many numbers less than 500 can you make using the digits 0, 1, 3, 5, 7, if no digit may be repeated? Identify the subproblems and solve each subproblem to find the answer.

b)   Let's change the problem slightly.

How many numbers less than 500 are there if the digits can be repeated? Identify the subproblems and solve each subproblem to find the answer to this question.

> The following problems will require some thought. While combinations, permutations, and factorial formulas are necessary and useful, you cannot do them without common sense and good problem solving skills. Discuss and debate choices of methods with your team.

IC-97.   How many permutations of the letters in the word SQUARE begin with SQ?

a)   What was different about this problem that you had to consider?

b)   What method did you use to solve this problem? Explain why you chose this method.

IC-98.   Five teenagers go to the movies. They want to sit together in a row with a student on each aisle (assume the row is 5 seats wide including 2 aisle seats).

a)   How many ways can they sit in the row?

b)   If Kris wants to sit in an aisle seat, how many ways can they all sit in the row?

c)   If Patrice wants to sit on an aisle seat with Beth next to her, how many ways can the five students sit?

IC-99.   **Anagrams**

a)   How many distinct ways can the letters in the word MASH be arranged?

b)   How many distinct ways can the letters in the word SASH be arranged? Be careful!

c)   How many distinct ways can the letters in the word SASS be arranged?

d)   What makes these counts different?

IC-100.   How many permutations of all the letters in the word PYRAMID do not end with D?

IC-101.   Your teacher gave you a list of ten questions to study for a test and told you that the test would consist of six questions chosen from the list. When you got home, you realized that you wouldn't have time to study for all ten questions, so you picked the seven that you thought were most likely to be on the test. When you got to school the next day, you found out that your teacher had randomly chosen six questions to put on the test.

a)   The teacher could have picked 4 from the 7 that you studied and 2 from the three you did not. Represent each of these in combination notation.

b)   To find the number of tests the teacher might have constructed this way, what should you do with these two results: Multiply? Add? Discuss this with your team.

c)   In how many ways could your teacher have randomly selected six of the ten questions? Express this in combination notation.

What is the probability that you will have studied:

d)   six of the selected questions?

e)   five of the selected questions?

f)   three of the selected questions?

g)   Assuming you get correct all the questions that you studied for and miss all the ones you did not study for, what is you expected score on the test?

IC-102. Consider this puzzle:

a) How many ways are there to arrange the letters in each of the two scrambled clues on the left?

b) How many ways are there to arrange the letters in each of the two scrambled clues on the right?

c) Unscramble each of the clues to find the letters in the circles.

d) How many ways are there to arrange the circled letters that complete the MISQUOTE?

e) Unscramble the circled letters to find the MISQUOTE.

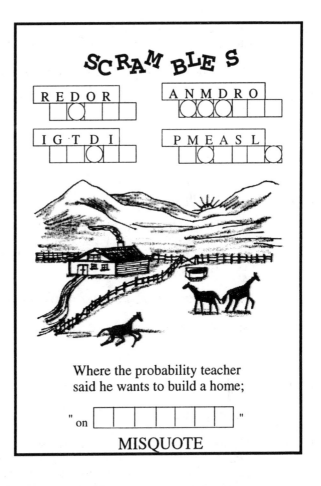

SCRAMBLES

R E D O R

A N M D R O

I G T D I

P M E A S L

Where the probability teacher said he wants to build a home;

" on ⬚⬚⬚⬚⬚⬚⬚ "

MISQUOTE

IC-103. A wildlife biologist is given the task of estimating the population of blacktail deer on Southfork Mountain. She uses a tranquilizer gun to capture, tag, and release unharmed 50 does and 15 bucks over a period of several months. She returns to the mountains the following year and makes the following observations:

"I saw 70 does this week and only 4 of them had tags."

"Of the 40 bucks I observed, 15 had been tagged."

a) Estimate the number of does on Southfork Mountain.

b) Estimate the number of bucks on Southfork Mountain.

IC-104.   We know that $_nC_r = \dfrac{n!}{(n - r)!r!}$ and $_nC_r = \dfrac{_nP_r}{r!}$, but these are not really different formulas. Show that they really amount to the same thing.

IC-105.   You are given a bag that you are told contains 8 marbles. You draw a marble, record its color, and put it back.

   a)   If you do this eight times and you don't record any red marbles, can you conclude that there aren't any red marbles in the bag? Explain.

   b)   If you do this 100 times and you don't record any red marbles, can you conclude that there are no red marbles in the bag? Explain.

   c)   How many times do you have to draw marbles (putting them back in each time) to be absolutely certain that there are no red marbles in the bag?

IC-106.   Simplify the following expressions so that they do not have negative exponents:

   a) $\dfrac{x^{-2} - y^{-2}}{x^{-1} + y^{-1}}$

   b) $(x^{-2} - 5y^{-1})^{-1}$

IC-107.   Sketch the graph of $y = 2^{(x+3)}$. Then write the equation of the graph that is four units to the right and five units down from this one.

IC-108.   Solve each inequality for x and represent each solution on a number line. Assume that $c > 0$ and $a > 0$.

   a) $|x - b| \le c$

   b) $|ax - b| \ge c$

IC-109.   Consider the system at right: How many solutions does this system have? Justify your answer.

$$x = (y - 3)^2 + 2$$
$$y = (x - 5)^2 + 3$$

IC-110.   Multiply each of the following. The first one is already done for you.

   a) $(x + y)^1 = x + y$

   b) $(x + y)^2$

   c) $(x + y)^3$

C-111. "These counting problems are driving me crazy," Alex complained as he tossed his book bag on the chair. "They don't have anything to do with real algebra." Alex had been to see his counselor and arrived after his team had started to work.

"I'm glad you said that," commented José. "Guess what we're doing today?"

"Impossible!" said Alex.

"Remember the last problem on last night's homework?" Marcia asked. "Today's first problem is to expand $(x+y)^4$ and $(x+y)^5$."

"I'm just going to use my answer from last night and multiply by another factor of $(x + y)$," Melvin suggested.

"I'm just going to add another bunch of branches to my tree diagram." José added.

"To your WHAT?" the others shouted all at once.

"To my tree diagram," said José. They all looked to see what he had.

"See, when you multiply $(x + y)(x + y)$, you multiply the x in the first factor by each term in the second factor, and you multiply the y in the first factor by each term in the second factor. So you get $x{\cdot}x$, $x{\cdot}y$, $y{\cdot}x$, and $y{\cdot}y$, just like in the tree above right.

"Then for $(x + y)^3$, everything in the first answer gets multiplied by x and also by y, so you just add another set of branches and count up: there is one x^3, three x^2y, three xy^2, and one y^3."

"Oh, cool," said Melvin. "Now I see why, in $(x+y)^3$, the total of the powers of x and y in each term is always 3."

a)   Explain Melvin's last statement.

Then Marcia said, "And I see why there are three x^2y branches! To get to the end of a branch, you start at the left, at the first junction, and choose x or y. Then at the second junction you choose x or y again, and then one more time. If you choose x twice and y once, you wind up with x^2y, and there are three ways to do that.

b)   Make a copy of the $(x + y)^3$ tree, and trace the paths that end in x^2y. Explain why there can only be three. Explain why there can only be one branch each of

x³ and y³. How many branches are there of xy^2? Explain how you can tell without going through the tree.

>>Problem continues on the next page.>>

José said, "To be honest, I'm not sure how I'm going to fit another layer of branches on my tree. Besides, we'll probably have to do $(x + y)^{20}$ or something. Maybe Marcia is on to a shortcut here. Let's see if we can figure out $(x + y)^4$."

c) In $(x + y)^3$, it took 3 x-y choices to get to the end of a branch, so all the branches ended in x^3, x^2y, xy^2, or y^3. What will the branches of $(x + y)^4$ end in?

Alex said, "It's pretty easy to see how many branches will end in x^4 and y^4. And I think I even see how many there will be that only have one power of x or one power of y, because this time it takes four choices of x or y to get through the tree."

d) What did Alex see? How many branches will end in x^4, y^4, x^3y, xy^3? If you're not sure, make the tree.

Now it was Melvin's turn to jump back in. "The x^2y^2 one is the tricky one. I'm making a list of all the ways to get it. I'll just say which two of the four choices are x, and let the other two be y. It could be choices 1 and 2, 1 and 3, 1 and 4, 2 and 3, 2 and 4, or 3 and 4. I think that's all of them. So there will be 6 x^2y^2."

e) Write out the expansion of $(x + y)^4$.

"Wait," said José, "Is making all these lists really going to be faster for $(x + y)^5$ than multiplying $(x + y)^4$ by $(x + y)$? And what about $(x + y)^{20}$? And why are we doing this in this unit anyw. . .WAIT! "

"I see it! In $(x + y)^5$, you go through five junctions to get to the end of a branch. To get, say, x^2y^3, you have to choose x at two of the five junctions. To find how many of those paths there are, we need to count how many different ways there are to pick two out of the five junctions to be the ones where you choose x, just like the list Melvin made: it could be junctions 1 and 2, 1 and 3, 2 and 4, etc. . . and we learned how to do that in this unit! And, we learned how to do it on our calculators!

f) Use what you've learned in this unit to find the coefficients of x^5, x^4y, x^3y^2, x^2y^3, xy^4, and y^5 in the expansion of $(x + y)^5$, and write out the expansion.

IC-112. Write the expansion for $(x + y)^8$. Use you calculators to find the coefficients

IC-113. Describe a method for figuring out the binomial expansion for $(x + y)^n$ without having to multiply factor by factor or draw a tree diagram.

IC-114. Five cards are dealt from a shuffled deck of 52 playing cards. A royal flush is the AKQJ10 all of the same suit. What is the probability of getting a royal flush?

IC-115. In several states, standard license plates have one digit (1 to 9), then three letters, then three digits (0 to 9). How many license plates of this type are possible? What is the probability of getting one containing ALG 2?

IC-116. Expand $(x + y)^7$.

IC-117. The array of numbers at right is known as Pascal's Triangle.

$$\begin{array}{c}
1 \\
1 \ 1 \\
1 \ 2 \ 1 \\
1 \ 3 \ 3 \ 1 \\
1 \ 4 \ 6 \ 4 \ 1 \\
1 \ 5 \ 10 \ 10 \ 5 \ 1
\end{array}$$

a) There are many patterns in the triangle, which continues indefinitely. Describe as many as you can find (at least 3).

b) Look at your work on expanding binomials (problems IC-106 and 107). What is the relationship between $(x + y)^n$ and the nth row of the triangle, if you count the 1 at the top as row 0?

c) Each row of the triangle can be figured out from the row directly above it. Find the rule.

d) Charlie wanted to find $_{10}C_3$ and he didn't have a calculator. But he knew $_9C_3$ and $_9C_2$. ($_9C_3 = 84$ and $_9C_2 = 36$.)

He had just finished calculating the number of two- and three-person committees that could be selected from the nine spirit club volunteers when the executive council informed him that they were only interested in three-person committees and that one more person had volunteered. He needed to calculate $_{10}C_3$ and he had left his calculator at a friend's house.

Then he had an inspiration! He thought, I already have the number of three-person committees the new volunteer will not be on because they would be selected from the other nine. What number is that? Give the answer in combination notation as well as a number.

AND I also know how many committees the new volunteer will be on because I can just add his name to each of my two-member committees. How many possible committees include the new volunteer?

Explain how Charlie calculated $_{10}C_3$ without a calculator (and without multiplying or dividing).

e) The answers to parts (b), (c), and (d) are all related. Explain how.

IC-118. How many distinct permutations are there of the word "**bookkeeper**?"

IC-119.   Consider the function $C(r) = {}_8C_r$.

    a)   What is an appropriate domain for this function?

    b)   What is the range?

IC-120.   If you put $100 in the bank at an annual rate of 3%, compounded monthly, how long will it take to be worth $1000?

IC-121.   What is the inverse of $f(x) = -x + 6$? Justify your answer.

IC-122.   Find all of the roots of $f(x) = x^3 + 3x$.

BUILDING A BETTER BIOME

> This is a large problem that will pull together systems of equations and sampling techniques. It will make a good portfolio entry, and it could serve as a summary problem because it brings together many ideas from throughout the course.

IC-123.   **The Bird Biome Investigation**

A biologist is trying to determine how the number of birds of three species, A, B, and C, in a particular biome compares to the optimum combined number that the region might support. She has tagged birds in the biome to estimate the numbers of each species already there. She had collected the information given below before an unfortunate encounter with a thundering herd of turtles landed her in the hospital. You have been given the task of completing the analysis of the region based on her notes.

    Week 1:   Three species of birds: A, B, and C. Estimate of food supply: approx. 3.5 kg of food per 10 m^2. Dimensions of biome are 325 m by 400 m.

>>**Problem continues on the next page.**>>

Week 2: Research has shown that each nesting pair of species A requires 30 kg of food (during the season) and defends an area of 60 m². Each nesting pair of species B requires 25 kg of food and defends an area of 100 m². Each nesting pair of species C requires 40 kg of food and defends an area of 300 m². In addition, species A and C prefer to build their nests in a particular type of pine tree, and there are only about 1100 of these trees in the biome. Neither will choose a tree that already has a nest.

Week 3: Caught and tagged 280 adult males of species A, 100 adult males of species B.

Week 4: Caught 140 adult males of species A—44 had tags. Caught 120 adult males of species B—48 had tags.

Week 5: Completed count of species C nests; a total of 12 active nesting pairs were found within the biome.

Questions you should consider but are not limited to (be sure to show all of your reasoning):

a)   Approximately how many pairs (assume that each adult male has a mate) of each species of birds are currently living in this biome?

b)   What is the optimal combination of pairs of birds that could live in this biome?

c)   How does the existing population compare with the maximum combined number of nesting pairs the biome can support?

d)   Summarize your results for parts (a), (b), and (c) in a letter to the biologist for whom you completed the work. In the letter you need to demonstrate mathematically your various conclusions. Then based on your results, think of at least two questions the biologist might want to explore further in relation to this biome. Be sure to include these questions in your letter. It is important to note that the mathematics does not give us answers here but can be helpful in identifying problems or new questions.

IC-124. If five cards are dealt from a shuffled deck of playing cards:

a)   What is the probability of getting a five card hand that is all red?

b)   Express your solution to part (a) in the form: $\dfrac{_aC_b}{_dC_e}$.

c)   What is the probability of getting a five card hand that is all clubs?

d)   Express your solution to part (c) in the form: $\dfrac{_aC_b}{_dC_e}$.

e)   What is the probability of getting a flush (5 cards from any one suit)?

IC-125. A license plate is composed of three letters followed by three numbers. What is the probability of getting a license plate containing **ALG 2** on it if:

a) it is okay to repeat the digits and the letters?

b) it is not okay to repeat the digits nor the letters?

IC-126. The new track coach has a very mathematical mind!

a) How many ways can the track coach pick a four-person 100-meter relay team from a group of nine sprinters?

b) How many ways can the coach organize the team that was chosen in running order?

IC-127. Expand the binomial: $(a + b)^8$

IC-128. Sketch both graphs below on the same set of axes. What is the solution to the system?

$$f(x) = (x - 3)^2 + 2 \quad \text{and} \quad g(x) = 2 + \log_2 (x - 2)$$

IC-129. An isosceles triangle has sides of lengths 10, 10, and 5 cm. What are the measures of the three angles?

IC-130. Here's a strange rule:

$$A \, \Omega \, B \, \Omega \, C = \sqrt[C]{A^B}$$

a) What is: $8 \, \Omega \, 2 \, \Omega \, 3$?

b) What is: $-1 \, \Omega \, 2 \, \Omega \, 4$?

c) If $A > 1$, when does $A \, \Omega \, B \, \Omega \, C = A$?

IC-131. If $m > n$, is $x^m > x^n$ for every positive x? Justify your answer.

C-132. Points are placed on a circle in such a way that $\overset{\frown}{AB} = 10°$, $\overset{\frown}{BC} = 20°$, $\overset{\frown}{CD} = 30°$, and so on around the circle, stopping once one complete revolution is made. Copy and complete the circle to the right. If two of the labeled points are chosen at random from the circle, what is the probability that the segment joining the points forms a diameter of the circle?

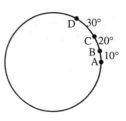

EXPLORING WITH COMBINATIONS

C-133. For the purposes of this problem, we will include the "trivial" subgroups: the one containing nothing, and the one containing all three things.

a) How many subgroups of any size can be made from a group of three things?

b) Generalize part (a): How many ways are there to choose n or fewer things from a group of n things? This is actually simpler than finding how many subgroups there are of a particular size. You can experiment with some other values of n (though you probably don't want to go beyond n = 5 if you're listing all the possibilities!) Or you can think of a decision chart. What decision must you make for each of the n things?

C-134. Duong noticed that $_1C_0 + _1C_1 = 2^1$. He tried $_2C_0 + _2C_1 + _2C_2 = 2^2$ and found that it worked also.

a) Does $_3C_0 + _3C_1 + _3C_2 + _3C_3 = 2^3$?

b) Does $_4C_0 + _4C_1 + _4C_2 + _4C_3 + _4C_4 = 2^4$?

c) Explain why $_nC_1 + _nC_2 + ... + _nC_n = 2^n$. How does this relate to the previous problem?

C-135. Jean Luc's favorite Asian restaurant has six dishes on its lunch menu. He wants to get their three item combo for lunch and is reminded by the counter-person that he can repeat a selection. How many different ways could he order lunch?

C-136. Make a quick sketch of each of the following functions:

a) $y = (x - 1)^2(x - 3)^3(x - 5)^2$

b) $y = -(x - 1)^2(x - 3)^3(x - 5)^2$

IC-137.   You roll three different colored dice and use the numbers on the dice to determine the lengths of the sides of a triangle. <u>Example</u>: 3, 3, 5 would be an isosceles triangle with base 5.

What is the probability of building a right triangle?

IC-138.   Given the function $h(x) = -2(x + 3)^2 + 2$:

a)   what are the intercepts?   b)   what are the domain and range?

IC-139.   Expand the binomial: $(y + z)^5$

IC-140.

> We have distinguished sequences from other functions by using t(n) rather than f(x). Another common way to denote a sequence is with subscripts; instead of t(n) we write t_n to mean the same thing. Sometimes the rule for a sequence only tells how to get each term from the ones that came before it; this is called a **RECURSIVE DEFINITION**. When defining a sequence this way it is also necessary to specify one or more of the beginning terms of the sequence. For example, the sequence 1, 3, 5, . . . could be defined by the rule $t_n = t_{n-1} + 2$; $t_0 = 1$. This says that the nth term is the previous, or (n - 1)st, term plus two, and the initial term is one.

For each of the following recursively defined sequences, list the first four terms, and state whether the sequence is arithmetic, geometric, or neither.

a) $t_n = t_{n-1} - 11$; $t_0 = 98$.   b) $a_n = 2a_{n-1} + 1$; $a_0 = 0$.

IC-141.   Last Autumn, Julia noticed something interesting as she blew up spherical balloons for Harris's birthday party.

a)   If the radius of the balloon is 4 cm, what is the volume of the balloon? In case you have forgotten, the volume of a sphere with radius r is $\frac{4}{3} \pi r^3$.

b)   If the radius of the balloon is 8 cm (**double** the size as in part (a)), what is the volume?

c)   Is the volume twice as big when the radius is doubled?

d)   Julia did figure out a pattern. What is it?

C-142.   Imagine a circle with radius 4 units and a center at (5, 6). This circle is rotated around the x-axis, always staying the same distance from the axis. It sweeps out a three dimensional figure. What shape is formed? Make a sketch.

C-143.   Your teacher has decided one person in your class can take one week off from doing homework. The lucky person has been narrowed down so it is between you and Newton. The teacher says, "I'm thinking of a number between 0 and 10. Whoever can choose the number closest to it gets the holiday from homework. Quickly, Newt yells out "Three!" Assuming he did not hit the number exactly, what number would you choose? Justify and explain your answer.

C-144.   Solve for x. Give answers in degrees or radians but think about the possible quadrants.

$$2 \sin x \cos x + \cos x = 0$$

UMMARY AND REVIEW

C-145.   **Unit 11 Summary Assignment**

a)   If you were going to write the test for this unit, what kinds of problems would you include? Describe each type of problem and explain why you would choose it.

b)   Find your favorite problem from this unit. If it is one you completed as a portfolio entry, describe the problem and explain what makes it your favorite.
Otherwise write out the complete question (or summarize the information), write out your complete solution process, and then explain what makes it your favorite problem.

c)   Find a problem that you still cannot solve or that you are worried that you might not be able to solve on a test. Write out the question and as much of the solution as you can until you get to the hard part. Then explain what it is that keeps you from solving the problem. Be clear and precise.

d)   What did you learn in this unit?

e)   Turn all this in to be included in your portfolio according to your teacher's instructions.

IC-146.   **Triangles By Chance: An Investigation**

Obtain three dice from your teacher. You may also want some string, linguini, a compass or some other building material. Roll the three dice and use the numbers on the dice to represent the lengths of sides of a triangle. Build (or draw) the triangle. Record the three numbers in a table according to the type of triangle formed (scalene, isosceles, equilateral). For example, if 3, 3, and 5 came up on the dice, you would record 3,3, 5 under the heading ISOSCELES since a triangle with sides of length 3, 3, and 5 is isosceles. Repeat this ten times, then add your information to the class list on the board.

Examine the data from the whole class and discuss it with your team. Based on the class results and on your discussion, estimate:

a)   the probability of being able to build an equilateral triangle.

b)   the probability of being able to build an isosceles triangle.

c)   the probability of being able to build a scalene triangle.

d)   the probability that no triangle is formed.

e)   Explain how you came up with each of your estimates.

f)   Calculate the **actual probabilities** for each part (a) through (d) above. Show and explain your reasoning for all of your work.

g)   Record your results to all of the above in either a report or on a poster based on your teacher's instructions. Examine the grading rubric to be sure you include everything your teacher expects.

IC-147.   The local theater is offering a "moviefest." Patrons can watch three different movies for the price of one and they can watch them in any order. In how many different ways can you arrange the order in which you see the three movies?

IC-148.   Next June Joanna is taking a vacation. She will make four stops while she is gone. They will be Pittsburgh, Washington, D.C., Philadelphia, and New York City. Joanna is not sure in what order to visit these places. In how many different ways can she organize her vacation?

IC-149.   Ms. Hart has three different math books, four different chemistry books and six different history books to arrange on a shelf.

a)   How many ways can she arrange all the books in any order?

b)   How many ways can she arrange the math books?

c)   How many ways can she arrange the chemistry books?

d)   How many ways can she arrange the history books?

e)   How many ways can she arrange the books if each subject is grouped together?

C-150.   How many <u>distinct</u> ways can you arrange the letters in the word CAR? POP?

C-151.   In an algebra class of 28 students, in how many different ways can a 4-student study teams be formed?

C-152.   A license plate is composed of a number followed by three different letters followed by three different digits. All letters and the numbers 0 through 9 can be used in any respective position. What is the probability of getting a license plate with your initials on it?

C-153.   What is the probability of getting a full house (three of one kind of card and two of another kind of card, assuming "kinds" are 1, 2, ..., Q, K) from five cards dealt from a shuffled deck of 52 playing cards? Express your answer in combination form.

C-154.   You are given a bag that you are told contains 8 marbles, 4 red and 1 each of four other colors. Express in the form $\frac{{}_aC_b}{{}_dC_e}$ the probability that two marbles, drawn together, will:

a)   be the same color.   b)   be different colors.

C-155.   A coin is flipped four times. What is the probability of getting two tails if the first two flips were two heads?

C-156.   Expand each binomial:

a) $(x - y)^3$ b) $(x - y)^4$

C-157.   **TOOL KIT CHECK-UP**

Your Tool Kit contains reference tools for algebra. Return to your Tool Kit entries. You may need to revise or add entries.

Be sure that your Tool Kit contains entries for all of the items listed below. Add any topics that are missing to your Tool Kit NOW, as well as any other items that will help you in your study of algebra.

- Decision Chart
- Factorial
- Recursive Definition
- Pascal's Triangle

- Permutations
- Combinations
- Binomial Expansion
- Other Counting Techniques

UNIT 12

Closest to the Pin
DESCRIPTIVE STATISTICS

Unit 12 Objectives
Closest to the Pin: DESCRIPTIVE STATISTICS

We see data represented in many forms. Whether we see it as a representation of an athlete's performance or the public's opinion on a particular issue, it is displayed as a daily part of our lives. We call these displays or numerical summaries of data "statistics." Advertisers often make references to statistics to persuade consumers to purchase their products, and political parties use statistics to persuade voters to support their candidates. In these examples the data is frequently collected or presented in a biased way in order to sway the reader. One of the goals of this unit is to analyze conclusions drawn from data with a critical eye. When you encounter a presentation based on statistics, you should first consider the way the data was gathered.

In this unit you will have the opportunity to:

- consider and discuss issues that might cause bias in data gathering and its reporting.

- use measures of central tendency (the mean and median) and measures of dispersion (the mean and standard deviation) to compare sets of data.

- convert data into z-scores, standard scores, and percentiles in order to make comparisons across data sets easier.

- use stem-and-leaf plots and box-and-whisker plots to display and compare sets of data.

Read the following problem and discuss with your team the question: "Now that we have accepted the job, what should we do?" Write down a few ideas.

DS-0. **CLOSEST TO THE PIN** The Hookenslise Corporation is having its annual golf tournament. Each year it gives away numerous prizes, including a new car. The corporate theme for the year has been, "Consistency and Hard Work Pay Off." In keeping with this theme, the corporate president wants this year's "Closest to the Pin Award" to go to the player who is consistently close to the hole on five designated par three holes. (This way they hope to award the prize to the "best" player, not merely the luckiest one.) They need to know how to make this determination. Your team has been hired to find the best method to analyze the data they have gathered so far.

PROBLEM SOLVING
REPRESENTATION/MODELING
FUNCTIONS/GRAPHING
INTERSECTIONS/SYSTEMS
ALGORITHMS
REASONING/COMMUNICATION

Unit 12
Closest to the Pin: DESCRIPTIVE STATISTICS

DATA GATHERING

DS-1.   In your teams, discuss how the following issues can bias a survey. Be prepared to share your thoughts with the class.

a)   Where was the survey taken?   b)   Who took the survey?

c)   How were the survey questions asked?   d)   When was the survey taken?

e)   What was the question?

DS-2.   **Closest to the Pin Lab** If you have not yet read problem DS-0, read it now.

To test your ideas, we need some data. Let's simulate the golf shots by tossing coins at a target. Your teacher has set up a target. From a distance of five feet, each team member should toss the coin five times.

a)   Measure each distance from the target to the final position of the tossed coin to the nearest centimeter. Measure from the center of the target to the center of the coin. Record all of your data on a chart as shown below. **Do not discard any toss.**

b)   For each set of data, calculate both the **MEAN** (average score) and the **MEDIAN** (middle score). Record the results on your chart. **Save this data; you will use it throughout the unit.**

Name	Toss 1	Toss 2	Toss 3	Toss 4	Toss 5	Mean	Median

DS-3.   Which average (the mean or the median) do you think best meets the needs of the corporation? Why?

DS-4. Have one team member record all of your tosses on the class histogram provided by your instructor. (A **HISTOGRAM** is a bar graph showing the frequency with which data values occurred.) Sketch the shape of the histogram.

DS-5. Data points that are quite removed from the rest of the data are called **OUTLIERS**. Does the class data have any outliers? What may have caused them?

DS-6. Is this an accurate model for the "Closest to the Pin" contest? What factors may cause some of your data to be biased?

DS-7. The following are test scores from a difficult chemistry test. Calculate the mean and median from each set of data:

a)   62, 68, 75, 60, 72, 62, 67   b)   60, 62, 96, 68, 72, 62, 67

c)   The highest score in the second set is 96. What effect does this score have on the mean and median for the set?

DS-8. Create a set of data in which:

a)   the median is <u>much</u> higher than the mean.

b)   the mean is <u>much</u> higher than the median.

DS-9. The Davidsons took a trip to Minneapolis and left on Friday afternoon in the middle of the rush hour traffic. Because of all of the traffic, they averaged 40 mph on the way to the city. They returned Sunday morning when traffic was much lighter. They averaged 60 mph on the way home.

a)   What was their average speed?

b)   The Davidsons live 120 miles from Minneapolis. How long did it take for them to drive to the city?

c)   How long did it take to return?

d)   Find the average speed by calculating rate = $\frac{\text{Total Distance}}{\text{Total Time}}$. Does this answer agree with your results from part (a)? If not, which one is correct?

e)   If the total distance from the Davidsons' home to Minneapolis were 300 miles, what would be the average speed?

f)   If the total distance were n miles, what would be the average speed?

DS-10. Brandon's little brother spilled orange juice
on his calculator and now he's stuck in
radian mode and the π button won't work.

He needs to evaluate $\pi + \cos \frac{\pi}{5}$. Explain
how he can still use <u>his</u> calculator to evaluate
the value.

DS-11. Read the information in the box below and add it to your Tool Kit.

SERIES AND SUMMATION NOTATION

A **SERIES** is the sum of the terms of a sequence. An example of a simple
arithmetic series in expanded form is $2 + 4 + 6 + 8 + 10$. A convenient way to

indicate a series is to use **SUMMATION NOTATION**: $\sum\limits_{n=1}^{5} \mathbf{2n}$. This

notation is read, "The sum of numbers of the form 2n as n goes from
1 to 5." The **INDICES**, n = 1 and 5, show that n is to be replaced

successively by 1, 2, . . . , 5. The symbol $\sum$ (the Greek letter sigma) means

that the terms resulting from successive replacements are to be added together,
that is, summed.

Therefore, $\sum\limits_{n=1}^{5} 2n = 2(1) + 2(2) + 2(3) + 2(4) + 2(5) = 30.$

---

a) Find $\sum\limits_{n=1}^{5} 3n.$

b) Find $\sum\limits_{n=1}^{4} (2n+1).$

DS-12. Dan Domain's teacher had him make several squares on centimeter paper. Then he had to
make a graph that compared the <u>side length</u> and the <u>surface area</u> of the squares.

a) Dan's teacher asked him to find a curve to fit
the data (shown at right), so Dan used a
quadratic. Is a quadratic a good choice? How
could you tell <u>without</u> looking at the graph?

b) After doing all that work, Dan's teammate
claimed that a parabola is not a very good
model, since a parabola is U-shaped and this
data isn't. What do you think?

c) Describe another example where the domain of
the situation is not the same as the domain of
the equation that models that situation.

DS-13.   Solve for c: $c + \sqrt{c + 1} = 5$

WHAT IS AVERAGE?

DS-14.   Using the data gathered from the "Closest to the Pin"
lab, find the mean and median for your team.

a)   Is it true that the mean for your team is the
average (mean) of the means of the
individual members? Will this always be the
case? Explain in a few sentences or using algebra to show why you came to this
conclusion. What kind of reasoning did you use, inductive or deductive?

b)   Is it true that the median for your team is the average (median) of the medians of the
individual members? Will this always be the case? Explain in a few sentences or
using algebra to show why you came to this conclusion.

DS-15.   For this simulation, your whole class represents our "population of interest," that is, the
corporation's golfers. Your team is a **sample** of that population. When we take the
mean of a sample, we hope that it will approximate the mean of the population. How
does your team's mean compare to the class mean that your teacher put on the board?

DS-16.   Do you think that every team in the class will have the same result? Explain.

DS-17.   We are going to gather all of the mean scores and the median scores and display them on
two new histograms. Your teacher has two master graphs. On the graph labeled
MEAN, record all of the mean scores from the individuals in your team. On the graph
labeled MEDIAN, record all of the median scores from the individuals in your team.

DS-18.   Look at the mean graph created by the class. Where is the graph centered? What is the
shape of the curve? How does it differ from the class histogram you sketched in
problem DS-4?

DS-19.   Look at the median graph. Where is the graph centered? What is the shape of the curve?
How does it differ from the class histogram you sketched in problem DS-4?

DS-20.   Suppose we had a class of 100 students. What would change for these two graphs?

DS-21. If each person did 100 tosses instead of just 5, what would change for the two graphs? Why?

DS-22. A teacher is trying to decide which 32-point exam to use. She randomly chooses five students to take both of the exams. The scores of the exams are shown below:

Form A: 20, 22, 24, 26, 28   **Form B:** 10, 22, 24, 32, 32

a) What is the mean for each form?

b) What is the median for each form?

c) Are the two tests equivalent? If not how are they different?

d) Which form do you think she should use? Why?

DS-23. The Hookenslise Corporation is in the midst of union negotiations. Labor claims that the company's average salary is $28,000 while management claims it is $32,000. If they are using the same set of data, how can their averages be different? How could such a large difference have occurred?

DS-24. Look back at your team data from the "Closest to the Pin" problem. How many scores (from your team) are below your individual median score? What percent of the scores are below that value?

DS-25. Find $\sum_{n=2}^{6} (3n - 2)$.

DS-26.   Read the information below about notation and add it to your Tool Kit.

> ### STATISTICAL VARIABLES
>
> In statistics there are some standard variables used to represent certain values. When data refers to the entire group (which is called the **POPULATION**) the variables are written using lower-case Greek letters such as μ (pronounced "mu") and σ (pronounced "sigma"). When the data refers to a **SAMPLE** from the population, the data is written using standard (English) letters.
>
> Examples:
>
> If the members of our class were our population then a subgroup consisting of every fifth member of our class would be a sample.
>
> If the set of all words written in English were our population, the words on page 25 of your history book could be a sample (although perhaps a biased one).
>
> The following are variables we have used so far:
>
>   **n**   total number of data values in your sample
>
>   **x**   an individual value from a set of data
>
> $\overline{\mathbf{x}}$ sample mean
>
>   μ   *(mu)* population mean
>
> Here are two variables that we will be using in the next few days.
>
>   **s**   sample standard deviation
>
>   σ   *(sigma)* population standard deviation
>
> Note: Σ is capital sigma, σ is lower case sigma.

DS-27.   Suppose the mean ($\overline{\mathbf{x}}$) SAT score for a random sample of students is 960.

a)   What does this tell you about the actual mean (μ) for all students who took the SAT?

b)   Would another sample have the same mean?

c)   For different samples, does μ change? Does $\overline{\mathbf{x}}$ change?

d)   How do $\overline{\mathbf{x}}$ and μ compare numerically?

DS-28.   Assuming n is an integer greater than 1 and A is a positive real number, which is larger: $\frac{A}{n}$ or $\frac{A}{n-1}$? Justify your answer algebraically.

DS-29.   Write the following series in expanded form and find the sum: $\sum\limits_{n=1}^{6}\left(\frac{1}{2}n+10\right)$

DS-30.   Simplify if possible; justify each step.

a) $\dfrac{2x - 3x^2}{4x^3}$ b) $\dfrac{2x^{-1} - 3x^{-2}}{4x^{-3}}$

SPREADS: RANGE, MEAN DEVIATION, STANDARD DEVIATION AND VARIANCE

DS-31.   Look back at problem DS-22.

a)   What makes the two tests different? Discuss in your team a method for describing the difference between the two sets of data.

b)   Find a way to numerically represent this difference.

DS-32.   Try your method for the following two sets of data. Does your method still help to distinguish between the two sets of data?

Set A: 10, 30, 39, 40, 43, 48, 70   **Set B:** 10, 20, 30, 40, 50, 60, 70

DS-33. One way to measure the spread of data is to calculate the **RANGE** (high score - low score), but the previous problem shows that this measure may not give a good sense of the spread.

Another method for measuring the spread is to calculate the average (mean) distance from the mean called the mean deviation. In general,

$$\textbf{MEAN DEVIATION} = \frac{\sum |(x - \overline{x})|}{n}$$

Use this formula to calculate the mean deviation for Set A in the previous problem. You may need to refer back to problems DS-11 or DS-26 to interpret the symbols used in the formula.

Note: Many statistical formulas that use Σ (summation notation) will not use indexed values. It is always assumed that all the data values (x) will be used in the formula. In this case, we know that there are "n" data values that need to be summed.

Using indexed values, the formula is written $\dfrac{\sum\limits_{i=1}^{n} |x_i - \overline{x}|}{n}$.

DS-34. Find the mean deviation for your tosses on the "closest to the pin" problem. Compare your result with those of the other members of your team. Who appears to be the most "consistent" player in your team?

DS-35. Notice how we used absolute value to calculate the mean deviation. What would happen if we did not use absolute value? Use your data to demonstrate.

DS-36.

Although the mean deviation gives a fairly reliable measure of the dispersion, the use of absolute value leads to problems with the development of more advanced mathematical computations. Therefore, the **STANDARD DEVIATION**, which uses squaring to retain positive differences is more generally used.

$$\sigma = \sqrt{\frac{\Sigma (x - \bar{x})^2}{n}}$$

In any set of data at least 75% of the points will lie within two standard deviations of the mean, and if the data are normally distributed 68% will be found within one standard deviation of the mean and 95% will be within two standard deviations. This information can be very useful in interpreting data and is another reason that people choose to use the standard deviation.

Calculate the standard deviation for your tosses on the "closest to the pin" problem. Once again, compare your result with those of the other members of your team. What does the standard deviation tell you about your data?

DS-37. Is the formula above equivalent to $\frac{\Sigma |x - \bar{x}|}{\sqrt{n}}$? Justify your answer with an explanation or a counterexample.

DS-38. How do the mean deviation and the standard deviation from your tosses compare?

DS-39. The set of data at right is organized in a frequency table. Although we do not know the source of the actual data, we can still make an estimate of the mean and other statistical quantities.

Class	Frequency
0 - 9	5
10 - 19	16
20 - 29	12
30 - 39	8
40 - 49	5
50 - 59	3
60 - 69	1

a) 4.5 is the best single value representative for the first class of data (0-9). Explain why you think that this would be true.

b) Using this quantity, make an estimate of the sum of all the scores in the first class.

c) Find the midpoint of each of the other classes and make estimates for the sum of all the scores in each class. Then find an estimate for the total of all of the scores.

d) How many total scores were there?

e) Make an estimate for the mean.

f) In what class will the median occur?

DS-40. Consider the following set of data: 8, 10, 15, 25, 34, 36

    a)   Find the mean.

    b)   Calculate the mean deviation.

    c)   Calculate the standard deviation.

    d)   How do your answers from parts (b) and (c) compare?

DS-41. Ms. Hilling teaches two geometry classes. On the last test both classes had a mean of 78 but the standard deviation for her first class was 8 while the standard deviation for her second class was 15. What does this information tell you about the performance of the two classes on that test?

> Still another measure of spread or dispersion or variation is the **VARIANCE**, which is simply the square of the **standard deviation.**
>
> $$\sigma^2 = \frac{\sum\left(x-\bar{x}\right)^2}{n}$$
>
> Sometimes it is more convenient to use the **variance** in making calculations.
>
> What is the **variance** for each of Ms. Hilling's two Geometry classes? Do you think this calculation gives you any better information?

DS-42. Remember Brandon's problem with his calculator? The π button still doesn't work but now it's stuck in degree mode. Explain how he can evaluate the problem $\pi + \cos\left(\frac{\pi}{5}\right)$ where $\frac{\pi}{5}$ is in radians.

DS-43. Ms. Shimizu brought in a big bowl of hard candy for her class. She walked around the room letting each student take a handful, but she started with the students with the smallest hands and went in order of increasing hand size.

    a)   Sketch a graph of this situation, comparing the number of pieces of candy in the bowl over time.

    b)   Is this situation an example of a discrete function or a step function or neither? Justify your choice.

DS-44. Kisha has graphed $y = x(6 - x)$ in a standard window.

a) What is the best name for the graph?

b) Jamal has bet Kisha that he can make the graph look like a horizontal line without changing, adding, or deleting functions. Kisha doesn't think he can do it, but Jamal is sure he can. What strategy does Jamal have in mind?

DS-45. Show that $\cos 2x \neq 2 \cos x$.

STATISTICS ON A CALCULATOR

DS-46. This problem introduces the STAT features on your calculator. Your teacher will provide a resource page. Enter the following set of data:

22, 8, 33, 19, 27, 23, 15, 35, 38, 16, 19, 24, 17, 37

a) Use your calculator to sort the data. Use this sorted list to find the median.

b) Use the 1-Var statistic feature and record all of the variables that are displayed. What do each of the variables stand for?

c) What is the mean of the data?

d) What is the standard deviation?

DS-47. Enter your team's data for "Closest to the Pin." Use the statistics features to calculate the mean and standard deviation for your team.

DS-48. Most graphing calculators will draw histograms from your statistical data. Use your calculator to draw the histogram. Change the x-scale to view different kinds of histograms.

DS-49. The frequency table at right represents all scores on a 10 point quiz.

a) Find the mean score.

b) Find the standard deviation of the scores.

c) Draw the histogram of the scores.

Score	Frequency
4	2
5	4
6	8
7	15
8	22
9	8
10	4

DS-50.

Data can be represented graphically in many forms. A useful organizational tool is the **STEM-LEAF PLOT**. In its simplest form for two digit data, the tens digits are listed vertically in numerical order in the first column. The ones digits are recorded to the right of the corresponding tens digit as you read through the list. Consider the data: 25, 38, 25, 30, 60, 42, 17, 22, 55, 69, 42, 100, 52, 12.

a) Complete the preliminary stem-leaf for this information. (The first five numbers have already been entered, in addition to all the tens digits.)

1	
2	5 5
3	8 0
4	
5	
6	0
7	
8	
9	
10	

b) Rewrite the stem-leaf in final form putting the ones digits on each line in increasing order.

1	2 7
2	
3	
4	
5	
6	
7	
8	
9	
10	

DS-51. While straightening up the living room, Calvert's mom came across a Spanish test on which he had earned a score of 42. Before she assumes that he failed the test, what questions does she need to ask him? List at least three.

DS-52. Your end-of-unit project is to write a report for the corporation that hired your team at the beginning of this unit. (Remember "Closest to the Pin?") Go back and reread the initial project and write down some ideas about completing parts of this project. Consider the statistical tools we have studied so far: mean, median, spread, and standard deviation. Your task is to devise a method to determine the most consistently accurate golfer. How do each of these statistical tools help you to develop your project?

444

DS-53. Tara's family took a casual drive through the country one Saturday. They drove slowly to enjoy the scenery, so they averaged 30 mph. On the way home, they took the same route, but because everyone was tired they drove at the speed limit of 55 mph.

a) What was their average rate for the whole trip (50 miles each way)?

b) What would be their average rate if they drove at the same speeds for 100 miles each way?

c) What conclusions can you make?

DS-54. Suppose you walk the 3000 miles from San Francisco to New York City at 3 mph. Then you fly back at 500 mph.

a) What is your average speed for the whole trip?

b) Explain, in words, why your average speed is much closer to 3 mph than to 500 mph. Use as few numbers as possible and absolutely no algebra in your explanation.

DS-55. Without a calculator, evaluate: $\left(\frac{4}{9}\right)^{3/2}$

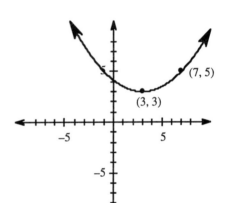

DS-56. Write an equation for the curve at right. Is it a function? Justify your answer.

DS-57. Solve for x, correct to three decimal places.

a) $27 = 6^x$

b) $27 = \dfrac{1}{6^x}$

c) $27 = \dfrac{1}{\left(\frac{1}{6}\right)^x}$

d) Show that $\dfrac{1}{\left(\frac{1}{6}\right)^x} = 6^x$.

DS-58.   Consider two sets of test data:

Test A	57	76	76	95
Test B	29	94	95	95

a)   Find the mean and standard deviation (σ) of each set.

b)   Who would have more reason to rejoice: the person who earned a 95 on Test A or on Test B? Explain using your results from part (a).

DS-59.

> If you earned 42 points out of 50 on a particular test, 42 is called your **RAW SCORE**. Raw scores are often converted to **Z-SCORES**, because then you can tell how far a particular score is from the mean. A z-score of 1 is 1 standard deviation above the mean. A z-score of 2.5 is $2\frac{1}{2}$ standard deviations above the mean.

a)   What does a z-score of 0 indicate?   b)   What does a z-score of -1 indicate?

DS-60.   A set of data has a mean of 92 and a standard deviation of 8.

a)   How many standard deviations above the mean is a raw score of 104?

b)   If a student has a raw score of 110, what is his z-score?

c)   What z-score corresponds to a raw score of 88?

d)   What raw score corresponds to a z-score of -1.75?

DS-61.   Consider the following scores on a geometry test: 75, 86, 94, 89, 80, 72, 17, 100, 56, 80, 91, 71, 79, 57, 94, 90, 58, 60, 100, 75, 83, 86, 53, 93, 92, 60, 81, 100, 94, 69, 89, 86, 42, 76, 75. Just from looking at the numbers, how do you think the class did on the test?

DS-62.   Find the mean and the standard deviation of the scores in problem DS-61.

DS-63.   What do you think caused the standard deviation to be so high? Test your hypothesis and share it with your team.

DS-64.   In some large classes, teachers use z-scores to assign grades. For example 1.5 standard deviations below the mean might be the highest F and 1.5 above the mean might begin the A's. According to this grading policy, which scores on the geometry test would fail the test? Which would get A's?

DS-65.   Would it be to your advantage if your teacher graded your next test on this type of a curve? Explain.

DS-66.   On a recent 250 mile trip, Felicia averaged 50 mph over the first 125 miles. What should be her average speed for the second half of her trip if she wants to average 60 mph over the whole journey?

DS-67.   Write possible equations for each of these four graphs. Notice that you will need to account for the scaling of the axes for graphs (c) and (d).

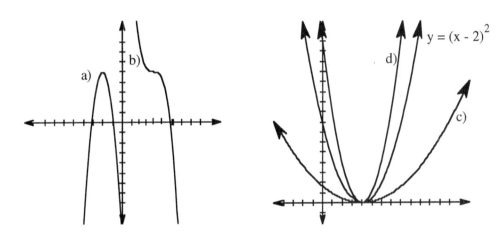

DS-68.   For the sequences listed below, state whether each is arithmetic or geometric, whether the terms are increasing or decreasing, and find a formula for the nth term after the initial term. The initial term for each sequence is in bold print.

a)   **1**, 3, 5, 7, . . .

b)   **1**, 3, 9, 27, . . .

c)   **10**, 5, $\frac{5}{2}$, $\frac{5}{4}$, . . .

d)   **16**, 12, 9, . . .

DS-69.   Given the points O(0, 0) and R(-5, -12):

a)   What is the equation of the circle centered at point O and passing through R?

b)   What is the measure of the angle formed by $\overline{OR}$ and the positive x-axis? Answer in both radians and degrees.

c)   Graph your circle in part (a) and $x^2 + y^2 = 25$ on the same set of axes. Shade the region between the circles.

d)   If we use these circles as a dart board and the dart is certain to hit randomly somewhere within the largest circle, what is the probability of hitting the shaded region?

DS-70.   The volume of an open-top box is 30 in³. The length of the base is twice its width.

a)   Sketch and label a diagram.

b)   Express the total outside surface area S in terms of the width x. Simplify.

PERCENTILES

DS-71.

A **PERCENTILE** ranking indicates the percentage of students who scored *below* that score. For example, if you are at the 90th percentile in your class, 90 percent of the students at your grade level have a GPA below yours. If there are 320 students in your class, how many would be at the 90th percentile or above? Add this definition to your Tool Kit.

DS-72.   Ryan had a score of 76 on the geometry test in problem DS-61. What is his percentile?

DS-73.

> Another representation of data is the **BOX AND WHISKER** diagram. This diagram shows the high and low values, as well as the values at the 75th, 50th, and 25th percentiles. The four groups between these percentiles are called **QUARTILES**. In the box and whisker diagram, the highest and lowest quartiles are the whiskers, and the middle two quartiles are the boxes.

The diagram at right represents the data 1, 3, 5, 6, 6, 7, 8, 9

The numbers 1, 4, 6, 7.5, and 9 have special significance on this box and whisker diagram. Why? Discuss this with your team What do each of the numbers represent?

DS-74. On your calculator, plot the data in the previous problem using a box and whisker diagram.

DS-75. What percentage of the data falls in each section: A, B, C, and D?

DS-76. Make a stem-leaf and a box and whisker diagram for the geometry test scores in problem DS-61. Use the box and whisker diagram to describe the performance of the class on that test.

DS-77. Compare your results for the preceding problem with your answer to problem DS-61. Which methods do you think provide the best description of the data? Why do you think so?

DS-78. Recall these two ways to write a general equation for a parabola:

$$y = a(x - h)^2 + k \qquad \text{and} \qquad y = ax^2 + bx + c$$

Veronica is confused. "If there are two different general equations for a parabola, how do you know which one to use and when?" Help her out by answering the questions below.

a) Are they really two different equations? Prove that you can always change one into the other by expanding $y = a(x - h)^2 + k$ so that it is in $y = ax^2 + bx + c$ form (multiply it out and combine like terms). Represent the values of a, b, and c in terms of a, h, and k.

b) Answer Veronica's question: How do you know which of these equations to use?

c) Does the 'a' represent the same thing in both equations? Do the 'k' and 'c' both represent the y-intercept? Explain your thinking.

DS-79. Driving from San Antonio to Dallas, Erin averaged 60 mph for the first 2 hours, 20 mph the next hour (rush hour), and 65 mph the final 3 hours of his journey.

a) Can you determine how fast he was going after one hour based on these data? If so, find his speed; if not, explain why not.

b) What was his average rate for the entire 6 hour trip?

DS-80. Consider the function $y = 3 \sin (x + \frac{\pi}{2}) - 4$.

a) How is its graph different from $y = \sin x$?

b) Sketch the graph.

DS-81. If $p = 3t - 5t^2$:

a) find p when $t = 0$.   b) find t when $p = 0$.

DS-82. Each labeled point on this graph is either a maximum or a minimum.

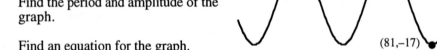

a) Find the period and amplitude of the graph.

b) Find an equation for the graph.

c) Use one of the given points to check your equation.

DS-83. Sketch a temperature vs. time graph of these situations (with time as the independent variable):

a) A cup of hot coffee is left on a table.   b) A glass of ice tea is left in the sun.

c) What kind of function would you use to model these situations? Give a reason for your choices.

DS-84. Solve $\dfrac{\sqrt{8m^2}}{\sqrt{2m}} = 6$.

DS-85. Find the equation of the line that passes through (-2, 5) and is perpendicular to $y = -5x + 2$.

DS-86.   Solve for x: $\frac{1}{x+2} - \frac{1}{x} = 2$.

DS-87.   Solve this system: $(x - 3)^2 + (y + 2)^2 = 100$ and $y + 2 = (x - 3)^2$

a)   Sketch the graph of the two equations on the same set of axes.

b)   Find the points of intersection algebraically and label them on your graph.

TRANSFORMATIONS OF Z-SCORES

DS-88.   A recent 90-point algebra test resulted in the following raw scores: 85, 63, 77, 56, 57, 80, 69, 46, 57, 86, 77, 67, 67, 90, 68, 89, 87, 43, 65, 57, 68, 47, 52, 75, 73. The instructor has asked for your help in analyzing the results.

a)   Organize the material in a stem-leaf plot.

b)   Use the stem-leaf plot to make a box and whisker diagram of the data. Mark the mean and the median on the plot.

c)   Write a summary of how you think the class did. Refer to the box and whisker plot.

DS-89.   Danielle's score on the above test was an 86. In what percentile did she fall? What was her z-score?

DS-90.   While z-scores are very useful because they indicate the distance from the mean, they have a psychological difficulty. Even if you know you scored 1 standard deviation above the mean, how does it feel to be told that you have a score of 1?

We can combat that problem by making a linear transformation of the data using $y = Ax + B$. Let y represent the new score, and x represent the old z-score. The equation would read: **New Score = A (z-score) + B.** $(y = mx + b)$

If you scored the mean, a score of 50 would feel better than a z-score of 0, so let's find a scoring system that lets 50 be the mean and 10 be the standard deviation.

a)   Explain why a z-score of 0 will be transformed to a new score of 50.

b)   Explain why a z-score of 1 will transformed to a new score of 60.

c)   If x represents the z-score and y represents the new score, we have two points: (0, 50) and (1, 60). Find the linear function that makes this transformation.

d)   In the equation that you found, what does the y-intercept represent? What does the slope represent?

DS-91.   SAT scores use a similar transformation. They use a mean of 500 and a standard
         deviation of 100. What is the linear transformation $(y = Ax + B)$ that converts z-scores to
         SAT score.

DS-92.   Aimee has been tutoring her brother,
         Logan, for the past two weeks. As an
         incentive, she promised to take him out
         to dinner if he earns an A on his next
         test. (His teacher has announced that to
         earn an A, one's z-score must be ≥ 1.5.)
         The day came and Logan scored 42 out
         of 60. If the class average was 30 with a
         standard deviation of 8, did Logan earn
         his dinner? Explain.

DS-93.   Take out your team data from our original "Closest to the Pin" problem.

         a)   Make a histogram and a box and whisker diagram of the individual scores.

         b)   Describe the advantages and disadvantages of each type of graph.

DS-94.   Multiply:

         a) $(a + b)(a^2 - ab + b^2)$ b) $(x - 2)(x^2 + 2x + 4)$

         c) $(Y + 5)(Y^2 - 5Y + 25)$ d) $(x - y)(x^2 + xy + y^2)$

         e) What did you notice about these products?

         f) Make up another multiplication problem that will follow the same pattern.

DS-95.   Parts (a) and (d) of the preceding problem represent a general pattern known as the **sum
         and difference of cubes**. Use this pattern to factor each of the following
         polynomials:

         a) $x^3 + y^3$ b) $x^3 - 27$

         c) $8x^3 - y^3$ d) $x^3 + 1$

         e) Make up another sum or difference of cubes problem and show how to factor it.

DS-96.   Use the sum or difference of cubes pattern and what you already know about factoring to factor the following as completely as possible.

a) $x^5 + 8x^2y^3$ b) $8y^6 - 125x^3$

c) Start with $x^6 - y^6$. This one is tricky. If you start it as the difference of two cubes you will not be able to factor it completely. Think of it as the difference of two squares and then factor the factors as the sum and difference of two cubes.

DS-97.   Add some notes to your Tool Kit about how to factor the sum and the difference of two cubes.

DS-98.   Find the equation of a cubic function that has $y = x^3$ as its parent, an inflection point at $(-6, -10)$, and that passes through the origin.

DS-99.   Write an equation for this curve. Then sketch the graph of the inverse of this graph and write its equation.

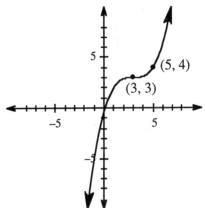

(5, 4)

(3, 3)

DS-100. Find the area of the circle that has circumference c.

DS-101. Find the domain and range for each function.

a) $f(x) = \dfrac{x}{x^2 - 4x}$ b) $f(x) = \dfrac{1}{\sqrt{x} - 5}$

SAMPLING TECHNIQUES

DS-102. How many drops of water do you think a penny can hold? Using your supplies, count the number of drops of water your penny can hold before it overflows. Record your results on a class stem-leaf plot, then make a box and whisker diagram.

DS-103. Look at the box and whisker diagram generated by this data. Why is the data so spread out? Discuss as a class **exactly** how you did the experiment. Did you all do it exactly the same way? What instructions could be given at the beginning of the experiment that would help make the results more uniform?

DS-104. As a class, decide on uniform instructions and repeat the experiment.

DS-105. Is the data more uniform this time around? Which experiment better answered the original question, "How many drops of water can a penny hold before it overflows?"

DS-106. When gathering data it is important that the question be clearly worded to eliminate conditions that would bias the results. (For example, the height from which you used the dropper.) Rewrite the instructions for the penny and water experiment with this in mind.

DS-107. In the last unit (problems IC-111 through IC-113) you developed a method based on counting combinations to write out the expansion of binomial expressions raised to powers without having to do all of the multiplication. Use your method to expand the following:

a) $(x - y)^6$ b) $(a + bc)^4$

DS-108. How can you use Pascal's Triangle to expand $(x + 2y)^3$?

a) What substitution can be made? Use it to expand the binomial.

b) Now try $(5x - 2y)^3$.

DS-109.

THE BINOMIAL THEOREM

The method of using combinations to write the expansion of expressions of the form $(x + y)^n$ is called the **BINOMIAL THEOREM**. When it is written out in general the notation for combinations makes it look very complicated.

$$(x + y)^n =$$
$$_nC_nx^n + {_nC_{n-1}}x^{n-1}y + {_nC_{n-2}}x^{n-2}y^2 + \ldots + {_nC_1}xy^{n-1} + {_nC_0}y^n$$

Add some examples to show how you can use the Binomial Theorem and Pascal's Triangle to your Tool Kit.

DS-110. Extend your copy of Pascal's triangle to the tenth row.

a) Explain how to figure out $_{12}C_5$ without writing out two more whole rows.

b) If you knew $_{19}C_4$ and $_{19}C_3$ how could you figure out $_{20}C_4$?

c) Show by writing out the numerical calculations using the formula $_nC_r = \dfrac{_nP_r}{r!}$ that your answer to part (b) is correct.

d) In general, why should $_{n+1}C_r = {_nC_r} + {_nC_{r-1}}$?

DS-111. Bias can take many forms. Sometimes it is created unintentionally by conditions in an experiment. Other times it is more intentional. For each example below, comment on its possible bias.

a) In a TV commercial an interviewer asks people on the street to name their favorite radio station. All five that he asked claimed WCPM as their favorite.

b) A university campus wants to increase fees in order to build a new recreation hall. It surveys students to determine support. Survey booths are placed outside the university gym. The resulting survey showed overwhelming support.

c) A study shows that many more accidents occur on I-95 during the day than at night. Is it therefore safer to drive at night?

d) An active citizens' group claimed that a nuclear facility was operating at below average standards and therefore should be shut down.

DS-112. A district attorney claims that local officials received $32,515 in bribes from organized crime. What problem do you see in this report? Explain.

Closes to the Pin: Descriptive Statistics

DS-113.   The streets in Squaresville are neatly laid out as shown in the diagram below. The city is sponsoring a race from 1st and A to 5th and E. They want to know how many "shortest-path" routes are possible.

a)   Since there is only one shortest path to get to 1st and B, write a little 1 at that corner. There is also only one way to get to 2nd and A, so write a little 1 at that corner.

b)   How many shortest paths are there to get to 2nd and B? Write the appropriate number at that corner.

c)   At each intersection on the grid, write the number of shortest paths a runner can take to reach it. Look for a familiar pattern in the numbers.

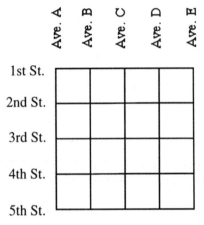

d)   Continue in this manner to solve the original problem.

DS-114.   What's the name of the pattern you used to solve the last problem?

DS-115.   What does it mean if someone has a negative z-score?

DS-116.   Solve for g: $\sqrt{2g+1} - 7 = -g$.

DS-117.   Write an equation for this curve.

a)   Make a statement about the end behavior of this function. What happens to y as x gets larger and larger?

b)   Write the equation of the vertical asymptote. What happens as x gets closer and closer to 3?

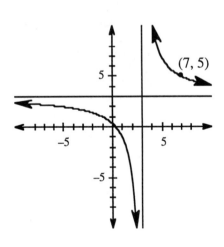

DS-118. Do not use a calculator and do not convert to exponential form. Instead, do the problems mentally.

a) $\log 1$

b) $\log 10^3$

c) $10^{\log 4}$

d) $10^{3\log 4}$

e) $\log 0$

f) $\log 10$

g) $\log \sqrt{10}$

h) $10^{(2/3)\log 27}$

i) $\log (-10)$

BIAS IN SAMPLING AND REPORTING

DS-119. On the square piece of paper provided by your teacher, write down an integer from 1 to 4. Tape it to the board to form a histogram.

DS-120. What numbers were picked most frequently? Discuss in your teams why this might have happened.

DS-121. Statistical results can be affected by psychological issues. In the previous activity, logic might have suggested that each number would be equally likely to be picked, but statistics shows us that this is not the case. Researchers who conduct experiments need to eliminate sources of bias for their statistical analysis to be meaningful. Discuss in your teams the potential causes of bias in the following samples.

a) Cola #2 did a taste test comparing itself to Cola #1. Participants were asked to pick their favorite drink—one labeled m and the other q. The majority of participants picked the drink labeled m, which was Cola #1.

b) A survey was conducted in the following manner: "The Bill of Rights guarantees the right to bear arms so that we can protect our families and our country. Recently, attempts have been made to enact stricter gun controls. Do you want these restrictions?"

c) Another survey was conducted in the following manner: "Last year over 15,000 people were murdered by handguns. That was 68% of all murders. Recently, attempts have been made to enact stricter gun controls. Do you want these restrictions?"

DS-122.   Another interesting oddity of statistics is called the
           "Simpson's Paradox." Consider the following
           example based on a recent case: The Cooson
           Corporation formed two new departments which
           required massive hiring. Department A had 500
           male and 250 female applicants. From this pool,
           they hired 250 men and 150 women. Department B
           had 100 male and 400 female applicants. They
           hired 25 of the men and 108 of the women. A few
           months later a suit was filed against them charging
           that their hiring practices discriminated against
           women. How could this be?   Let's take a closer
           look.

    a)   What percentage of the total males who
          applied were hired? What percentage of the
          total females who applied were hired?   Which group appears to be favored?

    b)   In Department A, what percentage of the males who applied were hired? What
          percentage of the females who applied were hired?   Which group appears to be
          favored?

    c)   In Department B, what percentage of the males who applied were hired? What
          percentage of the females who applied were hired?   Which group appears to be
          favored?

    d)   What is the paradox?

    e)   Is the suit justified? Explain briefly.

DS-123.   Uri's friend's father needs to have surgery. Hospital Alpha has a 100% success rate with
           that procedure, but has only performed it five times. Hospital Beta has a performed the
           operation 400 times and has an 90% success rate. Which hospital would you
           recommend? Explain.

DS-124.   Let $f(x) = 2^x(x^2 + 4)$. Find the roots of $f(x)$.

DS-125.   On a test with a mean of 66 and a standard deviation of 15, a z-score of 1 corresponds to
           what raw score?

DS-126.   If Josh received a percentile ranking of 20% on a standardized test, what percentage of
           test takers scored above him?

DS-127. Decide whether each of the following is always, sometimes, or never true when the variables represent real numbers. For the ones that are sometimes true explain when.

a) $\frac{1}{x} + \frac{1}{y} = \frac{1}{x+y}$

b) $\sqrt{a^2 + b^2} = a+b$

c) $\sqrt{x^2} = x$

d) $\sqrt{x^2} = -x$

e) $2^x = 0$

f) $(4 - x)^2 < 0$

g) $(x + y)^2 = x^2 + y^2$

h) $\sqrt{x^2} = |x|$

i) $\frac{x}{2} + \frac{y}{3} = \frac{x+y}{5}$

j) $\frac{x}{2} + \frac{y}{4} = \frac{x+y}{6}$

k) $\frac{1}{x} + \frac{1}{y} = \frac{x+y}{xy}$

DS-128. Expand $(a - 2b)^4$ using Pascal's Triangle.

DS-129. During the same week of the 1996 presidential campaign, one poll claimed Clinton had a 20% lead over Dole while another claimed that Clinton had only a 6% lead. If both statistics are accurate, how is this possible?

DS-130. Simplify $(a^{-1} - b^{-1})^{-1}$.

DS-131. Solve for x if $-2\pi \le x \le 2\pi$.

a) $4 \sin^2 x = 1$

b) $3 \tan^2 x = 1$

DS-132. A bag of popping corn contains $\frac{2}{3}$ white kernels and $\frac{1}{3}$ yellow kernels. Only $\frac{1}{2}$ of the white kernels will pop, whereas $\frac{2}{3}$ of the yellow ones will pop. A kernel is selected at random from the bag, and pops when placed in the popper. What is the probability that the kernel selected was white?

DS-133. Reread the "Closest to the Pin" problem from the beginning of the unit. It's time to start writing your report. Be sure to use the statistical methods you have learned in this unit to support your decision.

DS-134. A test was given that had some extreme scores. The median was 52 and the mean was 63. Were the extreme scores very high or very low? Explain.

DS-135. In a labor dispute using the same set of data, management reported an average company salary of $68,000, while labor reported an average company salary of only $48,000. Both averages were accurate. How is this possible? Explain the discrepancy.

DS-136. Bill and Karen have a $5 bet on who will have the better grade on a physics test. Unfortunately they take the test from two different instructors and each instructor made up her own test! Bill had a score of 53 where the test had a mean score of 42 with standard deviation of 12. Karen earned a score of 118 where the mean score was 102 with a standard deviation of 19. Who should win the bet? Explain.

DS-137. A music company wants to know the music preference of people in Cleveland. Their surveyor asks people who are walking out of a business office building, "What is your favorite type of music?" What kind of problems may arise that will not produce accurate results? (List as many problems as you can.)

DS-138. A group of 30 students took a college placement test with the scores listed below. Make a box and whisker diagram for the data.

42	58	89	74	87	83	96	38	65	48
62	85	80	71	90	24	77	63	68	85
88	80	73	78	71	84	73	56	67	75

DS-139. If Eugene had a score of 83 on the college placement test in the previous problem, find both his percentile in the class and his standard z-score.

DS-140. The mean for the set of scores in problem DS-138 is 71 and the standard deviation is approximately 16.4. The teacher wants to assign new scores to the tests so that the mean is 100 and the standard deviation is 20.

a) The original score of 71 will now be _____.

b) An original score of 90 will now be _____.

c) If the new score is 78, what was the original score?

DS-141. Expand $(2 - 3x)^3$ and simplify your answer.

DS-142. For the final exam in this course we are considering two options. You can take a 100-point test worth 15% of your grade or a 300-point test worth 10% of your grade. Which testing option would have a greater impact on your grade? Explain.

DS-143. Solve this system of equations: $x^2 + y^2 = 16$
$$y = x^2 - 4$$

DS-144. Find the area of the triangular region formed by the intersection of the graphs of the inequalities at right:

$$y \le -\frac{1}{2}x + 5$$
$$y \ge x - 1$$
$$y \le \frac{5}{2}x + 5$$

DS-145. A cannon shoots a cannon ball into the air. The barrel of the cannon is located 6 feet above the ground. After 2 seconds the ball is 102 feet above the ground. After 4 seconds it is 70 feet above the ground. Find the equation of the parabola that models the path of the cannon ball.

DS-146. An exponential function has an asymptote at $x = -10$. If the graph goes through the points $(2, 8)$ and $(4, 30.5)$, find the equation of the function.

DS-147. **TOOL KIT CHECK-UP**

Your Tool Kit contains reference tools for algebra. Return to your Tool Kit entries. You may need to revise or add entries.

Be sure that your Tool Kit contains entries for all of the items listed below. Add any topics that are missing to your Tool Kit NOW, as well as any other items that will help you in your study of algebra.

- Mean and Median
- Series and Summation Notation
- Mean Deviation
- Stem-Leaf Plot
- Percentile
- Binomial Theorem

- Outliers
- Statistical Variables
- Standard Deviation
- Raw Scores and Z-Scores
- Box-and-Whiskers and Quartiles
- Histogram

UNIT 13

Return of the Bouncing Ball and Other Topics
REVISITING AND EXTENDING EARLIER TOPICS

Unit 13 Objectives
Return of the Bouncing Ball and Other Topics: REVISITING AND EXTENDING EARLIER TOPICS

The topics of this unit extend and build on topics you studied in Units 2, 4, and 7. This unit has three main parts. The first part builds on sequences from Unit 2, moving on to sums of arithmetic and geometric sequences and introducing the idea of an infinite sum. Formulas for sums lead to an introduction to proof by induction. The second part extends the work you started in Unit 4 with parabolas and circles to include ellipses and hyperbolas. The third topic draws upon your expertise in factoring polynomials and uses the factor theorem, which is central to Unit 7 to develop a method for dividing polynomials.

In this unit you will have the opportunity to:

- Learn formulas for computing sums of arithmetic sequences and both finite and infinite geometric sequences.

- Learn a new method of proof called mathematical induction.

- Learn about two more conic sections, the ellipse and the hyperbola, and the relationship of their geometric properties to their equations.

- Add division of polynomials to your Tool Kit for finding the roots of polynomial functions.

One of the problems we will solve in this unit will be to find the vertical distance traveled by a bouncing ball.

RE-0.   **RETURN OF THE BOUNCING BALL** A ball with a rebound ratio of 0.6 (each bounce is 0.6 times as high as the previous one) is dropped from a height of 10 meters and allowed to bounce repeatedly. When the ball hits the ground for the 10th bounce, what vertical distance has it traveled? If the ball continued to bounce and bounce and bounce . . ., what vertical distance would it travel?

PROBLEM SOLVING
REPRESENTATION/MODELING
FUNCTIONS/GRAPHING
INTERSECTIONS/SYSTEMS
ALGORITHMS
REASONING/COMMUNICATION

Unit 13

Return of the Bouncing Ball and Other Topics:
REVISITING AND EXTENDING EARLIER TOPICS

SUMS OF ARITHMETIC SEQUENCES

RE-1.   Becky's grandfather said that if
she does all her homework he
will give her money to help her
buy a used car when she gets
her driver's license.
Grandfather has noticed that
Becky is very diligent at the
beginning of each semester but
becomes less consistent as the
weeks go on, so he has decided
to add an incentive for
persistence. He will give her $5
the first week, $7 the next
week, $9 the next, etc., adding

$2 to each week's gift as long as she does every assignment. As soon as she misses one,
he will start over at $5 per week. Becky thinks this is a wonderful plan and she starts
dreaming about how much money she will have. She knows she can go a long time
without missing an assignment with this as an incentive. She wants to know how much
she will have if she gets through the 9th and 10th grades with a perfect homework record.
That's 70 weeks all together!

Becky begins adding: $5 + 7 + 9 + 11 + ...$

Grandfather sees what Becky is doing and says, "Let me show you a trick I learned in
high school. Sometimes it's helpful to write out all the parts of a problem before you do
any calculations. The 70th payment will be $5 + 69(2) = 5 + 138 = 143$, so the sum of all
70 payments looks like this:

$$5 + 7 + 9 + 11 + ... + 139 + 141 + 143."$$

Then Becky's Grandfather suggested, "Now add the values for the first and last weeks.
What do you get?"

Becky quickly answered, "$5 + 143 = 148$."

"Good, now add the amounts for the second week and the next-to-last week."

"$7 + 141 = 148$. Hmmmm . . . and $9 + 139 = ... 148$! And I see why! As the lower
term goes up by 2, the upper one goes down by 2, and the <u>total</u> stays the same!"

"Excellent! So what is the total?"

>>Problem continues on the next page.>>

"Well, now I see everything in terms of pairs that make 148," said Becky, and she made the diagram at right. "Since there are 70 numbers being added, there are 35 pairs, so the total must be 35 times 148!"

"That's easy enough to do:
35(148) = \$5180. Wow! I can buy a cool old car for that much. Thanks, Grandfather."

a)   Use Grandfather's method to find the sum:

12 + 19 + 26 + . . . + 257   (There are 36 terms in the sum.)

b)   Use Grandfathers method to find the sum of the sequence t(n) = -11 + 4n from n = 1 through n = 100.

c)   Add the following information to your Tool Kit:

SUM OF AN ARITHMETIC SEQUENCE

If t(n) is any arithmetic sequence, then the sum of the first k terms of the sequence is given by the formula:

$$t(1) + t(2) + \ldots + t(k) = \frac{k}{2}[t(1) + t(k)]$$

Note that t(1) is counted as the first term here. If we think of the sequence as starting with t(0), then the sum of the first k terms is

$$t(0) + t(2) + \ldots + t(k - 1) = \frac{k}{2}[t(0) + t(k - 1)]$$

In general the formula can be stated as, "First term plus last term, times half the number of terms."

The sum of terms of a sequence is called a **SERIES**.

RE-2.   Find the sum of the integers from 100 through 1000.

RE-3.   Let p = 2 + 5i and q = 3 - 4i. Calculate the following values and simplify to a + bi form:

a)   p + q

b)   p - q

c)   p · q

d) $\frac{p}{q}$

RE-4.   Twelve horses raced in the Petaluma Derby. In how many different orders could they finish?

RE-5.   Suppose someone multiplied out the polynomial $(x + 2)^{30}$. What would be the coefficient of x^{11}?

RE-6.   Solve for x in **degrees**.

a) $2 \sin x = -1$ b) $\cos^2 x + 5 \cos x + 4 = 0$

RE-7.   A line segment is drawn from point A(3, 2) to point B(-21, 0). Find the coordinates of the midpoint.

RE-8.   In Unit 3 you compared the depreciation of a Mazda Miata and a Honda Civic EX. The depreciation functions were:

$$M(x) = 19800(0.78)^x$$
$$H(x) = 16500(0.82)^x$$

In Unit 3 you used graphing and estimation to figure out when the value of the two cars would be the same. This time solve the system of equations to find out when they will have the same value (to the nearest month).

GEOMETRIC SERIES

RE-9.   In her math class Becky learned about the speed of exponential growth, so she decided to see if Grandfather would agree to a different plan.

"What if instead of increasing my incentive by $2 per week, you increased it by 10% each week?"

Grandfather wasn't born yesterday, however. "First you have to figure out the most this change could cost me."

So Becky began to add again, but this time she took Grandfather's advice and wrote out everything before doing anything:

$$5 + 5(1.1) + 5(1.1)^2 + 5(1.1)^3 + \ldots + 5(1.1)^{68} + 5(1.1)^{69}$$

"I don't suppose you remember a trick for this one, Grandfather."

>>**Problem continues on the next page.**>>

"As a matter of fact, I might. Take your total and call it S. Now multiply that by 1.1 and tell me what you see."

"OK, $S = 5 + 5(1.1) + 5(1.1)^2 + 5(1.1)^3 + \ldots + 5(1.1)^{68} + 5(1.1)^{69}$,

so $(1.1)S = 5(1.1) + 5(1.1)^2 + 5(1.1)^3 + 5(1.1)^4 + \ldots + 5(1.1)^{69} + 5(1.1)^{70}$.

That looks almost like S again, but with the first term missing and an extra one on the end. So I can substitute $S - 5$ for all of the terms except the last one:

$$(1.1)S = (S - 5) + 5(1.1)^{70}$$

And now I can solve for S!" And she did.

$$(1.1)S - S = -5 + 5(1.1)^{70}$$

$$(0.1)S = -5 + 5(1.1)^{70}$$

$$S = \frac{-5 + 5(1.1)^{70}}{0.1} = \$7887.47$$

a) Use Grandfather's method to find the sum: $1 + 3 + 9 + 27 + \ldots + 3^{19}$.

b) Grandfather said he would agree to this plan only if Becky could write a formula fo the sum of any geometric sequence. Fill in the missing steps to help her:

$$S = a + ar + ar^2 + ar^3 + \ldots + ar^{(n-1)}$$

(The series stops at $n - 1$ power because there are n terms, but the first one is no multiplied by r.)

$rS = $ _____

$rS = $ _____ (Substitute $S - a$.)

$rS - S = $ _____

but $rS - S$ can be factored:

$rS - S = S($ _____ $)$, so

$S = $ _____

RE-10. Find the sum of the first 20 terms ($t(0)$ through $t(19)$) of the sequence $t(n) = 16(1.5^n)$.

RE-11. **RETURN OF THE BOUNCING BALL**
A ball with a rebound ratio of 0.6 (each bounce is 0.6 times as high as the previous one) is dropped from a height of 10 meters and allowed to bounce repeatedly. When the ball hits the ground for the 10th bounce, what vertical distance has it traveled?

UNIT

RE-12.   Add the following information to your Tool Kit. Then solve the problem below.

SUM OF A GEOMETRIC SEQUENCE

The sum of the first n terms of a geometric sequence,

$$a + ar + ar^2 + ar^3 + \ldots + ar^{n-1}$$

is called a **GEOMETRIC SERIES** and is given by the formula

$$S = \frac{a(r^n - 1)}{r - 1}$$

Find the sum of the sequence $t(n) = 1.4(0.8^n)$ for $n = 0$ through $n = 49$.

RE-13.   Look at the differences between successive terms in the quadratic sequence
1, 3, 7, 13, 21, . . . What kind of sequence do the differences form? Use the formula
for an arithmetic series to find the 75th term in the original quadratic sequence.

RE-14.   Use another method to find $t(75)$ in the quadratic sequence in problem RE-13.

RE-15.   12 students will be chosen at random from the 900 students at Rolling Meadows High
School to serve as the Judicial Board for minor student infractions.

a)   How many different Judicial Boards are possible?

b)   Mariko hopes to be on the Board. How many of the possible boards include her?

c)   What is the probability that Mariko is chosen for the board?

RE-16.   One angle of a triangle has measure 70° and the side opposite it has length 37.2 ft.
Another angle of this triangle is 30°. Find measures of the rest of its parts.

RE-17.   For the following system: $x^2 + y^2 = 25$
$y = x^2 - 36$

a)   Find the intersection of the graphs.

b)   Find the algebraic solution of the system.

RE-18.   Find the equation of the line tangent to the circle $(x - 1)^2 + (y + 2)^2 = 25$ at the
point (4, 2).

RE-19. 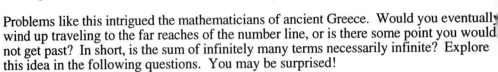 Of course we know that the ball in problem RE-11 would not bounce forever, but imagine that it could. Or instead of pretending that a ball could bounce forever, imagine starting at 0 on a number line and following this rule: move 20 units to the right, and then continue making moves to the right, with each move being 0.6 times the previous move.

Problems like this intrigued the mathematicians of ancient Greece. Would you eventually wind up traveling to the far reaches of the number line, or is there some point you would not get past? In short, is the sum of infinitely many terms necessarily infinite? Explore this idea in the following questions. You may be surprised!

a) You can use the formula for the sum of a geometric sequence to investigate this issue. The formula can also be written $S = \frac{a(1 - r^n)}{1 - r}$. Explain or show why this form is equivalent to the version in your Tool Kit.

b) The formula for the distance traveled after 10 moves (or the distance traveled by the ball after 10 bounces) could be written in this form:

$$S = \frac{20(1 - 0.6^{10})}{1 - 0.6} = \frac{20(1 - 0.00605)}{0.4}$$

Write the formula for the distance traveled after 20 moves in the same form.

c) Calculate the quantity 0.6^n for n = 10, 20, 30, 40, and 50. What number is being approached? It may help to write out the values in decimal, rather than scientific, notation in order to answer. What number is the quantity $\frac{20(1 - 0.6^n)}{0.4}$ getting very close to as n gets very large? If the ball could bounce forever with a rebound ratio of 0.6, essentially how far would it travel?

d) When we have a geometric series with a multiplier, or common ratio, which is between 1 and -1, adding infinitely many terms does not result in an infinite sum. Instead there is a specific number that the sums <u>approach</u> as the <u>number</u> of terms being added gets larger and larger. This number is called the **sum of the infinite geometric series**. The sum is finite because the term r^n in the formula $S = \frac{a(1 - r^n)}{1 - r}$ approaches 0, resulting in the following formula. Add it to your Tool Kit.

INFINITE GEOMETRIC SERIES

For an **INFINITE GEOMETRIC SERIES** with an initial value a and common ratio r, with $-1 < r < 1$, the sum is given by the formula

$$S = \frac{a}{1 - r}.$$

---

e) A contest offers to pay the winner's family a monthly stipend forever, that is, as long as the winner has a living descendent, the stipend will be paid from an annuity account. The stipend is $10,000 the first month and it decreases by 1% each month. How much money must be set aside to pay the winning family?

RE-20.   A retired hiker decides to spend his days walking around the country. On the first day he walks 25 miles. On the following days he finds that he cannot keep up that pace, and that on average he travels 5% less each day than on the previous day. If he walked in a straight line, how far from his starting point would he travel?

RE-21.   Candice has two parents, four grandparents, eight great-grandparents, etc. If Candice traces her family tree back for 15 generations (with Candice as the 16th generation), how many direct ancestors will she have identified?

RE-22.   A deck of 40 playing cards has cards numbered one through ten, with each number appearing in red, blue, green, and yellow. How many different ways are there to have three of one number and two of another?

RE-23.   Find the sum of terms a_0 through a_{80} for the sequence $a_0 = 10$, $a_n = -0.95a_{n-1}$.

RE-24.   When a closed container is heated the pressure inside will build. A closed cylinder is heated in such a way that the pressure doubles every hour. If the pressure builds to 100 times its starting pressure, the container will explode. When will it explode?

RE-25.   A 125-foot redwood tree is leaning 20° off vertical toward the north. How long will its shadow be when the noon sun is 68° above the horizon?

RE-26. In studying geometry you learned about deductive proof. After assuming a few very basic facts, called postulates, all the other true statements, called theorems, can be proved by logical argument, based on the postulates and the theorems that have already been proven. Mathematicians have also proved theorems for algebra. Many can be proven by deductive methods similar to those you used in Geometry, but some require different methods. One of these methods is called **PROOF BY MATHEMATICAL INDUCTION**. Here's an example.

If you use the formula for the sum of an arithmetic series to find the sum of n counting numbers, you get the following result:

$$1 + 2 + 3 + \ldots + n = \frac{n(n + 1)}{2}$$

The validity of this formula for every n = 1, 2, 3, . . . can be proven by mathematical induction. The proof by induction consists of two steps. Think of the formula as representing a sequence of statements:

$$1 = \frac{1(1 + 1)}{2}$$
$$1 + 2 = \frac{2(2 + 1)}{2}$$
$$1 + 2 + 3 = \frac{3(3 + 1)}{2}$$
$$\vdots$$

We can easily prove that any of these specific statements is true. Then we prove deductively that *if* any of these statements is true, *then* the next one must also be true. Since the 1st is true, so is the 2nd, hence the 3rd, the 4th, and all the rest.

We can see that the first statement is true. We call this the anchor. Next, suppose that one of the statements, say, the kth one, is true. In other words, suppose there is some value of k for which it is true that

$$1 + 2 + 3 + \ldots + k = \frac{k(k + 1)}{2}$$

(Note: this statement makes it appear that k is greater than 3, because we wrote out the first three terms to show the pattern, but the process will apply to any k = 1, 2, 3, 4, . . .)

Our goal is to transform this equation algebraically into the next one (n = k + 1). Then we can conclude that if the kth statement is true, so is the (k + 1)st. Before we start transforming, it helps to see what the (k + 1)st equation looks like. To do that we substitute (k + 1) for n in the formula, and we get

$$1 + 2 + 3 + \ldots + (k + 1) = \frac{(k + 1)[(k + 1) + 1]}{2}, \text{ which simplifies to}$$
$$1 + 2 + 3 + \ldots + (k + 1) = \frac{(k + 1)(k + 2)}{2}.$$

>>**Problem continues on the next page.**>>

This equation is the target. We need to know that if the kth equation is true, so is this one. Note that the target statement can also be written

$$1 + 2 + 3 + \ldots + k + (k + 1) = \frac{(k + 1)(k + 2)}{2}$$

since the term before $(k + 1)$ is k. Compare this statement to the sum of the first k positive integers.

$$1 + 2 + 3 + \ldots + k = \frac{k(k + 1)}{2}$$

If we assume the above statement is true, then, we can add the quantity $(k + 1)$ to both sides. We get the following equation:

$$1 + 2 + 3 + \ldots + k + (k + 1) = \frac{k(k + 1)}{2} + (k + 1)$$

And this must also be true because we just added the same thing to both sides of a true equation. Now we can apply the properties of algebra to the right hand side of this equation, which does not have that annoying ellipsis (. . .).

$$
\begin{aligned}
\frac{k(k+1)}{2} + (k+1) &= \frac{k(k+1)}{2} + \frac{2(k+1)}{2} \\
&= \frac{k^2 + k + 2k + 2}{2} \\
&= \frac{k^2 + 3k + 2}{2} \\
&= \frac{(k+1)(k+2)}{2}
\end{aligned}
$$

So now we have:

$$1 + 2 + 3 + \ldots + k + (k + 1) = \frac{(k + 1)(k + 2)}{2}$$

And this is the target statement that says that the formula is true for $n = k + 1$.

To summarize: we got to the $(k + 1)$st equation by adding the same thing to both sides of the kth statement, so if the kth equation is true, then so is the $(k + 1)$st.
In the case of $k = 1$, we *know* the statement is true, and now we know automatically it is also true for $(k + 1)$, which equals 2. But that makes it true for $k = 2 + 1 = 3$, $k = 3 + 1 = 4$, and all the rest. Here is a summary of the method.

>>Problem continues on the next page.>>

PROOF BY INDUCTION

Mathematical induction is used to prove that a given formula is true for any natural number ($n = 1, 2, 3, \ldots$). It consists of the following steps:

1. Verify by substitution that the formula is true for $n = 1$.

2. Write the general statement of the formula for $n = k$.

3. Algebraically transform the statement for $n = k$ into the statement for $n = k + 1$.

   (Before doing Step 3, it is helpful to see what the statement for $n = k + 1$ should look like by substituting $(k + 1)$ in place of n in the original formula.)

These steps complete the proof.

Prove the following formulas by induction:

a) $2 + 4 + 6 + \ldots + 2n = n(n + 1)$

b) $5 + 8 + 11 + \ldots + (3n+2) = \dfrac{n(3n + 7)}{2}$

c) $1^2 + 2^2 + 3^2 + \ldots + n^2 = \dfrac{n(n + 1)(2n + 1)}{6}$

RE-27. Prove by induction: $1 + 3 + 5 + \ldots + (2n - 1) = n^2$

RE-28. What is the fourth term in the expansion of $(x - 3)^{12}$?

RE-29. A bag contains 4 red pens, 6 green pens, and 2 blue pens. If three pens are chosen at random, what is the probability that one of each color is picked?

RE-30.   The graph of g(x) is shown at right. Sketch the graph of:

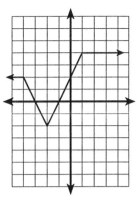

  a)   g(x) - 3   b)   g(x + 4)

  c)   2·g(x)   d) $\frac{1}{2}$g(x - 2)

  e)   g($\frac{1}{2}$x)

RE-31.   A quadratic function has roots of 3 - 2**i** and 3 + 2**i**.
          What is its equation?

RE-32.   Factor completely: $5x^7y - 320xy$.

RE-33.   Remember the "sleeping parabolas" of Unit 4? Write the equation for the following
          sideways parabola in graphing form and sketch its graph.

$$x = 2y^2 - 12y + 13$$

ELLIPSES

RE-34.   When you first graphed the circle $x^2 + y^2 = 25$ you may have used x- and y-intercepts or
          the graphing calculator.

  a)   What are the four intercepts?

  b)   What equations would you type into the graphing calculator to see the graph?

  c)   What are the center and radius of the graph?

RE-35.   Now consider the equation $4x^2 + y^2 = 25$.

  a)   What are the four intercepts?

  b)   Use the graphing calculator to graph this equation. Verify that your intercepts are
        correct.

  c)   This shape is called an **ellipse**. How many points are needed to make a good
        sketch of this shape?

RE-36.   For the ellipse $x^2 + 4y^2 = 25$ find four points and sketch the graph. How is this ellipse different from the previous one?

RE-37.   An ellipse is basically a circle that has been stretched vertically or horizontally. Would the ellipse $4x^2 + 25y^2 = 25$ be stretched vertically or horizontally? Find the intercepts and draw the graph.

RE-38.   Here is another equation of an ellipse: $\frac{x^2}{4} + \frac{y^2}{9} = 1$

a)   Is it easier or harder to find the intercepts in this case?

b)   You neither need to use the graphing calculator nor to rearrange the equation to find the intercepts. To find the x-intercepts, substitute $y = 0$ and you can determine the x-intercepts by inspection. Find the x-intercepts and then use the same idea to find the y-intercepts.

c)   How do the x- and y-intercepts relate to the equation in this form?

RE-39.   In the previous problem you found that the x-intercepts were (±2, 0) and that the y-intercepts were (0, ±3). Find the intercepts and sketch these graphs.

a) $\frac{x^2}{16} + \frac{y^2}{5} = 1$ b) $5x^2 + 4y^2 = 100$

c)   Which form of the ellipse equation made it easiest to predict the intercepts?

RE-40.   Write an equation to represent each ellipse.

a)   x-intercepts ±3; y-intercepts ±6   b)   x-intercepts $\pm\sqrt{10}$; y-intercepts ±1

RE-41.   Use what you know about locator points and what you have learned about graphing ellipses to graph:

a) $\frac{(x-2)^2}{16} + \frac{(y-3)^2}{25} = 1$

b)   What are the coordinates of the four relocated intercepts? These points, at the top, bottom, left, and right extremes of the ellipse, are called its **vertices.**

c)   Substitute two of the four points into the equation to show that they check.

RE-42.   Graph the following equations. Some of them will need to be rearranged into a more useful form.

a) $\dfrac{(x+2)^2}{9} + \dfrac{(y-3)^2}{4} = 1$

b) $\dfrac{x^2+2x+1}{16} + \dfrac{y^2+6y+9}{25} = 1$

c) $4(x^2-10x+25) + 9(y^2-8y+16) = 36$

RE-43.   Find the equation for each ellipse:

a)

b)

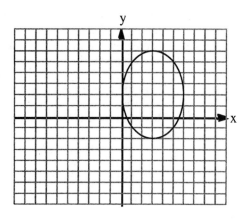

RE-44.   Prove by induction that for n = 1, 2, 3, . . . ,

$$\dfrac{x^n - 1}{x - 1} = x^{(n-1)} + x^{(n-2)} + \ldots + x + 1$$

RE-45.   Ernie and Lisa were solving g(x) = 17. Ernie's answer was $-3\pm\sqrt{\tfrac{17}{2}}$; Lisa's answer was $\dfrac{-6\pm\sqrt{34}}{2}$. Without using your calculator, show that both could be correct and figure out what quadratic function g(x) they could have started with.

RE-46.   In $\triangle ABC$, if AB = AC and m$\angle ABC = 70°$ then what is m$\angle BAC = $?

RE-47.   At the start of the previous section the problems were quadratic equations that contained sums of squares and their graphs were either circles or ellipses. We now want to look at quadratic equations involving differences of squares such as $4x^2 - 9y^2 = 36$ or $\frac{x^2}{9} - \frac{y^2}{4} = 1$.

Although the equation looks very similar to the ellipse, the graph is very different.

a)   Rearrange either equation so that it can be entered into the graphing calculator. Verify your new equation with your teacher and then enter the equation into the calculator. Be careful to use parentheses as necessary.

b)   Copy your graph on graph paper. You should have two convenient x-intercepts, no y-intercepts, and you can use the table from your calculator to get more points on the "branches."

c)   This shape is called a **hyperbola.** There are two branches that resemble a sideways V with a rounded tip. Each tip is a **vertex** of the hyperbola. What are the x-intercepts? How could you determine them from the equation?

d)   As the x-values get farther from 0, the hyperbola appears more and more like two straight lines. In fact there are two lines called **slant asymptotes** that the hyperbola gets closer and closer to. Make a table of values and use your calculator to look at the ratios $\frac{y}{x}$ for large values of x. What fraction(s) do they seem to be approaching? This number and its opposite are the slopes of the asymptotes. We can use the asymptotes and the intercepts to make a reasonable sketch of the graph without using the calculator.

RE-48.   Consider the hyperbola $\frac{x^2}{4} - \frac{y^2}{25} = 1$.

a)   From your experience in the previous problem, predict what the x-intercepts and the slopes of the asymptotes will be. Graph the asymptotes and use them along with the intercepts to sketch the hyperbola by hand.

b)   Solve the equation for y and graph it with your graphing calculator.

c)   Check to see if the x-intercepts and the slopes of the asymptotes match your predictions. Describe how the x-intercepts and slopes of the asymptotes are determined by the equation.

RE-49.   To understand why the hyperbola approaches a slant asymptote, we'll begin with an experiment. Pick a number between 50 and 100 and find the square root of that number. Now subtract 25 from your original number and take the square root of that value. Compare the two square roots. Now repeat the process several times, beginning with larger numbers. Use numbers in the following ranges: 100 to 150, 150 to 200, 250 to 300, 500 to 1000, 1000 to 10,000, above 10,000 . You may divide this work among your team and share the results. Make a table showing the results. What do you observe?

Now look at the equations that were entered into the calculator:

$$y = \pm\sqrt{\frac{25x^2}{4} - 25}$$

a)   Use the pattern you described above to estimate, *without a calculator*, the values of y for x = 1,000,000.

b)   Find a formula that tells the approximate values of y for large values of x, and simplify this expression. How is this equation related to the graph of the hyperbola?

RE-50.   Graph each hyperbola without using the graphing calculator. Begin by graphing the x-intercepts and asymptotes to guide you.

a) $\frac{x^2}{16} - \frac{y^2}{9} = 1$ b) $9x^2 - 4y^2 = 36$

RE-51.   If the terms are reversed so that $\frac{y^2}{16} - \frac{x^2}{9} = 1$, the graph no longer has x-intercepts.

a)   Why is this true?

b)   Solve this equation for y.

c)   Draw the graph. Identify the intercepts and slope of the asymptotes.

RE-52.   Using the intercepts and slope of the asymptotes as a guide, graph each hyperbola without using the graphing calculator.

a) $\frac{y^2}{4} - \frac{x^2}{25} = 1$ b) $x^2 - y^2 = 9$

RE-53. Use what you know about locator points and what you have learned about graphing hyperbolas to graph each of following. The following suggestions may help to organize your work.

First find the locator point. Be careful that you do not get the coordinates of the locator point reversed. Next determine the orientation (up/down or left/right) to locate the vertices. Then, starting at the locator point, use the slope to sketch the asymptotes as a guide for each branch of the graph.

Some of the equations may need to be rearranged into a more useful form

a) $\dfrac{(x-2)^2}{9} - \dfrac{(y+3)^2}{4} = 1$ b) $\dfrac{y^2-2y+1}{4} - \dfrac{x^2+6x+9}{25} = 1$

c) $4(x^2-10x+25) - 16(y^2+6y+9) = 64$

RE-54. Find the sums of following sequences:

a) $t(n) = 3(-2)^n$, $n = 1$ through $n = 50$

b) $t(n) = -100 + 13n$, $n = 0$ through $n = 100$

RE-55. Find an equation for the ellipse with vertices at (-4, -5), (1, 7), (6, -5), and (1, -17).

GENERAL QUADRATIC EQUATIONS

RE-56. A **GENERAL QUADRATIC EQUATION** is an equation of the form $ax^2 + by^2 + cx + dy + e = 0$ in which a and b may not both be equal to zero. Depending on the values of the coefficients, the equation will graph as a parabola, a circle, an ellipse, or a hyperbola. In special cases it may also be two lines, a single point or no graph at all. Examine each of the following equations and predict what shape it will be when graphed. Give reasons for your answers.

a) $3x^2 - 3y^2 = 18$ b) $4x^2 + 9y^2 - 24x + 18y + 9 = 0$

c) $16x^2 - 4y = 0$ d) $x^2 + y^2 - 2x - 6y - 9 = 0$

e) $-2x^2 + 4y^2 - 8x - 20y + 61 = 0$ f) $8y^2 + 96y - 2x + 289 = 0$

$$ax^2 + by^2 + cxy + dx + ey + f = 0$$

is a general equation that would include all possible 2-variable quadratic relations.

In RE-56 we are considering a special case of this equation where there is no xy term.

E-57.   To graph the ellipse $4x^2 + 9y^2 + 16x - 18y - 11 = 0$ we will need to rearrange the terms and complete the square so that the features can be recognized.

In this case we have four x-squares to complete and nine y-squares to complete.

a)   Show how to change to equation above into the equation below.

$$4(x^2 + 4x) + 9(y^2 - 2y) - 11 = 0$$

b)   Show how to change to equation above into the equation below.

$$4\left[(x + 2)^2 - 4\right] + 9\left[(y - 1)^2 - 1\right] - 11 = 0$$

c)   Show how to change to equation above into the equation below.

$$4(x + 2)^2 + 9(y - 1)^2 = 36$$

d)   Show how to change to equation above into the equation below.

$$\frac{(x + 2)^2}{9} + \frac{(y - 1)^2}{4} = 1$$

e)   Find the locator point and vertices. Draw the graph.

E-58.   Write the original equation on your paper and fill in the steps between the ones given for rearranging the following hyperbola into graphing form. For each of steps (a), (b), and (c), write a sentence describing what was done to the equation above it to get that equation

$$25x^2 - 4y^2 - 150x - 8y + 121 = 0.$$

a) $25(x^2 - 6x \quad) - 4(y^2 + 2y \quad) + 121 = 0$

b) $25[(x - 3)^2 - 9] - 4[(y + 1)^2 - 1] + 121 = 0$

c) $25(x - 3)^2 - 4(y + 1)^2 = 100$

d)   Finish the rearrangement.

e)   State the locator point, the coordinates of the vertices, and the slope of the asymptotes.

f)   Sketch the hyperbola.

E-59.   Show and justify each step to rearrange the parabola $x^2 - 2x - 8y + 17 = 0$ into the graphing form $(y - 2) = \frac{1}{8}(x + 1)^2$

RE-60.   For each of the following equations, identify the curve, write the equation in graphing form, and list the following information: center, vertex or vertices, and asymptotes, if any.

   a) $9x^2 - 16y^2 - 32y = 160$ b) $y^2 - 2y + 3x = 5$

   c) $16 + 6x - x^2 - y^2 = 0$

RE-61.   Find the equation of a hyperbola with vertices at $(0, \pm5)$ and asymptotes $y = \pm2x$.

RE-62.   Find the infinite sum: $0.9 + 0.09 + 0.009 + 0.0009 + \dots$

RE-63.   Why does the formula for an infinite geometric series contain the condition that $-1 < r < 1$? Look back at how the formula was derived. What is different when $|r| > 1$?

RE-64.   Find the equation of an ellipse with vertices $(-2, -3)$, $(10, -3)$, $(4, -2)$, $(4, -4)$.

GEOMETRIC PROPERTIES OF PARABOLAS AND ELLIPSES

RE-65.   Many people think that "parabola" is a name for all curves that are "sort of U-shaped." In fact, parabolas have geometric properties which are unique to curves whose parent graph is $y = x^2$ (or $x = y^2$). On graph paper, make a large, careful graph of

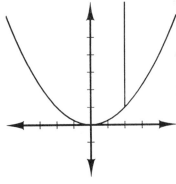

$y = \frac{1}{4}x^2$, for $-5 \le x \le 5$ (or your teacher may provide a resource page). Use a straightedge to draw several vertical lines from the top of the graph down to the parabola (see diagram). Imagine each of the lines as a beam of light striking the parabola, or as the path of an object "falling" toward the parabola from the top of the page. Suppose that the light will reflect or the object will bounce when it hits the parabola. For each vertical line segment, use your straight edge to draw a ray showing the path of the reflection from the parabola to the y-axis; the incoming ray and the outgoing ray should make equal angles with the parabola. Describe what you notice.

E-66.

> The point at which the reflected rays intersect is called the **FOCUS** of the parabola. If you drew the lines accurately in the previous problem, they will all intersect at the point (0, 1). The distance p from the vertex to the focus is called the **FOCAL LENGTH** of the parabola, and it is determined by the stretch factor. Repeat the process from the previous problem with the parabola $y = \frac{1}{2}x^2$ to estimate the focal length for that parabola.

E-67.

> What happened to the focal length when the stretch factor doubled from one-fourth to one-half? Here are some other parabolas and their foci (plural of focus): $y = x^2$, focus (0, 0.25); $y = 3x^2$, focus (0, $\frac{1}{12}$); $y = \frac{1}{8}x^2$, focus (0, 2). Find a formula relating the focal length, p, and the stretch factor, a.

E-68.   The reflective property of parabolas make them very useful. Reflecting mirrors and dishes are made in the three-dimensional shape called a paraboloid whose cross-sections are parabolas. In a high-beam light the bulb is placed at the focus, causing the out-going rays of light to be parallel. In a satellite dish, the antenna is placed at the focus where all the incoming electromagnetic waves converge. Find the equation of the parabola shown in the cross-section of the satellite dish in the drawing at right.

1.5 ft.

RE-69.

Ellipses also have unique geometric properties; not every oval is an ellipse. Suppose an ellipse has its center at the origin, with x-intercepts at (±a, 0) and y-intercepts at (0, ±b), where a > b. Then there are two points on the x-axis at (±c, 0), with $c^2 = a^2 - b^2$, which are called the **FOCI OF THE ELLIPSE**. To understand the geometric properties of the ellipse, imagine a pool table in the shape of an ellipse, with only one pocket, located at one focus. If you place a ball on the other focus and hit it *in any direction*, it will bank off the rail and go into the pocket. In addition, no matter where the ball hits the rail, it will always travel the same distance in reaching the pocket.

a) An ellipse has equation $\frac{x^2}{16} + \frac{y^2}{9} = 1$. What are the coordinates of the foci?

b) Where should the foci be in the ellipse $\frac{x^2}{9} + \frac{y^2}{16} = 1$?

c) **Extension:** Make a careful sketch of an ellipse and draw lines to show the path of a ball hit from one focus in a variety of directions. What is the distance traveled by the ball to the pocket at the other focus?

RE-70. Find the coordinates of the focus of each parabola:

a) $y = 3x^2 - 12x$

b) $x^2 + 7x - 3y - 5 = 0$

RE-71. Find the coordinates of the foci of each ellipse:

a) $\frac{x^2}{16} + \frac{y^2}{36} = 1$

b) $9x^2 + 25y^2 - 225 = 0$

c) $4x^2 + 16y^2 - 8x - 12 = 0$

RE-72. A ship exits its home port with a heading N23°E and travels this direction for 2 miles where it stops at a neighboring island. It leaves the island with a heading of S45°E and travels for 8 miles. The ship begins to have engine problems and needs to return back to its home port. What heading does it need to take and how far will it need to travel to get to the home port?

Note: N23°E means moving 23° towards the East from a North heading. Headings are given with a starting position of North or South followed by the number of degrees heading toward the east or west.

E-73. Solve the system: $\frac{x}{4} + \frac{y}{3} = 1$

$$2x - \frac{y}{3} = 17$$

CCENTRICITY

E-74. Did you ever know anyone who was eccentric? In mathematics, eccentric means "out of round," and eccentricity is a measure of how far an ellipse is from being round. To define this we need some terminology.

EQUATIONS FOR ELLIPSES

The line through the two ends of the ellipse in the long direction is called the **MAJOR AXIS** of the ellipse, and the distance from the center of the ellipse to one end of the major axis is called the **SEMI-MAJOR AXIS**. If a is the semi-major axis, c is the distance from the center to either focus, and (h, k) is the center, the equation of the ellipse can be written

$$\frac{(x-h)^2}{a^2} + \frac{(y-k)^2}{b^2} = 1, \text{ if the major axis is horizontal, or}$$

$$\frac{(x-h)^2}{b^2} + \frac{(y-k)^2}{a^2} = 1, \text{ if the major axis is vertical.}$$

The formula for **ECCENTRICITY** in either case is: $e = \frac{c}{a}$, where $c^2 = a^2 - b^2$.

---

a) Find the eccentricity of the ellipses in problem RE-71.

b) Find the eccentricity of the ellipse in problem RE-41, part (a).

c) Find the equation of an ellipse whose major axis is 10 units long with an eccentricity of 0.8.

d) Suppose an ellipse has eccentricity = 0. What would it look like? Where would the foci be? Would it still be true that a ball hit from one focus would rebound to the other focus?

EQUATIONS FOR HYPERBOLAS

A hyperbola has relationships similar to those of an ellipse. The line connecting the vertices of the two branches is called the **TRANSVERSE AXIS**, and the letter a is used to represent the distance from the center to either vertex. In this case, if the center of the hyperbola is at the origin, the equation can be written in the form:

$$\frac{x^2}{a^2} - \frac{y^2}{b^2} = 1$$

(We use a^2 and b^2 for the numbers in the denominators because we see the square roots of those numbers on the graph.)

The vertices are $(\pm a, 0)$ and the asymptotes have equations $y = \pm\frac{b}{a}x$. The foci are on the transverse axis, in this case the x-axis, at $(\pm c, 0)$, with c given by the equation

$$c^2 = a^2 + b^2.$$

The eccentricity is again a measure of the shape of the curve; the larger the eccentricity the more quickly the branches spread apart. The formula is again

$e = \frac{c}{a}$ (since c > a, the eccentricity of a hyperbola is always greater than 1; ellipses have eccentricity less than 1). If the vertices are on the y-axis, the equation

becomes $\frac{y^2}{a^2} - \frac{x^2}{b^2} = 1$ and everything else is the same <u>except</u> the asymptotes have

slopes $\pm\frac{a}{b}$.

To shift the center (or locator point) to (h, k) replace x and y in the equations with (x − h) and (y − k), respectively, and adjust the equations of the asymptotes to go through the point (h, k) instead of (0, 0).

Find the eccentricity and the coordinates of the foci for each hyperbola in problem RE-52.

RE-76.   Even though they knew no algebra, the ancient Greek mathematicians knew about circles, ellipses, hyperbolas and parabolas. They called these curves the **conic sections** because they are created by the intersection of a cone with a plane. (To the Greeks a cone had two sections which extended infinitely, as shown in the drawing at right.) When placed in a 3-dimensional coordinate system as shown below, the "double cone" has an equation of the form $z^2 = ax^2 + by^2$. For this question, let $a = b = 1$, so $z^2 = x^2 + y^2$. Planes in 3-space have equations of the form $ax + by + cz = d$.

>>Problem continues on the next page.>>

a) The equation $z = 4$ is a plane parallel to the x-y plane (formed by the x- and y-axes), so it only intersects the upper section. Show that the intersection of this plane with this cone is a circle by finding the equation of the intersection of the plane $z = 4$ with $z^2 = x^2 + y^2$.

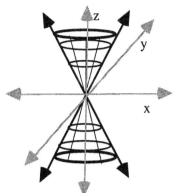

b) The equation $x = 2$ is a plane parallel to the y-z plane   Show that the intersection of this plane with this cone is a hyperbola by finding the equation of the intersection of the plane and the cone.

c) What will be the intersection if the plane in part (a) is tilted slightly? Don't try to do the algebra; just see if you can visualize it.

d) What will be the intersection if the plane in part (b) is tilted just to the point where it only intersects one branch of the cone? Do not try to do the algebra here either.

RE-77. Find the coordinates of the foci and the eccentricity of each ellipse in problem RE-42. Find the approximate value for the eccentricity for each ellipse and explain how the size of the eccentricity is related to the shape of the ellipse.

RE-78. Find the coordinates of the foci and the eccentricity of each hyperbola in problem RE-53. Calculate the approximate value of the eccentricity for each hyperbola and explain how the eccentricity of the hyperbola is related to its shape.

RE-79. For each of the following equations, identify the curve, write the equation in graphing form, and list the following information: center, focus or foci, asymptotes, and eccentricity.

a) $2x^2 + y^2 - 4x + 6y - 7 = 0$

b) $3y^2 - x^2 + 12y = 0$

c) $12x^2 + 8y^2 + 48x - 48y + 24 = 0$

RE-80. Andy and Laurie were challenged by their teacher to factor the expression $x^3 + x^2 - 5x + 3$. For a while they were stumped, but then Andy got an idea.

"Think about the function $y = x^3 + x^2 - 5x + 3$. If we knew the roots, we could find th factors."

"I see one easy root," said Laurie. "If $x = 1$, you get 0."

"Great, now we know that one of the factors is $(x - 1)$, but what are the chances we car guess the other roots?"

"Maybe we don't have to," said Laurie. "Maybe we can use what we know about multiplying polynomials to figure out the other factor. That would be a quadratic, and v know how to factor those."

"Great idea," said Andy, "You start."

"Okay, let's try this: we know we need x^2 in the other factor to make x^3, so let's multiply by that $(x - 1)(x^2) = x^3 - x^2$ and compare it to $x^3 + x^2 - 5x + 3$."

"It's a start; we got one term right, and the next one wrong. Can we fix that without messing up the x^3?" Andy asked.

"Yes," Laurie responded, "If we add terms with powers less than 2 to the x^2 we multiplied by, the cubed term won't be affected. What we need is two more x^2. Whatever we put in will be multiplied by x, so let's put in $2x$ and see what we get.

$$(x - 1)(x^2 + 2x) = x^3 - x^2 + 2x^2 - 2x = x^3 + x^2 - 2x$$

"How does that compare to $x^3 + x^2 - 5x + 3$?" asked Laurie.

"Cool. Now we have the first two terms right, and I'll bet we can fix the x term, too. We need another $-3x$, so let's put in -3:"

$$(x - 1)(x^2 + 2x - 3) = x^3 + x^2 - 2x - 3x + 3$$

"That's it!" they yelled in unison. "The -3 not only made the x term right, it also gav us the constant term we needed."

Then they factored the quadratic to get: $(x - 1)(x - 1)(x + 3) = x^3 + x^2 - 5x + 3$ and they had met the challenge.

a) Why is it appropriate to call the process they discovered for finding the missing quadratic factor **POLYNOMIAL DIVISION**?

b) Use their process to divide $x^3 + 4x^2 - 7x - 10$ by $(x - 2)$.

RE-81.   Andy and Laurie were talking about the polynomial division process they developed.

"There has to be a better way to organize the information," said Andy.

"It reminds me of the generic rectangles we used to multiply polynomials in Algebra 1," replied Laurie.

"Oh yeah. . .?"

"Well, look at the multiplication problem

$(x + 4)(2x^2 - 7x + 9) = 2x^3 + x^2 - 19x + 36.$

Do you see how all the terms that have the same power of x are along a diagonal?"

"Yes, and the highest and lowest powers appear only once, in the upper left and lower right corners."

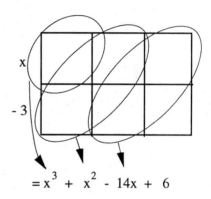

"Right, and we can use that pattern to organize the information in division. Watch. Suppose you want to divide

$(x^3 + x^2 - 14x + 6)$ by $(x - 3).$

We know the upper left has to be x^3, the diagonals add up to x^2 and -14x, and the lower right is 6.

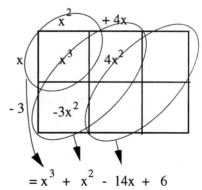

$= x^3 + x^2 - 14x + 6$

"And since we need x^3 in the upper left, we know that x^2 goes above the 1st column as the multiplier. That puts $-3x^2$ in the lower left"

"Okay, and since that diagonal has to add up to $1x^2$, we need $4x^2$ in the middle of the top row, and to get that we need $+4x$ above the second column as the multiplier."

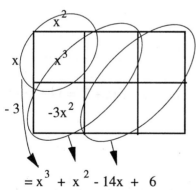

$= x^3 + x^2 - 14x + 6$

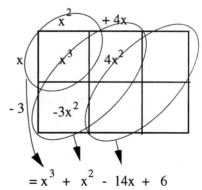

$= x^3 + x^2 - 14x + 6$

"Now we're rolling. That puts -12x in the middle of the bottom row, and since that diagonal has to equal -14x, we get -2x in the upper right..."

"And that means put -2 at the top of the last column, which gives us +6 in the lower right!"

"So the answer is $x^2 + 4x - 2$. Good job!"

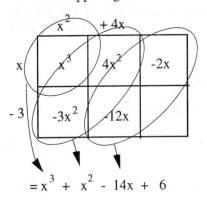

$$= x^3 + x^2 - 14x + 6$$

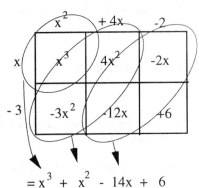

$$= x^3 + x^2 - 14x + 6$$

Use the generic rectangle method for the following problems.

a)   Divide $2x^3 + x^2 - 19x + 36$ by $(x + 4)$.

b)   Divide $x^4 - x^3 - 11x^2 - 5x + 4$ by $x^2 + 2x - 1$.

RE-82.   Divide $6x^3 - 5x^2 + 5x - 2$ by $(2x - 1)$.

RE-83.   The next problem was to divide $x^4 - 7x^2 + 3x + 18$ by $x + 2$.

"Wait," said Andy, " there's no x^3 term!"

"That's easy," Luís chimed in, "Just add in $0x^3$."

Use Luís's idea to complete the division problem.

RE-84.   Sarina wondered, "What will happen if the divisor does not divide evenly, that is, if it is not a factor of the other polynomial?" Each of the following division problems will have remainders, but you can use the same method to do the division.

a)   Divide $2x^4 - x^2 + 3x + 5$ by $x - 1$.

b)   Divide $x^5 - 2x^3 + 1$ by $x - 3$.

RE-85.   Latisha had graphed the polynomial $y = x^3 - 5x^2 + 8x - 6$ during class and she remembered that it had one real root when $x = 3$. Explain how you could use division to find the other roots and find them.

RE-86.   A parabola has vertex (-3, -7) and focus (-3, -7.1). Find its equation.

RE-87.   Find the locator point and sketch the graph of $y^2 - 2x^2 + 28x + 2 = 0$. Find the
          coordinates of the foci and equations of the asymptotes, if any, and state the eccentricity.

RE-88.   Consider the functions $y = \sin x$

                                                  $y = 3 \sin 2 \left(x - \frac{\pi}{2} \right)$

          a)   Explain the effect of each **bold** number in the second function on the graph of the
                first function.

          b)   Make a sketch of both graphs on the same set of axes. Be sure to show your scale.

RE-89.   Suppose that $|x| < 1$. Consider the sum $1 + x + x^2 + x^3 + x^4 + x^5 + \ldots$

          a)   Use the formula for the infinite geometric series to find the sum.

          b)   Use multiplication to verify that this formula is correct.

          c)   When dividing polynomials, you began by getting the highest power term right and
                then correcting the lower power terms in order. It can also be done the opposite
                way: starting with the constant term and going up. Use this process to divide 1 by
                (1 - x), and see what happens. The table is set up to get you started. Since the
                product must equal 1, all the diagonals must add to 0.

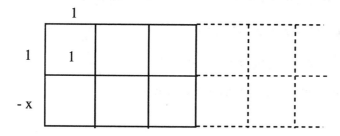

RE-90. As they got used to using the generic rectangle to divide polynomials, Andy and Laurie started noticing some patterns.

"Look back at RE-81 part (a)," said Laurie. "The coefficients in the answer are the same as the numbers in the top row of the rectangle!"

"Hey, I'll bet we could save ourselves some writing!" said Andy, who never liked to write things down. "Look. All I have to write are the numbers."

x	2	-7	9	0
+4	8	-28	36	

"Then you know the answer will start with $2x^2$ because you are dividing $2x^3$ by x. S you can just write the answer $2x^2 - 7x + 9$ and no remainder."

a) "That's pretty slick," said Laurie, "will it work for RE-81(b)?" Try it yourself.

b) Using just the numbers see what happens when you divide $\left(x^4 - x^3 - 11x^2 - 5x + 4\right)$ by $\left(x^2 + 2x - 1\right)$.

c) Now try $\left(x^4 - x^2 + x - 5\right) \div (x - 1)$. Remember the x^3 term is $0x^3$.

RE-91. **TOOL KIT CHECK-UP AND UNIT SUMMARY**

For this unit your summary could just as well be your Tool Kit . For each of the topics listed you should include the general formula or description as well as at least one example.

- Formula for an Arithmetic Series

- Formula for a Finite Geometric Series

- Formula for an Infinite Series

- Description of Proof by Induction

- General Equation for Conics

- Standard Equation for an Ellipse and the Relationship of its Coefficients to its Graph

- Standard Equation for a Hyperbola and the Relationship of its Coefficients to its Graph

- Eccentricity

- Asymptotes

- Division of Polynomials

RE-92. END OF COURSE SUMMARY

The most useful way to summarize the course for yourself and to prepare for future mathematics courses will be to CLEAN UP YOUR TOOL KIT! Get it ready to use in your next mathematics course. At this point you should probably give it a complete overhaul. Review your entries, unit by unit, and check with your team to make sure you have covered all the important concepts. Then get rid of all the entries that you no longer need because they are tools you use so regularly that you hardly have to think about them. Keep a succinct set of notes and examples for topics you are most likely to forget or mix up.

Many of the ideas we have studied are interconnected. Many of your old entries may be consolidated under new headings.

In cleaning up your Tool Kit unit-by-unit you should review your strengths and weaknesses and make a note of any problems that have caused you difficulty over the year. For these problems, choose some examples and work through them now. If you are still having difficulty with any of them, now is the time to ask the questions that will help clear up that difficulty.

Some Ways to Get Started and Some Answers

CF-7.   c)   0, 1, 2, 3, or 4

CF-8.   (-2, -1), (3, 4)

CF-12.   all except (c), (f), and (g) are polynomials

CF-14.   a)   x = -26   b)   x = $\frac{15}{4}$

CF-19.   use the quadratic formula

CF-20.   parabolas, lines, and cubics are polynomials

CF-23.   x = -1 or 5

CF-32.   b)   5   c)   3

CF-35.   20 days; arithmetic

CF-46.   area = 25 sq. units

CF-54.   a)   x = 3

CF-63.   Fred is correct.

CF-64.   first find AB

CF-72.   a)   (1 + 2i, -3 + 4i), (1 - 2i, -3 - 4i)

CF-73.   c) $5 + i\sqrt{6}$

CF-75.   express 16 and 8 as powers of 2

CF-78.   c)   -16

CF-79.   a) $\frac{x+3}{2}$

CF-85.   b)   34   e)   3 - 2i

CF-86.   a)   4 - i

CF-87.   c)   -22 + i

CF-89.   a)   perform the inverse operations in the reverse order

CF-91.   b) $\frac{3}{16}$

CF-92.   a)   be sure to use some negative numbers

CF-100.   (1 + 2i, 2 + 4i), (1 - 2i, 2 - 4i)

CF-101.   solve in terms of b using the quadratic formula

CF-103.   a)   Center: (3, 7), radius: 5

         b)   Center: (0, -5), radius: 4

CF-111.   a)   (3, 0), (0, 0), (-3, 0)

CF-114.   a) $b^2 - 4ac = -7$; complex

CF-115.   b)   1, i, -1, -i

CF-116.   b)   i

CF-118.   x + y = 685, 5x + 8.5y = 5000, so 450 adult tickets would have allowed them to meet their goal.

CF-119.   b)   x: -3, $\frac{15}{2}$ (dbl root); y: 675

CF-120.   b) $2x^2 + 12x + 18$

CF-127.   assuming each ball takes up the space of a 3.7 cm cube, the cost is over $19,600

CF-128.   c)   about 0.004

CF-131.   b) $(x - (-2 + \sqrt{3}))$ and $(x - (-2 - \sqrt{3}))$

         c) $2 - \sqrt{3}$ and $2 + \sqrt{3}$

         d) $(x - \sqrt{10})(x + \sqrt{10})$

         e) $(x - \frac{3 + \sqrt{37}}{2})(x - \frac{3 - \sqrt{37}}{2})$

CF-139.   23.1 meters

CF-141. $\frac{8}{12}$

CF-143.   b) $4 \pm 3i$

CF-152.   d)   average is 3; x coordinate of vertex

CF-156. $(x + 4)^2 + (y - 7)^2 = 16$

CF-157. $\frac{2(x-5)^2}{3} + 1$

UNIT 8

CT-5. $2x^2 - 4x = 2(x^2 - 2x)$; complete the square in the parentheses, but remember what you add inside the parentheses is multiplied by 2.

CT-6. $y = 6x - x^2$

CT-8. x: none, y: (0, 88)

CT-9. a) 30-60: hypotenuse = 2, leg = $\sqrt{3}$; isosceles: hypotenuse = $\sqrt{2}$, leg = 1

CT-10. b) 176.88

CT-11. $26 + i$

CT-17. 45-45: $\frac{1}{\sqrt{2}}$, $\frac{1}{\sqrt{2}}$

CT-18. 17.46°

CT-19. 4; double root at x = -1, simple roots at -4 and 2, both ends go up.

CT-21. Write expressions for: how far the officer has traveled after x hours, and how far Sally is from where the patrol car started x hours after it started traveling.

CT-26. a) $\frac{\sqrt{2}}{2} \approx 0.707$

CT-27. a) subtract π from 4 to see how far into the third quadrant you are, then divide that by π to see what fraction of the lower semi-circle the angle with the negative x-axis is. That number times 180° is the angle you need.

CT-30. d) distance = $\frac{300}{360}(2\pi)$

CT-41. The area below the parabola and above the line y = 2x – 5.

CT-43. Transform the equation so that the fractions which have x in them are on the same side, then use a common denominator to add them together.

CT-44. ≈ 82.4 ft.

CT-49. The graph includes points (0, -1.5), ($\frac{\pi}{2}$, -0.5), (π, 0.5), ($\frac{3\pi}{2}$, -0.5), (2π,–1.5). Now write an equation to represent this graph.

CT-50. use method from CT-40

CT-53. a) x: $\frac{-3 \pm \sqrt{6}}{3}$, y: 1

b) x: $\frac{5 \pm i\sqrt{31}}{4}$, y: -7

CT-54. average of roots = $\frac{5}{4}$.

CT-62. a) amplitude of 3, period of 4π

CT-63. The period is 1.
a) locator (0, 0), period 1
b) locator (0, 0), period 2, amplitude 3
c) locator (0, 1), period 1, amplitude 3

CT-66. b) $\frac{5 \pm \sqrt{57}}{4}$ c) no solution

CT-68. a) y = sin (x + $\frac{\pi}{2}$) or y= -sin (x -

d) y = sin $\frac{1}{3}$(x - $\frac{\pi}{2}$)

CT-71. a) x ≈ 2.5121

CT-74. 4.73% annual interest

CT-76. a) x = 4 or -2

CT-81. a) (0.3420, 0.9397)

T-84.　a)　180°　　　　c)　$\frac{\pi}{6}$ radians

　　　e)　$\frac{5\pi}{4}$ radians

T-85.　b)　$-18x^3y + 6x^5y^2z$

T-86.　$y = \sqrt[3]{2x} - 1$

T-87.　$f(x) = 2(x - 4)^2 + 2$

T-99.　　sine:　0, π, 2π; 0°, 180°, 360°
　　　cosine:　$\frac{\pi}{2}$, $\frac{3\pi}{2}$; 90°, 270°

T-100.　b)　locator ($\frac{\pi}{2}$, 1), period = $\frac{2\pi}{3}$

T-101.　a)　2i

T-108.　$y = 2 + 4 \sin x$

T-109.　a)　210°　　e)　$\frac{9\pi}{2}$

T-111.　c)　≈ 394 million

T-113.　$y = -\frac{3}{3125}(x - 125)^2 + 15$

T-118.　a)　factor out x

T-123.　a)　$\frac{1}{5}$　　c)　　27

T-133.　Sketch graphs of the two functions.

T-134.　c)　$\frac{200\pi}{3}$ ≈ 209.44 sq. units

T-136.　a)　7　　　　b)　6

T-142.　solve one equation for x^2, and
　　　substitute for x^2 in other equation

T-143.　negative orientation, double roots
　　　at (-2, 0), (0, 0), and (2, 0)

T-144.　$y = \frac{(x-5)^2}{12} + 1$

T-151.　locator points (π, -2) (4π, -2)
　　　asymptotes x = -π/2, 5π/2, 11π/2

T-152.　$\pm\sqrt{\frac{8}{9}} = \pm\frac{2\sqrt{2}}{3}$

T-156.　(-1 + i, 3),(-1 - i, 3)

UNIT 9

ST-6.　a)　36.12 cm.

ST-10.　a)　a cone

ST-12.　(6, -2, -8)

ST-20.　a)　96.9 sq. units

ST-22.　x ≈ 2.714, h ≈ ±4.199

ST-24.　a)　$y = x^{2/3}$

ST-33.　a)　$y = 1368(0.9366)^x$

ST-34.　$\frac{ab}{a+b}$

ST-36.　a)　$\frac{1}{4}$

ST-38.　b)　$(\pm\sqrt{7}, 3), (0, -4)$

ST-46.　a)　56.3°

ST-48.　incorrect order of operations;
　　　a ≈ 57.23

ST-52.　≈ 1465.74 sq. feet

ST-53.　a)　$-2 + 2i\sqrt{3}$

ST-60.　No, the lot is ≈ 7367.19 sq. ft.

ST-62.　a)　z ≈ 20.05°

ST-64.　b)　$b^2 - 4ac > 0$

ST-65.　b)　$\frac{4}{x^2-4}$

ST-66.　c)　(10 - 0.5n)(10 - 0.5n)(10 - n)

ST-73.　≈ 899.28 feet

ST-74.　b)　$5.46

ST-75.　Start by factoring into $x(x^2 + 4) = 0$.

ST-77.　CD is $12.99; Cassette Tape is $
　　　7.79

ST-79.   a) 2^{2x} b) $2^{(x-1)}$

ST-91.   a) 84 cm^2

ST-92.   b) 270 gm

ST-93.   b) $\dfrac{x^3-2x-2}{x^2+x}$

ST-95.   b) 50°, 3.13, 8.59

ST-104.   m∠A = 29.7°, m∠B = 116.6°,
            m∠C = 33.7°

ST-105.   b) $y = \log_2(\frac{x}{4})$

ST-106.   (a) and (b) only

ST-107.   a) 0.2

ST-117.   c) k > 4

ST-119.   a) locator $(\frac{\pi}{4},-2)$ amp=1, period 2π

ST-120.   m∠A ≈ 119.6°,   m∠B ≈ 38.4°,
            m∠C ≈ 22.0°

ST-128.   c) z ≈ 7.75 or 1.17
            m∠Z ≈ 118.4° or 7.6°
            m∠Y ≈ 34.6° or 145.4°

ST-130. $\sqrt{800} = 20\sqrt{2} ≈ 28.28$

ST-131. $1 = 3^0$

ST-132. $\dfrac{1}{(\sin x)(\cos x)}$

ST-133.   b) $\dfrac{-1 \pm \sqrt{13}}{6}$

ST-137.   a)   x ≈ 24.49   b) x ≈ 17.15
            c)   x ≈ 30.90°

ST-138.   b)   cos x is a common factor

UNIT 10

PM-4.   a) (4, -4)

PM-6.   a) $(x + 3)^2 -2$

PM-8. $x^2 - 6x + 25 = 0$

PM-9.   b) $\frac{\pi}{3}, \frac{5\pi}{3}$ c) $\frac{\pi}{4}, \frac{5\pi}{4}$

PM-19.   a) $\frac{3 \pm \sqrt{51}}{2}$ b) -13

PM-20.   b) Multiply each equation by the
            common denominator to
            remove the fractions.

PM-21.   a) one answer is (2, 8)

PM-23.   Perpendicular slopes are opposite
            reciprocals; $y = -\frac{x}{3}$

PM-25.   a) $x = \frac{a+b}{c}$

PM-32.   b) $(x + 3)^2 + (y - 4)^2 = 25$

PM-33.   one equation is
            0.15x + 0.22y = 513.01

PM-35.   306.3 feet

PM-38.   Square both sides carefully

PM-47.   c) 15.5°

PM-48.   Use the descriminant $b^2 - 4ac = 0$.

PM-51.   b) (3, 4) and (5, 0)

PM-52.   a) 3a - 4b = 5, 3b + 4a = 6;
            $a = \frac{39}{25}= 1.56$, $b = -\frac{2}{25}= -0.08$

PM-53.   a) 3 + 4i

PM-54.   a) $\begin{bmatrix} 12 & -3 \\ -2 & 1 \\ -7 & -1 \end{bmatrix}$

PM-61.   1148 cu. cm.

PM-62.   Refer back to PM-23.

PM-63.   b) $(-\frac{2}{5}, 19.2)$ $y = 5(x + 0.4)^2 +$

PM-66.   b) 120°, 240°   c) 45°, 225°

M-72.   b) The sides of the diagram are labelled x; $\frac{1-x}{2}$; and $\frac{1-x}{2}$.

M-74. ≈ 1.29

M-76.   Use slope to determine the angle.

M-78.   a) $\frac{x+1}{x^2}$

M-84.   a) start at (0,0); amp =2; period = 2π
         b) start at (0,0); amp =1; period = π
         c) start at (0,0); amp =2; period = 2π
         d) same graph as (c)

M-88. $6.36

M-90.   a) $7\sqrt{6}$ b) $10\sqrt{3} + 10\sqrt{2}$

         c) $\frac{\sqrt{2}}{2}$

M-97. $y = -\frac{5}{12}x + 19$

M-98.   e) $x = 0, -2, \frac{4}{3}$

M-105.   b) $a + b + c = 1, 4a + 2b + c = 3$, $9a + 3b + c = 6$

M-106.   b) [0.1 0.2 0.6 0.1]; after one day there is a 10% probability that she will be well, a 20% probability that she will be in good condition, a 60% probability that she will still be critical, and a 10% chance that she will have died.

M-116.   a) $T = \begin{array}{c} \\ \text{rain} \\ \text{none} \end{array} \begin{array}{cc} \text{rain} & \text{none} \\ \begin{bmatrix} 0.7 & 0.3 \\ 0.2 & 0.8 \end{bmatrix} \end{array}$

         d) Find $D_4 = D_0(T^4)$ and look at the "rain" column entry, which $\approx 37.5\%$.

M-117.   d) 0.875

M-120.   a) 0.6764   b) 82.8%

IC-9.   0.190

IC-10.   c) 8.3

IC-13. $y = 5, z = 3$

IC-14.   b) $\frac{5\pi}{12}$

IC-15.   b) only one

IC-27.   Blue weighs 8 g and red weighs 16 g.

IC-28. $\frac{5}{x+4}$

IC-29. $\frac{x}{x+2}$

IC-30.   b) $\left[\frac{16\pi}{9}\right]$ c) 140°
         e) 1530°

IC-32.   rectangle with vertices (2, 0), (3, 1), (-1, 3), (0, 4); area = 6 square units

IC-33.   c) It is not changing; $\approx 68.20°$

IC-40. $\frac{1}{10!}$

IC-44.   c) 56

IC-46. $\frac{19}{29} - \frac{4}{29}i$

IC-59.   a) 1326   b) P(2 diamonds) = 0.0588

         c) $\frac{_{13}C_2}{_{52}C_2}$

IC-60.   a) 21

IC-65. $-\frac{9}{2}$

IC-67.   a) i

IC-75.   a) 1000

IC-76.   a) 0.45

IC-78.   a) Experiment with n = 3, 4, 5. What is the pattern? Why?

IC-79.　$\frac{\pi}{6}$ and $\frac{5\pi}{6}$ or 30° and 150°

IC-88.　a)　120

IC-92.　x = 2　or　x = -1

IC-93.　9.10

IC-95.　≈ 10.8 m

IC-103.　a)　875

IC-106.　a)　the answer is **not** $\frac{x^1 + y^1}{x^2 - y^2}$

　　　　b)　the answer is **not** $x^2 - 5y$

IC-110.　b)　$x^2 + 2xy + y^2$

IC-114.　0.000001539

IC-116.　$x^7 + 7x^6y + 21x^5y^2 + 35x^4y^3 + 35x^4y^3 + 21x^5y^2 + 7x^6y + y^7$

IC-117.　b)　The coefficients of $(x + y)^n$ are the elements of the nth row of the triangle.

IC-118.　151,200

IC-120.　78 months

IC-122.　Factor out　x　to begin.

IC-124.　a)　0.0253

IC-125.　b)　$\frac{1}{156000}$

IC-130.　a)　4

IC-137.　Only 3, 4, 5 makes a right triangle; how many ways can that occur?

IC-144.　First factor out cos x.

UNIT 12

DS-9.　a)　50 mph is not the answer. Continue with parts (b) through (d) to calculate the correct average speed.
　　　f)　48 mph

DS-11.　b)　24

DS-13.　c = 3

DS-23.　They are using two different averages. Which group is using the median?

DS-25.　50

DS-29.　sum = 70.5

DS-30.　b)　$\frac{2x^2 - 3x}{4}$

DS-39.　b)　22.5

DS-54.　a)　5.96 mph

DS-56.　$y = a(x - 3)^2 + 3$; substitute (7, 5) for (x, y) and solve for　a.

DS-57.　b)　x ≈ -1.839　　c)　x ≈ -1.839

DS-66.　The answer is not 70.

DS-67.　c)　$y = 0.2(x - 2)^2$

DS-69.　a)　Find the radius first.
　　　b)　247.403° or 112.597°; 4.318 rad or 1.966 rad
　　　d)　≈ 0.85

DS-81.　b)　0 or $\frac{3}{5}$

DS-84.　9

DS-85.　The y-intercept is 5.4.

DS-86.　-1

DS-87.　b)　(-0.08, 7.51), (6.08, 7.51)

DS-94.　b)　$x^3 - 8$

DS-95.　c)　$(2x - y)(4x^2 + 2xy + y^2)$

DS-96.　a)　Notice that x^2 is a common factor.
　　　b)　$8y^6 = (2x^2)^3$, and $125x^3 = (5x)$ so this is a difference of cubes.
　　　c)　Step one is $(x^3 - y^3)(x^3 + y^3)$; both factors can be factored again.

S-101.   a) Factor the denominator; what
              do the factors tell you?
          b) D: [0, 25) and (25, ∞);
              R: $f(x) \leq -\frac{1}{5}$ or $f(x) > 0$

S-113.   c) There are 10 paths to 3rd and D.

S-116.   g = 4

S-118.   d) 64   g) 0.5   i) no answer

S-127.   d) Sometimes, when $x \leq 0$
          i) S, when $y = \frac{-9}{4}x$

S-128.   The fourth term is $-32ab^3$.

S-131.   b) same as for part (a)

S-143. $(\pm\sqrt{7}, 3)$, (0,-4)

S-144   24 sq. units

S-145.   Use the points (0, 6), (2, 102), (4, 70),
          and the equation $y = ax^2 + bx + c$.

NIT 13

E-2.   495,550

E-3.   d) -0.56 + 0.92i

E-4.   479,001,600

E-6.   b) Solve $y^2 + 5y + 4 = 0$, then let
              $y = \cos x$.

E-8.   3.64 yrs.

E-12.   6.9999

E-13.   5551

E-14.   Use the general equation
          $y = ax^2 + bx + c$, substitute for x
          and y and solve for a, b, and c.

E-15.   b) $_{899}C_{11} \approx 7.3 \times 10^{24}$

E-16.   19.8, 39.0, 80°

RE-17.   b) $\frac{1 \pm i\sqrt{43}}{2}$

RE-18.   The tangent line is perpendicular to
          the radius.

RE-20.   500 miles

RE-22.   2160

RE-23.   This is a geometric sequence with
          80 terms and sum 5.2087.

RE-25.   90.2 ft.

RE-28. $-5940x^9$

RE-29.   0.3273

RE-31. $y = x^2 - 6x + 13$

RE-32.   Remember to factor out the
          common factor 5xy first.
          Then factor the difference of two
          squares, but don't stop yet.
          You can factor each of those
          factors again.

RE-33.   Remember to start by factoring out
          the 2 so $x = 2(y^2 - 6y + \quad) + 13$.
          And when you complete the
          square, what are you really adding
          to the whole expression?

RE-41.   (2, -2), (2, 8), (-2, 3), (6, 3)

RE-42.   b)   center (-1, -3), length 8 units,
               height 10 units

RE-43.   a) $\frac{(x+2)^2}{16} + \frac{(y-1)^2}{4} = 1$

RE-44.   First show that the relationship
          works for n = 1, and possibly n = 2
          and n = 3 to convince yourself.
          Then write
          $\frac{x^k - 1}{x - 1} = x^{k-1} + x^{k-2} + \ldots + x + 1$
          and add x^k (which is the next term
          or k+1st term) to both sides. The
          rest is careful algebra.

RE-46.   40°

RE-52.   a) $(0, \pm 2)$; $y = \pm \frac{2}{5} x$; up/down
         b) $(\pm 3, 0)$; $y = \pm x$; left/right

RE-53.   a) center $(2, -3)$; vertices $(5, -3)$,
             $(-1, -3)$; asy: $y = \pm \frac{2}{3}(x - 2) - 3$

RE-54.   a) $\approx 2.25 \times 10^{15}$ b) 55,550

RE-60.   a) hyperbola, center $(0, -1)$
         b) sleeping parabola
         c) circle, radius 5

RE-70.   a) $(2, -11\frac{11}{12})$

RE-71.   a) $(0, \pm \sqrt{20})$ c) $(1 \pm \sqrt{3}, 0)$

RE-73. $(8, -3)$

RE-77.   b) $(-1, 0)$ $(-1, -6)$, e = 0.6

RE-78.   a) $(2 \pm \sqrt{13}, -3)$, e = $\frac{\sqrt{13}}{3}$

RE-79.   a) ellipse, center $(1, -3)$, e = $\frac{\sqrt{2}}{2}$

         b) hyperbola, center $(0, -2)$, e = 2

RE-82. $3x^2 - x + 2$

RE-83. $x^3 - 2x^2 - 3x + 9$

RE-84.   a) $2x^3 + 2x^2 + x + 4$ with
             remainder 9

         b) $x^4 + 3x^3 + 7x^2 + 21x + 63 + \frac{190}{x-3}$

RE-87.   asymptotes $y = \pm \sqrt{2}(x - 7)$, e = $\sqrt{3}$,
         foci $(7 \pm 5\sqrt{6}, 0)$

RE-89.   a) $\frac{1}{1-x}$

RE-90.   c) The remainder is -4.

RE-91.   b) $x^4 - x^3 + 2x^2 - 7$

About the Index

Each entry of the index is in alphabetical order and is referenced by the problem number in which it is discussed. In some cases, a term or idea may be discussed in several of the following problems as well. The problems are listed by two-letter code that references the unit and the problem number. Whenever possible, terms are cross-referenced to make the search process quicker and easier. For example, *cos x* could also be found under the heading *trigonometric functions*.

Table of Unit Labels

Unit 1	EF	Sharpening Pencils: Exploring Functions
Unit 2	BB	The Bouncing Ball: Sequences
Unit 3	FX	Fast Cars and Depreciation: Exponential Functions
Unit 4	PG	The Gateway Arch: Parabolas and Other Parent Graphs
Unit 5	LS	The Toy Factory: Linear Systems
Unit 6	CC	The Case of the Cooling Corpse: Logarithms and Other Inverses
Unit 7	CF	At the County Fair: Polynomials and General Systems
Unit 8	CT	The Circle of Terror: Circular Functions
Unit 9	ST	Sunken Treasure: More Trigonometry
Unit 10	PM	Policy Making and Probability
Unit 11	IC	The Ice Cream Shoppe: Probability, Counting, and Sampling
Unit 12	DS	Closest to the Pin: Descriptive Statistics
Unit 13	RE	Return of the Bouncing Ball and Other Topics: Revisiting and Extending Earlier Topics

Index

THIS BOOK IS THE PROPERTY OF:

Book No._____

ISSUED TO	Year Used	CONDITION	
		ISSUED	RETURNED

PUPILS to whom this textbook is issued must not write on any page or mark any part of it in any way, unless otherwise instructed by the teacher.